COLONIAL JUSTICE
Justice, Morality, and Crime in the Niagara District,
1791–1849

COLONIAL JUSTICE

Justice, Morality, and Crime
in the Niagara District,
1791–1849

DAVID MURRAY

Published for The Osgoode Society for Canadian Legal History by
University of Toronto Press
Toronto Buffalo London

© Osgoode Society for Canadian Legal History 2002

Printed in Canada

ISBN 0-8020-3749-6

Printed on acid-free paper

National Library of Canada Cataloguing in Publication

Murray, David Robert
Colonial justice : justice, morality, and crime in the Niagara district,
1791–1849 / David Murray.

Includes bibliographical references and index.
ISBN 0-8020-3749-6

1. Criminal justice, Administration of – Ontario – Niagara Peninsula –
History – 18th century. 2. Criminal justice, Administration of – Ontario
– Niagara Peninsula – History – 19th century. 3. Criminal justice,
Administration of – Moral and ethical aspects – Ontario – Niagara
Peninsula – History. I. Osgoode Society for Canadian Legal History.
II. Title.

KEO176.M87 2002   364'09713'38   C2002-902116-2

University of Toronto Press acknowledges the financial assistance to its
publishing program of the Canada Council for the Arts and the
Ontario Arts Council.

University of Toronto Press acknowledges the financial support for its
publishing activities of the Government of Canada through its
Book Publishing Industry Development Program (BPIDP).

For My Family

Contents

Foreword

In many ways, the acquisition of historical knowledge is a cumulative process and one scholar moves forward from the building blocks provided by another. Although recent years have seen the publication of several good books and articles on the legal history of Upper Canada, these works in some ways are premature in that they offer overviews and interpretations before attempting to assess how the courts and legal structures actually functioned 'on the ground.'

Fortunately there does exist for early Ontario a relatively rich archival heritage which historians are beginning to tap into to create local studies which will allow us to arrive at a more encompassing synthesis. For no part of Upper Canada do richer records exist than for the Niagara District. In *Colonial Justice* Professor David Murray of the University of Guelph uses these records and demonstrates how necessary and revealing the local study can be as the essential precursor to more general interpretation.

David Murray argues that, as a colony, Upper Canada was obliged to adopt the essential elements of the British legal system. But just how did a system designed for a much more sophisticated society function in the wilds of early Canada? Focusing on the border District of Niagara, he offers some surprising and intriguing answers as he demonstrates how deeply legal processes affected Canadian life and how Niagara's criminal justice system actually functioned. Based primarily on court records, *Colonial Justice* integrates the stories of individuals caught up in the toils of justice, such as that of fugitive slave Solomon Moseby, with larger themes relating Upper Canadian social developments to contemporary legal issues and criminal trials.

The purpose of The Osgoode Society for Canadian Legal History is to encourage research and writing in the history of Canadian law. The Society, which was incorporated in 1979 and is registered as a charity, was founded at the initiative of the Honourable R. Roy McMurtry, a former attorney general for Ontario, now Chief Justice of Ontario, and officials of the Law Society of Upper Canada. Its efforts to stimulate the study of legal history in Canada include a research support program, a graduate student research assistance program, and work in the fields of oral history and legal archives. The Society publishes volumes of interest to the Society's members that contribute to legal-historical scholarship in Canada, including studies of the courts, the judiciary and the legal profession, biographies, collections of documents, studies in criminology and penology, accounts of significant trials, and work in the social and economic history of the law.

Current directors of The Osgoode Society for Canadian Legal History are Robert Armstrong, Jane Banfield, Kenneth Binks, Patrick Brode, Brian Bucknall, Archie Campbell, Kirby Chown, J. Douglas Ewart, Martin Friedland, Elizabeth Goldberg, John Honsberger, Horace Krever, Vern Krishna, Virginia MacLean, Wendy Matheson, Roy McMurtry, Brendan O'Brien, Peter Oliver, Paul Reinhardt, Joel Richler, James Spence, Richard Tinsley, and David Young.

The annual report and information about membership may be obtained by writing: The Osgoode Society for Canadian Legal History, Osgoode Hall, 130 Queen Street West, Toronto, Ontario. M5H 2N6. Telephone: 416-947-3321. E-Mail: mmacfarl@lsuc.on.ca.

R. Roy McMurtry
President

Peter N. Oliver
Editor-in-Chief

Acknowledgments

I have benefited from the assistance of many people during the long gestation period of this book. First and foremost, the moral support provided by my family, to whom this book is dedicated, especially my wife, my children and my grandchildren, as well as my daughter-in-law and son-in-law, has meant more than words can ever acknowledge. My brother, Don, has kept encouraging me to complete the book, a role he inherited from our father. Peter Oliver, the editor of this series, has been unfailingly supportive while helping continually through his constructive criticism to make this a better book. The anonymous reviewers of the manuscript identified a number of areas where changes were necessary both to clarify and to sharpen the argument. Susan Lewthwaite also read the manuscript with a helpful critical eye.

In addition to the published scholarship on the history of the Niagara region, which extends back over a two hundred year period and provides a key foundation for this book, I have also used the unpublished scholarship contained in a number of theses. I should like to acknowledge the valuable contributions of the graduate students who wrote them, in particular the work of Ann Alexandra McEwen, Frances Ann Thompson and W.J. Blacklock whose studies on the legal history of the Niagara District have been of immense assistance to me.

Some time ago I was fortunate to have Mark Cortiula read some of the Niagara newspapers on microfilm for me. I have also benefited from the knowledge of Kathy Hanneson, Chris Lee, and Alexandra

Holbrook of the University of Guelph to solve some computer related problems. They have each given invaluable help when it was needed. The staff at the Ontario Archives and the National Archives have always been ready to assist whenever I have called upon them, as have the staff at the University of Guelph Library. I am particularly indebted to Catharine Shephard who first introduced me to the court records of the Niagara district and helped me to interpret them.

My colleagues in the Department of History at Guelph have listened patiently when I expounded the ideas that appear in the book and when asked they have always gone out of their way to assist with advice and helpful suggestions. Working with supportive and very able colleagues has made my academic experience at Guelph a very fulfilling one. I am grateful to each one of them for their individual and collective efforts to create an environment in which teaching has been valued and scholarship encouraged.

The staff at the University of Toronto Press have helped to speed this book through the publication process. I am particularly indebted to Allyson May for her careful editing of the manuscript. I remain solely responsible for the content of the book and for any errors or omissions it contains.

DAVID MURRAY
Guelph, Ontario
March 2002

COLONIAL JUSTICE
Justice, Morality, and Crime in the Niagara District, 1791–1849

Introduction

From its creation as a separate colony in 1791, Upper Canada maintained the English system of law, law-making, and law enforcement. The first legislation passed by the newly elected Assembly introduced English laws and established trial by jury as the right of every colonist. Upper Canada's first lieutenant governor, John Graves Simcoe, had a clear vision of the British colony he wanted to see created in the western half of what had been Quebec. The colony was to demonstrate the superiority of British institutions, especially to the Americans. As his biographer characterized it, Upper Canada was to be 'a model of England overseas.'[1] The men appointed to legal positions in the colony, in addition to possessing 'Integrity and Ability,' should possess 'the most Influence' and exert it 'on behalf of Britain.' What Simcoe called 'the Pure Administration of Justice' was a key tenet of a colony designed to reproduce English society and institutions.[2]

The rule of English law was at the apex of the ideals Simcoe cherished and for Simcoe, as for his English contemporaries, the rule of law was rooted within a state-sanctioned Christian religion. Blackstone had written in his *Commentaries* that 'Christianity is part of the laws of England'[3] and Simcoe lost no opportunity to exhort the colony's legislators to build colonial justice on a firm foundation of Christian morality. In a speech closing the first session of the newly elected Legislative Assembly in 1792, he told the legislators that they had a duty to promote 'the regular habits of piety and morality, the surest foundation of all public and private felicity.'[4] This was not mere political rhetoric. Simcoe's words emanated from genuine conviction. He reiterated his beliefs in a letter to Henry Dundas, the home secretary and one of Prime Minister Pitt's closest confidants: 'the best security that all just Government has for its existence is founded upon the Morality of the People, and ... such Morality has no true Basis but when based upon religious principles.'[5]

In the spring of 1793 Simcoe issued a proclamation to all the inhabitants of the colony, 'for the Suppression of Vice, Profaneness and Immorality.' Christian ministers were ordered to read this proclamation four times a year in their churches and it was to be read as well at the opening of all court sessions. Ministers were urged to convince their parishioners to avoid anything that was 'contrary to the pure Morality of the Religion of the Holy Gospel of Jesus Christ,' and to practise 'piety and virtue.'[6] In a speech to the Legislative Assembly at the end of May 1793, Simcoe urged legislators to provide 'for the due support of Public Justice, for the encouragement of Morality, and the punishment of crime, which are necessary to the Existence of Society.'[7] At a time when the excesses of what he saw as 'tyrannical democracy' in the republican United States and revolutionary France seemed to pose the greatest danger to Britain, Simcoe was convinced of the need to inculcate the principles of eighteenth-century English government, along with its hierarchical stratification, to secure the foundation for this new British colony and an antidote to the seductive influences of American republicanism. Only if English principles were firmly planted could the colony succeed and prosper.

In Upper Canada as in Britain law enforcement was a function of local government. Although a separation of the powers of justice and executive government is evident from the middle of the nineteenth century, the system first established in the Canadian colonies rested on a long history of intermingled powers. At the local level, these powers were wielded by the magistrates. Norma Landau concluded that for the English justice of the peace, 'the office of justice yoked politics to administration.'[8] The same situation prevailed in Upper Canada during the early colonial period, and it ensured the pervasive influence of law and legal processes in the life of the local community. But where in England 'the county is ... the most useful and natural geographical unit of study if the work of the criminal courts is to be the central focus,'[9] the primary judicial unit in Upper Canada was the district. Following the union of the Canadas in 1840, the District Councils Act of 1841 transferred some of the functions of local government to newly created municipal councils. But the districts remained the primary units of local government and law enforcement in Upper Canada until they were dissolved in 1849 and their functions divided among counties and emerging urban centres.

The intermingling of administrative and judicial powers at the local level, especially by the magistrates in the court of quarter sessions created some unique problems in the colony. The districts tended to be larger geographic units than the English counties, and they were far more sparsely settled. Since the cost of local justice had to be borne by the district inhabitants, justice in the colonies imposed a heavier tax burden than it did in England. The men responsible for raising the taxes and for determining how the money was spent were, moreover, the magistrates responsible for the administration of justice. Thus the system possessed inherent structural inequities which the magistrates were ill-equipped to resolve.

Colonial Justice adopts the three themes of Simcoe's 1793 speech – justice, morality, and crime – as the organizing framework for a study of the criminal justice system in the Niagara district. As the anthropologist Clifford Geertz has written, 'the law is a craft of place'; it works 'by the light of local knowledge.'[10] How far local characteristics can affect the operation of the criminal justice system is one of the questions this book seeks to answer. Jim Phillips, discussing Canadian legal history, argues that 'the role played by law and legal institutions in different places at different times was fundamentally determined by local material, social and intellectual conditions.'[11] Clive Emsley, writing about crime and society in England, similarly suggests that 'the economic, political and social structure of a society creates a framework in which the criminal justice system functions ...'[12] Local conditions in the Niagara district moulded the environment in which the transplanted English system of law emerged in the new colony and they certainly influenced how it was administered.

The English system of justice was implanted at different times throughout North America, but there are observable differences in its administration. For example, we do not find in Niagara the same preoccupation with honour that Edward Ayers discovered in his study of crime and punishment in the American South.[13] Understanding how the legal process functioned at a local level can shed new light on the administration of British colonial law. (Local studies have only recently been undertaken by legal historians of Upper and Lower

Canada.)[14] *Colonial Justice* also tries to integrate the stories of ordinary individuals and their experiences with the legal administration, in the belief that certain individual cases can better illuminate how the justice system actually worked.

Exploring the administration of criminal justice in this one district of Upper Canada allows us as well to test a dominant paradigm of Upper Canadian legal history, according to which the criminal justice system was shot through with corruption and partiality. It has been argued that by the 1820s and 1830s the colony had become almost the polar opposite of Simcoe's vision. This led, in the words of Robert Fraser, to 'the internecine war over the administration of justice in the 1820s.'[15] Fraser calls 'the charge of partiality levelled against the administration of justice' in Upper Canada 'the most important theme in Upper Canadian legal history,' and maintains that whether or not the charge is true remains to be resolved. The subject 'awaits further research.'[16] Through an intensive examination of how justice actually worked in one district of Upper Canada we can begin to find answers to the question raised by Peter Oliver: whether British colonial justice in Upper Canada 'dealt fairly and humanely with those ordinary persons who supplied the courts with their regular business.'[17] As Oliver observes, even if 'ordinary criminal cases were adjudicated honestly and impartially,' this by itself would not refute the existence of a thoroughly corrupt legal system in Upper Canada. It would, however, suggest the need for a rethinking of our approaches to the legal history of this period.

The corruption argument does not rest upon a thorough examination of the legal system in each of Upper Canada's districts, but rather upon an amalgam of charges made by opponents of the regime and a study of some notorious cases of apparent injustice at the assize levels, particularly those with obvious political overtones. These cases have led to the conclusions that, 'by contemporary British (notwithstanding William Pitt the younger) and even pre-revolutionary American standards, British North American governments interpreted and applied the law in a relentlessly repressive fashion,' and that colonial governments 'wielded greater executive control over the administration of justice.'[18] Out of this repressive and heavy-handed use of executive power emerged a legal system riddled with partisanship and unfairness.[19] Whether this characterization of the legal system of Upper Canada is accurate and if so, whether it applies to the whole system and over the entire colonial period remains highly debatable. Any conclusions depend in part upon more focused local studies.

Even the picture of a legal system tightly controlled by the executive may, upon examination, require revision. Most of the legal business of the colony was conducted in the lowest courts, the courts of quarter sessions, and here the local magistrates were in charge. More serious criminal cases, and the instances of legal abuses cited by those who view the administration of criminal justice in Upper Canada as corrupt, were heard at the assize level before professional judges who toured the colony. At the assize level, and in cases with political overtones, the executive government could and did use its formidable array of powers to influence the outcome in important cases. But what happened in the less serious criminal cases resolved by the magistrates? Do we find examples of repressive acts occurring at quarter sessions as well? Norma Landau stresses the autonomy of justices of the peace in England: 'Neither the central government nor Parliament told them what to do, closely supervised their activity, or even insured that they act at all.'[20] If the Niagara JPs displayed the same degree of independence in the exercise of their powers, the argument for a monolithic and repressive system of justice in Upper Canada becomes more difficult to sustain.

If we are to understand the historical evolution of Canadian criminal justice, we need to look more carefully at how it actually operated in early communities. Did the practice of justice mirror the theory? The existence of a relatively complete set of court files for the Niagara district from 1828 on, combined with scattered court records for the period 1792–1828, a number of collections from persons prominent in the district, and a rich legacy of secondary historical works makes possible an analysis of the judicial system in one of the original settled districts of Upper Canada.[21] The Upper Canadian and Niagara court records permit an examination of the operation of the justice system, beginning at the local level, where most of the colonists first came into contact with it.

This book focuses upon the Niagara district criminal justice system as it functioned primarily through the court of quarter sessions, seeking to determine how the system operated in practice and whether or not it had become hopelessly corrupt by the 1830s. Part one introduces the Niagara district and examines the social and political structure of its justice system. Chapters 2 and 3 attempt to put a human face on the men who served as magistrates, sheriffs, jurors, and constables, but they also assess the importance of institutions like the colonial jury and the early constabulary. Part two contains three chapters on the theme of Christian morality, examining sabbath-breaking in the Niagara district, the treatment of 'lunatics' and the moral dilemma they presented, and, in chapter 6, the role played by the court of quarter sessions in social welfare. Christian morality was seen, certainly by the elite, as the moral foundation of the legal and social order well into the nineteenth century. How well was the Christian moral code upheld in the lower courts? Part three consists of four chapters on crime and punishment across the colonial period. Chapter 7 places the crimes and punishments of the Niagara district in context. It is followed by three thematic chapters. Chapter 8 examines women as victims of wife-beating and the treatment of African Canadians by the colonial justice system. Chapter 9 looks at a series of crimes and punishments, from smuggling to banishment, each of which was profoundly affected, even shaped, by the frontier with the United States. Chapter 10 examines attitudes towards fugitive slaves through an analysis of the abortive extradition of Solomon Moseby, a slave who escaped from Kentucky in 1837 and found refuge in Niagara.

1

The Paradise of Upper Canada

The Niagara peninsula has always been both a land bridge between British North America (and later Canada) and the United States, and a water crossing point or portage between Lake Erie and Lake Ontario. It developed as a conjunction of land and water routes, and as a gateway for settlers leaving the United States for British North America following the American Revolution. Bisected by the Niagara escarpment, the early Niagara peninsula was noteworthy for its agricultural potential, especially in the area bordering Lake Ontario and the Niagara river. The immediately available water power was another attraction for early settlers, allowing the establishment of water-driven saw and grist mills.

The Niagara peninsula was first subdivided into ridings, following an English precedent, but was later divided into sixteen townships. In 1792 the county of Lincoln was created, encompassing the current counties of Lincoln and Welland. The names of the townships within it copied those found in Lincolnshire in England. The Niagara district, which came into being by proclamation on 1 January 1800, became the administrative and judicial entity for the peninsula and in this early period the district shaped the life of the community within it. Names like Grimsby, Grantham, Louth, Wainfleet, and Humberstone had already been selected by Simcoe to emphasize the English heritage of this new Upper Canadian region.[1] The Niagara community, however, would develop in its own unique manner.

Figure 1.1. The Niagara district (after Gourlay, 1822)[2]

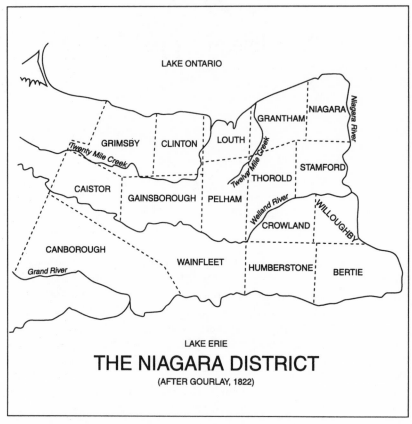

LAKE ONTARIO

NIAGARA

GRANTHAM

GRIMSBY   CLINTON   LOUTH

Twenty Mile Creek

Niagara River

STAMFORD

THOROLD

CAISTOR

GAINSBOROUGH   PELHAM

Welland River

CROWLAND

WILLOUGHBY

CANBOROUGH

Grand River

WAINFLEET   HUMBERSTONE   BERTIE

LAKE ERIE

THE NIAGARA DISTRICT
(AFTER GOURLAY, 1822)

Unlike much of the rest of nineteenth-century Upper Canada, Niagara was a relatively old and settled region. British forms of justice had been quickly established after the creation of the colony in 1791 and the naming of Newark (Niagara) as its first capital. Neither the War of 1812, the economic depression following it, nor the tension leading up to the 1837 Rebellion affected the town of Niagara's role as the district centre. Until 1849, when the district was abolished and the system of county government established, local government continued to be centred on the town of Niagara, and Niagara remained the centre for the judicial system of the region until well after the middle of the nineteenth century. The administrative and judicial structure created in 1791 lasted with very few changes until the union of 1840, imposed by Britain, brought Upper and Lower Canada together. Even then it would take another ten years to dismantle the structure.

It was the political importance of the region, especially for the emerging colony of Upper Canada, which first focused the attention of British colonial officials. From the end of the American Revolution the Niagara region has served as a political frontier, marking the boundary with the United States. That boundary was depicted initially as a British colonial boundary, denoting the division between the colonies which upheld the monarchy and British institutions and the American Republic, which had rejected the British Empire. Later the region would evolve to become a vital link in Canada's boundary with the United States, marking the dividing line between the separate national states and their individual traditions.

Following the American Revolution the Niagara river became the American frontier, a political boundary which shaped the development of the regions on both sides of the river in the early years of the Upper Canadian colony.[3] The location of the first capital of Upper Canada at Newark, which regained its name of Niagara in 1798, was determined by the location of the American frontier.[4] The subsequent transfer of the capital to York in 1796, following the signature of Jay's Treaty in 1794 and the British withdrawal from Fort Niagara in 1796, deprived the Niagara region of its former prestige and attendant economic and political power. The move was a response to the potential military threat posed by the United States and foreshadowed the War of 1812.

During the nearly fifty years of Upper Canada's existence as a separate British colony, the Niagara peninsula remained remarkably stable in its administrative structure. As the administrative centre, Niagara (now Niagara-on-the-Lake) was the town where land holdings were registered, licences obtained, and where the district court and jail were located. In 1816 an administrative reorganization led to the creation of the Gore district by carving out chunks of both the Niagara and the Home districts. Hamilton, the capital of the Gore district, began to assume a much more prominent role and soon surpassed Niagara as the real economic and political centre of the region. Even by 1840, when Upper Canada consisted of sixteen administrative districts, the remainder of the Niagara district was essentially unchanged, incorporating the present counties of Welland, Lincoln, and Haldimand.

The Niagara peninsula was one of the first Upper Canadian regions to experience European settlement from Loyalists fleeing the American revolution, from other American settlers following the Revolution, and from British immigration, and its population grew rapidly in the 1790s and in the first decade of the nineteenth century. The first township, also called Niagara, was surveyed in 1789; the two neighbouring townships along Lake Ontario, Grantham and Louth, were surveyed in 1791 and 1795, respectively. The remaining townships had been surveyed for land grants by 1813 and the settlement of each was fairly well advanced by the War of 1812.[5] Isaac Weld, who visited Niagara in 1795, observed that 'few places in North America can boast of a more rapid rise than the little town of Niagara.'[6] The district's population has been estimated at 6,000 in the mid-1790s and nearly double that, at 11,000, ten years later.[7] By 1805–6, the Niagara district was the most populous of Upper Canada's regions, containing nearly 25 per cent of the colony's estimated total of almost 46,000 inhabitants.[8] Along with population came relative wealth. Immediately prior to the war, the Niagara district collected more tax revenue than any other of the colony's administrative districts.[9]

The Niagara district suffered proportionately far more than the rest of Upper Canada from the War of 1812. A traveller described what he had seen in 1815: 'everywhere I saw devastation, homes in ashes, fields trampled and laid waste, forts demolished, forests burned and blackened, truly a most pitiful sight.'[10] The town of Niagara had been burned to the ground, as had the village of St Davids. The once prosperous merchants of the Niagara peninsula, the colony's 'Shopkeeper Aristocracy,' suffered serious financial losses. Robert Hamilton, the most powerful member of this merchant clique and the chief office holder in the peninsula, saw his firm's decline begin well before the War of 1812, but the war finished his business.[11] Some members of the elite sought public office to offset the losses from their former sources of livelihood and to enable them to maintain as far as possible their prewar standard of living. But these losses had serious economic consequences not only for the elite but for those who had been dependent on them. People in the Niagara district submitted a third of the claims for war damages in the colony and these claims amounted to nearly half of all the colony's losses (47 per cent).[12] The claims were not paid out until the 1820s and the peninsula's former economic prosperity was seriously impaired.

Table 1.1
Population of Niagara District, 1825–1841

Year	Population	Year	Population
1825	18,990	1834	27,347
1826	19,059	1835	28,636
1827	18,913	1836	30,447
1828	20,177	1837	32,296
1829	20,617	1838	25,897
1830	20,916	1839	29,953
1831	21,974	1840	32,504
1832	24,181	1841	34,577
1833	24,772		

Population growth too had been interrupted by the war. Robert Gourlay estimated the population of the Niagara district in 1817 at 12,500.[13] By 1828 it had risen to just over 20,000 people, scattered among some twenty settlements and towns. Niagara, with a population of 1,262, was one of the largest towns, but Grantham (later St Catharines) was already outpacing it with 1,727 inhabitants. The remainder of the population was spread out evenly among the other townships. The larger ones averaged 1,500 people, the smallest two contained just under 300 people. Over half the district population in 1828 was under sixteen.[14] By 1817, other districts of Upper Canada had surpassed Niagara in total population and in 1821 Niagara ranked sixth out of ten Upper Canadian districts in population size.[15] During the 1820s, as illustrated in Table 1.1, Niagara had one of the lowest rates of population growth in the colony.[16] In the 1830s, when other districts of Upper Canada grew rapidly, the population of the Niagara district expanded more slowly. It then fell following the Mackenzie Rebellion and only began to rise again in the 1840s.

Between 1812 and 1851 the population of the Niagara region grew by 380 per cent, reflecting the commercial and industrial expansion following the construction of the Welland Canal. This population growth, however, was only half that of the London district and 20 per cent of that of the Western district.[17] Niagara had certainly grown, but other parts of Upper Canada were growing at a faster pace. Robert Gourlay had written in 1817 that the Niagara district 'is now generally cleared, inhabited and cultivated.' But settlement remained sparse in many parts of the district,[18] although the completion of the first Welland Canal in 1829 stimulated more settlement in the interior. The 1830s saw another huge wave of British immigration into Upper Canada, but Niagara received a disproportionately small share of it and many of those who arrived moved on after the Rebellion of 1837. The population of the district barely exceeded 53,000 in 1850, a small fraction of Upper Canada's total population of 950,000.[19] Population and political influence were linked, and Niagara's relative importance in the colony steadily declined from its peak in the first two decades of the colony's existence.

Contemporaries were struck by the ethnic, racial, and religious diversity of the population of the Niagara district. Thus William Lyon Mackenzie, describing an election crowd in Niagara in 1824, wrote: 'There were Christians and Heathens, Menonists and Tunkards, Quakers and Universalists, Presbyterians and Baptists, Roman Catholics and American Methodists; there were Frenchmen and Yankees, Irishmen and Mulattoes, Scotchmen and Indians, Englishmen, Canadians, Americans and Negroes, Dutchmen and Germans, Welshmen and Swedes, Highlanders and Lowlanders ...'[20] The soldiers of Butler's Rangers who had taken up some of the Niagara district's land were followed by Loyalist settlers from New York, Pennsylvania, and New Jersey, and the American character of the early Niagara settlement was intensified as other American settlers continued to arrive. Some of the Loyalists brought slaves, and other African Americans arrived seeking refuge from slavery. The African American, or African Canadian component as they later became, of the district population may have reached 1 or at most 2 per cent of the total population in the 1820s and 1830s.

Niagara also saw the migration of Mennonites, Tunkers, and Quakers into the region. Their numbers were never large, but identifiable settlements of Tunkers, or River Brethren, as they were known from their original settlements along the Susquehanna river in Pennsylvania, grew up in Pelham and Bertie townships.[21] As early as 1792 Quaker settlements were also thriving in Pelham and Bertie townships and they remained an established element of Niagara's colonial society throughout the early nineteenth century.[22] These groups, like the Mennonites, found a colony willing to make allowances for their professed pacifism. But the dominant religious group in the district were the Methodists. By 1802 the Niagara circuit, with over 600 members, required the services of three Methodist circuit riders; by 1810 the number of adherents had grown to 1,150. The War of 1812 caused a serious decline in membership, but before long a revival occurred. By 1828 Methodist membership had risen to over 2,800 in the peninsula, requiring some fourteen ministers in seven circuits.[23] These heterogeneous religious groups looked to British institutions and British law to protect their religious freedom, despite the fact that religious discrimination was imbedded in British legislation.

Class differences were not as sharply etched in this newly settled area as they were in England or, indeed, as Governor Simcoe hoped they would become. Although a strong sense of rank existed, there was an equal belief in upward social mobility.[24] The elite, comprising well-off farmers, merchants, and leading office holders, aspired to gentry status even if the term 'gentry' did not have the same economic or social meaning in Niagara as it did in England. If commercial wealth had been an adequate substitute for landed wealth, the gentry aspirations of the Niagara elite might have been achieved – Robert Fraser identified the Niagara 'commercial compact' that developed around Robert Hamilton in the years prior to 1812 as coming closest to genuine gentry status. But their lack of landed wealth meant that the colonial elites could not achieve the same standing in their society as the English gentry, which proved a constant source of frustration.[25] Below the elite were the largest number of the settlers, independent, small-scale farmers or tradesmen; at the margin of this colonial society were servants, paupers, and landless labourers.

By 1818 Niagara was a relatively settled farming region, with most of its occupants either employed in farming or in small merchant operations. The northeast part of the district, along the Niagara river and surrounding the village of Niagara, had been settled first. Here the leading villages of Niagara and Queenston accounted for perhaps 1,000 of the district's population, or nearly 10 per cent. Gourlay's 1817 report indicates that this part of the district had the highest population density. Population density declined towards the interior of the district and was lowest in the southwestern part bordering the Lake Erie shore, as Figure 1.2 illustrates.[26] Bertie township, located in the southeast part of the district and also bordering Lake Erie, had a relatively high population density. Settlement of the district's interior in any numbers had to await the construction of the Welland Canal and the improvement of drainage.

Figure 1.2. Niagara District Population Density, 1817

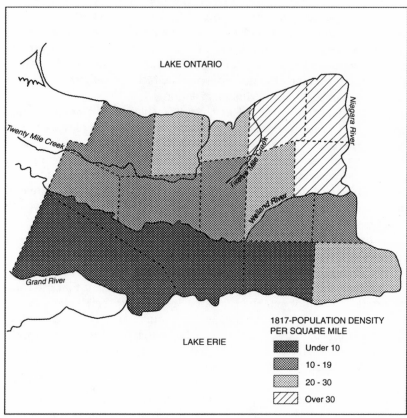

The Niagara peninsula was completely settled by 1850, and by that date it had a system of roads that facilitated transportation throughout the region.[27] This year also marks the end of the pre-railway era, and in many ways the end of the colonial system of government which had been instituted in 1791, in that the districts were abolished and the Niagara region was reorganized into a county system of government in the early years of the 1850s.

Construction of the Welland Canal, begun in 1824, transformed the Niagara peninsula in a number of ways. The first canal, completed in 1829, was extended to Lake Erie in 1833 and a second canal was constructed in the 1840s. The construction process brought many changes to the district. From the mid-1820s construction sites, shanties, and boarding houses sprang up alongside the canal works. Shops and taverns followed the labourers and soon canal settlements began to appear. Hundreds of immigrant wage labourers were recruited, whose presence added to the ethnic and religious heterogeneity of the district's population. Teams of Irish labourers, or navvies, grouped by their originating Irish region, moved from one construction project to another. The Welland Canal attracted Corkmen and Connaughtmen, and with them came regional and religious rivalries that could erupt in localized violence and, on occasion, notably in the 1840s, in larger riots.[28] The workers laboured for very low or subsistence wages and often had to wait lengthy periods to be paid. Since many had dependent families, the precariousness of their wages meant that they tended to live in poverty or on its edge.

Many of the first Irish canal workers eventually settled in St Catharines, stimulating the growth of the town, which would soon succeed Niagara as the centre of the peninsula. By 1832 20 per cent of the population of St Catharines was Roman Catholic and most of the Catholics were Irish. By 1851 25 per cent of St Catharines' population was Irish and a similar percentage of another canal settlement, Thorold, likewise claimed Irish background. The Welland Canal construction process thus introduced a Roman Catholic population to what had been a predominantly Protestant region.[29] It may also have attracted African American immigrants, who formed an identifiable minority of St Catharines's population by the 1840s.

The canal also marked a shifting of power and influence from the town of Niagara and the Niagara river inland to St Catharines. As H.V. Nelles remarks, 'the canal had changed the entire centre of gravity – politically, socially and economically – of the peninsula.'[30] The shifting power balance within the peninsula was a minor echo of the larger change occurring on the other side of the Niagara river.

It soon became clear that Niagara and her sister communities on the Niagara river – Queenston, Chippewa, and Fort Erie – could not compete successfully with Buffalo and Tonawonda on the American side, especially after completion of the Erie Canal in 1825. Even Canadian shippers soon found the Buffalo-New York route cheaper to use than the overland portage. While construction of the Welland Canal strengthened the overall economy of Upper Canada and benefited the Niagara region, the Canadian canal remained subsidiary to its American competitor. Donald Creighton describes the Welland Canal as 'simply an auxiliary of the Erie system.'[31]

Buffalo's rise to prominence was particularly rapid. The town was initially laid out by the Holland Land Company in 1801–3; the sale of lots began in 1803; and by 1812 the town's population had reached about 400. After the burning of Niagara by the Americans in the War of 1812, the British retaliated by pillaging the American side of the frontier and burning Buffalo.[32] But Buffalo quickly recovered. The Erie Canal stimulated a dynamic economic growth that soon enabled Buffalo to become the dominant city on the New York side of the Niagara river. From some 2,500 in 1825 Buffalo's population grew to over 81,000 by 1860, making the city the tenth largest in the United States on the eve of the Civil War. Its commercial ascendancy was based primarily on the shipment of grain from the American mid-west. Dwarfing other communities in the Niagara region on both sides of the frontier, Buffalo had emerged as 'the great natural gateway between the East and West.'[33]

From its initial eminence as the capital of the new colony, and in direct contrast to Buffalo, the town of Niagara steadily declined in political and economic importance. Prior to 1812, Niagara had been described as 'the most refined and modern settlement on the frontier.'[34] After the war, the town was unable to regain her political or economic status. A St Catharines paper gleefully reprinted the following description of a fading Niagara in 1826: 'The town of Niagara which but a short time since wore the appearance of a flourishing and fashionable city, is fast dwindling into decay. The Welland canal and the withdrawing of the troops from that town to York, have had as destructive an effect upon the inhabitants as a hurricane would have upon a cotton plantation.'[35] St Catharines had not yet replaced Niagara as the dominant city of the district and its new county town, but even in the 1820s its ambitions to supplant Niagara were plain. By 1851 there were five urban centres in Upper Canada with populations of 5,000 or more. Niagara was not one of them. It was now firmly established in the second rank, one of seven communities with populations between 2,500 and 5,000.[36]

Successive generations of visitors and writers have described the Niagara district as a paradise. Next to the overwhelming power and sublime effect of the Falls themselves, the Garden of Eden image of the land captivated many of the people who travelled through it. The Scottish radical, Robert Gourlay, writing after the War of 1812 and making a case for a canal across the Peninsula, rhapsodized that the Niagara region 'was intended for a paradise ... in point of climate, soil, variety, beauty, grandeur and every convenience, I do believe it is unrivalled.'[37] Francis Hall, travelling through the region in 1816–17, was equally struck by its agricultural richness. He found the 'unbroken succession of luxuriant orchards, corn-fields and farmhouses a rare and interesting sight in Canada.'[38] John Howison, who toured the area in 1819, termed it 'the most valuable part of Upper Canada.'[39] Another British traveller to Upper Canada, Anna Jameson, observed some two decades later that 'the land around Niagara is particularly fine and fertile, and it has been longer cleared and cultivated than in other parts of the province.'[40] The Upper Canadian revolutionary William Lyon Mackenzie, who knew the region well, glowingly described the lands on the Canadian side of the Niagara river as 'fair and fertile; the orchards loaded with peaches, apples, pears, quinces, plums and other fruit of the choicest kinds; and the fields filled with grain – yet does the population remain nearly stationary [and] lands rise but slowly in value.'[41] He offered no opinion as to why this apparent paradox should endure. The image of Niagara as a biblical paradise, also evident in place names like Jordan, continued in histories of the region. Marjorie Freeman Campbell's *Niagara, Hinge of the Golden Arc* quotes a life-long resident of Niagara as saying, 'The Niagara peninsula ... has always seemed to me like the promised land that lay beyond the River Jordan ...'[42]

If some commentators focused on the natural riches of the region, others lamented the poverty they found. The fate of the town of Niagara seemed to symbolize that of the region as a whole. American travellers noted critically what they perceived as endemic poverty on the Canadian side of the frontier, clear evidence for them of the inferiority of the British colony. The *St Catharines Farmer's Journal*, in December 1826, reprinted a letter from an American traveller describing what he had seen as he rode from Welland to Oswego Creek: 'I never witnessed such an appearance of poverty as in this day's ride. The houses generally, are mere huts, although situated in old settlements, which ought ere this to have shown that appearance of comfort and embellishment which an American, after the first few years of his necessary hard labour in clearing his land always studies to produce. This negligence on the part of the inhabitants of this neighbourhood, made an unfavourable impression, as I could not attribute it to any other cause than a want of industry and refined taste.'[43]

Americans were not the only ones who came to this conclusion. Patrick Shirreff, a Scottish farmer who toured the region in 1833, contrasted what he saw on the two banks of the Niagara River: 'Queenston and Niagara are mean, dirty-looking villages, apparently without trade, and very unlike the clean, bustling places on the opposite side of the river ... the houses and fences were inferior to those of any district yet seen, and instead of the youthfulness and never-ceasing activity of the States there seemed the listless repose of doating age.' To Shirreff, even the animals reflected this national difference. 'The brute creation partook of the change – horses, cattle, sheep and pigs, being inferior to those on the opposite of the frontier.' He concluded, 'if governments affect the state of countries, politicians would do well to visit both sides of the river Niagara.'[44] There was no doubt in his mind that if Niagara, 'the paradise of Upper Canada,' was so inferior to the settlements on the American side of the river, the rest of Upper Canada was bound to be that much worse. Shirreff was particularly critical of the lack of enterprise among the Niagara settlers. The earliest settlers were the least enterprising. If they could make a living for themselves, that was sufficient.

Shirreff was not the only British traveller to comment on the paradox Niagara presented. Anna Jameson, who toured the area in the mid-1830s, wrote: 'In spite of its local advantages, as a frontier town and the oldest settlement in Upper Canada, Niagara does not make progress. The population and the number of houses have remained nearly stationary for the last five years.' She was told that 'the country is beautiful in summer, taxes are trifling, scarcely felt, and there are no poor-rates; yet ignorance, recklessness, despondency and inebriety seem to prevail.'[45] When Jameson subsequently visited Buffalo, she was struck even more by the contrast: 'compared to our sleepy Canadian shore, where a lethargic spell seems to bind up the energies of the people, all here is bustle, animation, activity.'[46]

The perceptions of travellers received official sanction in the Durham Report in 1839, as Lord Durham too contrasted economic activity on either side of the frontier: 'on the American side all is activity and bustle ... on the British side of the line, with the exception of a few favoured spots, where some approach to American prosperity is apparent, all seems waste and desolate.'[47] It galled him that on the U.S. side there was 'every sign of productive industry, increasing wealth and progressive civilization.' Why could not the British colonies exhibit the same economic dynamism? Durham's vision of a more entrepreneurial and competitive Upper Canada was sharpened by his visit to Niagara. His secretary, Charles Buller, wrote, 'When from the Canadian shore [Durham] looked across the entrance of Lake Erie, and saw the noble buildings and crowded harbour of Buffalo, he longed to divert the stream of commerce to the British shore, and by means of the Welland Canal to give to Canada the trade between the Great Lakes and the sea.'[48] That vision never became reality. An argument made by one of Durham's predecessors, Sir Francis Bond Head, would not have allayed any of his anxiety. Head agreed that the Upper Canadians may have been 'poorer in purse' than Americans, but 'the moral picture,' he claimed, 'is beyond all description in our favour.'[49]

In the aftermath of the Rebellion of 1837 the Niagara region suffered from a new series of economic reverses. Its population declined as many elected to move elsewhere. One of Niagara's magistrates wrote this gloomy account in 1839: 'Hard times these – Crops shrunk – No Cash. What is to become of our country? Her Majesty the Queen had better employ us all as Soldiers – then we should be sure of Rations at all events.'[50] Another Niagara magistrate was even more pessimistic. Jacob Keefer, the Thorold magistrate, wrote to William Hamilton Merritt in February 1839, 'any one must see that we are losing *population* and population is said to be wealth. The cry, "let them go, their places will soon be filled with better men," does not work well; their places are *not* filled either by better nor worse.'[51] The economic decline of Niagara in the nineteenth century seemed to put its earliest years, the so-called capital years, into sharper relief.

While the natural beauty of the Niagara area was evident to people from the earliest settlement period, as it has been to visitors ever since, that beauty could not disguise the more rapid economic development on the American side of the river. Niagara Falls attracted thousands of tourists in the first half of the nineteenth century, but these people flocked in only to see the Falls.[52] Few remained as settlers. Patricia Jasen comments that 'if ever there was a golden age of tourism at Niagara, perhaps by 1825 it was already coming to an end.'[53] Some tourists visited the battlefields of the War of 1812, but the Falls remained the primary attraction. Ironically, it was the completion of the Erie Canal in 1825 which brought the age of mass tourism to Niagara.

On the Upper Canadian side of the Niagara river the frontier proved to be more of an economic obstacle than a benefit. The all-American route of migration and commerce along the Erie Canal rapidly displaced the older, historic route which had portaged across the Niagara isthmus. Even in Upper Canada, migrants were more likely to proceed west along the Dundas Street highway than to use the traditional

Niagara route. J. Wreford Watson argues that 'the political frontier made the response to change much slower and more difficult on the Canadian side and tended to retard the social development of the Canadian settlement, even if it quickened the industrial growth. Moreover, it created discordant junction between the United States and Canadian patterns of transportation, which threw the Canadian city [Niagara] off centre.'[54] It took some time for the Niagara river to evolve from a frontier of conflict to a bridge of contact between two independent nations. And by the time this transformation had been effected the economic and political power on the Canadian side had shifted irrevocably from Niagara to Toronto and Hamilton. In the meantime, on the other side of the river Buffalo and New York quickly and irreversibly established their economic predominance over the Niagara region and, indeed, over Upper Canada as a whole.

Despite the region's eventual political and economic decline, Niagara's stable administrative and legal edifice in the first half of the nineteenth century makes it an excellent historical laboratory in which to examine the operation of the Upper Canadian criminal justice system. Janet Carnochan begins her history of Niagara by suggesting that 'to know the history of Niagara is to know much of the history of Upper Canada.'[55] Studying the criminal justice system in Niagara may therefore yield insights about the colony as a whole. By reducing the scale of observation to a single administrative district and by using an historical microscope to reveal the individuals ensnared by the legal process, this book reveals aspects of the criminal justice system hidden or overlooked in macro studies of Upper Canada. The sometimes stark light shed by the legal documents helps to illuminate this rural and pre-industrial society as it struggled to define the meaning of British justice in a British North American environment, and in a frontier society heavily affected by both the proximity and growing predominance of the United States. Referring primarily to Niagara, William Kirby states that 'obedience to the teachings of religion and to the law, and respect for the magistrates appointed by the King, were marked features of the people who made Upper Canada the noble country that it is.'[56] This was certainly what the Loyalist descendants wanted to believe. But was it really true?

PART ONE

Justice

Upper Canada's legal structure was specifically designed to incorporate all English law as of 17 September 1792, the date of the opening of the first Legislature of Upper Canada, as the law of Upper Canada. That law would thereafter be modified by laws passed by the Legislature. But English legal and moral principles were to guide the Upper Canadians as they implemented the English legal code.

The key officials of the justice system, the judges, sheriffs, and magistrates, were appointed directly by the lieutenant governor and held office at the pleasure of the Crown. They were in every sense royal officials, agents of the Crown who were accountable only to the Crown's representative and not directly responsible to the people. Their mandate certainly included enforcing the laws passed by the colonial Legislature as well as English law as of 1792, but the Legislature itself had no official say in their appointment. Nor did it possess powers either to censure them or to remove them from office.

The criteria for selection of justice officials did not include competency, although contemporary belief equated wealth and property with competency. The magistrates of each district were selected from men who had attained a certain level of wealth or property. As John Weaver has remarked, magistrates had to be 'men of substance.'[1] Magistrates and sheriffs, like all agents of the Crown, had also to be men of unquestioning loyalty to Britain. During the colonial period, when the law was deemed to be exclusively a masculine enterprise, none of the agents was female.

Colonial justice also depended on constables appointed from the local citizenry and men who served as jurors on grand and petit juries. The laws were enforced through a system of courts similar to that found in England. Less serious cases were processed in the court of quarter sessions, and the more serious cases were held over for the yearly assizes, to be heard in the Court of King's Bench presided over by one of the colony's senior judges. In the colonial period the court of quarter sessions also served as the vehicle of local government. Tensions between the central government of the colony and the periphery were most evident in the assize courts, but justice in the court of quarter sessions, in terms of both the cases that came to court and the decisions reached, was predominantly local. The local nature of much of colonial justice in the Niagara district is the focus of the following chapters.

2

Courts, District Rulers, and Crown Servants

Courts of General Sessions of the Peace and a Court of King's Bench had been created in Quebec following the Conquest, which made their extension to Upper Canada both logical and natural even before the Constitutional Act formally divided the Canadas in 1791. Simcoe modelled the justice system in Upper Canada upon the English one and had his chief justice create a bill designating a Court of King's Bench as a superior court of civil and criminal jurisdiction. The resultant Act was passed in 1794.[1] The trials in this court occurred at assizes held in the capital of each district under commissions of oyer and terminer and general gaol delivery issued by the lieutenant governor to the judges of the Court of King's Bench. Assizes were held once a year until 1837, and then twice yearly. The courts of General Sessions of the Peace, more commonly known as quarter sessions, continued in Upper Canada on the same English model and followed English law until September 1792, when Upper Canadian statutes began to be added. The quarter sessions operated as the primary courts in each district of the colony. A law was passed in 1801 to remove any doubts about the legal authority of these courts and to confirm their powers by colonial statute as well as inherited British law.[2] Justices of the peace from the district presided at the quarter sessions. The magistrates also served as commissioners of the Court of Requests, which

were established within divisions of each district and given civil juris-
diction in cases of small debt recovery not exceeding 40 shillings.[3] The
Courts of Requests were crucial to the operation of the fledgling colony.
They met twice a month on Saturdays and these 'Saturday courts'
were often where local people could find a justice of the peace.[4] The
Courts of Requests were reorganized in 1833, only to be abolished in
1841 and replaced by Division Courts presided over by the District
Judge.

The ancient English commission of the peace empowered justices of
the peace to act alone on some issues, to act with one or more fellow
magistrates on others, and to act collectively as the court of general
sessions or quarter sessions on still others. These powers and the court
of quarter sessions evolved into 'a sort of legal constitution' which
was inherited by the new colony of Upper Canada. The court of quarter sessions in England was seen as 'the supreme county authority,'
and it quickly became the supreme district authority in Upper Canada.[5]
In Upper Canada, as in England, it soon proved impossible to distin-
guish among the administrative and judicial functions of the justices.
This can be seen in a statute passed in 1819 entitled, 'An Act for
establishing a Police in the Town of Niagara.'[6] The Act does not mention police in its text, but it does invest the quarter sessions magistrates with all the powers to regulate municipal affairs in the town of
Niagara, from its lighting to the inspection of weights and measures
and the rules for the operation of the town market; to function in other
words as 'a police.'

The court of quarter sessions normally met four times a year in the
town of Niagara, the district capital, although it could meet more
often in special sessions if the magistrates desired. By no means all of
the JPs regularly attended the court sessions. James Wilson, who examined the quarter sessions in the district of Johnstown, in the eastern
part of the colony, found that a group of magistrates he called 'Working Justices' formed the core of local government in that district.[7] A
similar conclusion can be drawn for Niagara. The real operation of the
court rested in the hands of a small number of magistrates, most of
whom lived in Niagara or St Catharines, or within close proximity. Of
the 117 justices named in the commission of the peace for Niagara in
1833 only ten showed up for the summer sessions in July 1838. Fourteen appeared for the adjourned sessions which met a month later.[8]

The number of magistrates who attended Niagara's quarter sessions
usually ranged from six or seven to twenty, a small fraction of the

total appointed. Even the so-called working justices could not always be relied upon to turn up on their own accord. In the summer of 1843, when not enough magistrates appeared to permit the court to function, the clerk of the peace wrote to six magistrates in the immediate vicinity of the town of Niagara, stating that their presence was required the following day.[9] Charles Richardson, the Niagara clerk of the peace, wrote to the provincial secretary in 1845, saying, 'notwithstanding the number of names in the Commission of the Peace for this District – It is a very difficult matter to obtain *two* at the Adjourned Sessions.'[10] The same situation prevailed in England, however. According to the Webbs, the judicial bench in the English courts of quarter sessions rarely consisted of more than three or four magistrates.[11]

The court of quarter sessions administered the non-judicial as well as the judicial functions of the district, including its finances, and magistrates were unable to keep separate their judicial and administrative roles. Frequently, and sometimes in surprising ways, their actions as penny-pinching local bureaucrats impinged on their functions as the King's local law enforcers. This confusion of functions effectively blurred the line between the executive and judicial powers of the government at the point where most people came into contact with them. The problems which emerged as the magistrates tried, often unsuccessfully, to reconcile their administrative responsibilities with their judicial mandate highlight one of the dilemmas of the premodern judicial system imported into the British North American colonies. Chronic financial shortage affected the local administration of justice.

The court of quarter sessions exercised so many powers that the magistrates have been seen as 'all pervasive' at the local level.[12] Local government administration took up most of the magistrates' time. According to one estimate, nearly 60 per cent of the business of the court of quarter sessions in one district of Upper Canada stemmed from local government rather than criminal administration.[13] Whether the same breakdown applied consistently across the colony is not clear, but the magistrates assembled in the courts of quarter sessions dealt with an astonishing range of matters, many of which became more complicated as the colony grew in the nineteenth century.

The quarter sessions court controlled the finances of the district, which meant in practice fixing the assessment rate, paying all fees and salaries, and covering the costs for things like censuses. Prior to 1841, when the District Councils Act transferred some of these functions to town councils, the court was also responsible for the appointment of officials in the district. Magistrates of the court had the authority to swear oaths and to issue licences of all kinds, from tavern licences to licences for church ministers. The court also oversaw the transportation of the district, authorizing both the building and repair of roads and bridges. At the same time, the court dealt with matters of criminal administration, from holding trials to overseeing the district jail, and with a range of what we might call social welfare issues.

A complete set of draft minutes from the Niagara court of quarter sessions allows us see how the court functioned when it was in session. These minutes of the spring session, 1838, demonstrate that the magistrates made no effort to separate their criminal and administrative duties,[14] which were jumbled together as the business arose. The court met in this session for four days. On the first day, after the grand jury had been sworn in, the first items of business were to grant a marriage licence to a minister and to administer an oath of allegiance. Six magistrates were then appointed as a committee of accounts to review the expenditures of the district. The court subsequently dealt with several petitions for public support of those defined as insane, first referring them to the grand jury and then authorizing payment of the funds recommended. After approving several licences for individuals wanting to operate taverns and appointing a street surveyor for the town of Niagara, the court turned to a case of larceny, referring the complaint first to the grand jury and, following an indictment, proceeding to trial. Over this four-day period the Niagara court dealt with eight criminal cases: six charges of larceny, one of assault, and one of riot. On each day other business was also fitted in, from monitoring the state of the jail and discharging a prisoner to granting licences, authorizing the payment of salaries, and discharging recognizances. The court also set the assessment rate for the district. Just as in England, where the administrative and judicial functions of the quarter sessions 'were so intermingled' that commentators found it impossible to disentangle them, the Niagara magistrates' primary concern was to despatch the business confronting the court, regardless of whether it was administrative or judicial.[15]

NIAGARA MAGISTRATES

The Webbs, in their monumental study of local government in England, labelled the justices of the peace 'the Rulers of the County.'

James Aitchison adapted the idea in his doctoral thesis on local government in Upper Canada, describing the Upper Canadian magistrates as 'the Rulers of the District.'[16] The district magistrates were the real rulers because, as non-elected officials, they constituted the court of quarter sessions, the local government of the district as well as the primary court of the criminal justice system. Often neglected or ignored in studies of the colonial period, they deserve to be better known. How were they appointed, and did they carry out their tasks effectively? Examining the magistrates of the Niagara district allows us to determine the identity of these local rulers and to see how they combined their judicial and administrative functions. These men were at once accountable to the representative of the Crown who had appointed them and deeply imbedded in their local communities, creating a tension which often manifested itself as they carried out their myriad tasks.

Magistrates were not required to be lawyers and in this early period of Upper Canadian history most were not. They were appointed on the basis of character and standing in the local community. From the earliest period this usually equated to possession of substantial property. The Act of 1842 setting out the qualifications for justices of the peace stated that they 'shall be of the most sufficient persons' in the district[17] and specified a property qualification of £300. In each district and community magistrates constituted a local elite, or local oligarchy, who were willing and, in some cases, eager to use their status and their powers as magistrates to enhance their positions, wealth, and influence. H.V. Nelles labelled the Niagara magistrates as 'a tightly knit oligarchy that supplied the community with religious, social, economic and political leadership.'[18] The localities in which they exercised their power and influence were sufficiently isolated in the colonial period that the magistrates were often unchallenged in their local domination.

These local oligarchs were also associated with each other in the judicial, political, economic, social, and military spheres, forming an interconnecting nexus of influence. Family connections strengthened links among the magistrates. Frances Ann Thompson found that fifty-three out of ninety-six magistrates commissioned in Niagara between 1828 and 1840 were connected by marriage or family.[19] Many of the key magistrates were appointed in the 1790s or early nineteenth century and held office for many years. Longevity in office added to their influence and power. It also provided a continuity of legal interpretation at the local level through periods of war, economic distress, and rebellion.

Bruce Wilson identifies the Niagara district as a place where 'trade, government and social regulation became inextricably intertwined.'[20] Robert Hamilton had established this pattern, creating a network of family connections. A number of relatives he helped to emigrate from Scotland were given junior positions in his rapidly expanding commercial empire, and as they gained wealth and prominence in their own right Hamilton then helped them to become magistrates. As J.K. Johnson notes, the position of magistrate served for many as 'a building block to which other or greater responsibilities could be added ...'[21] In Niagara, men who were magistrates or otherwise part of the district's legal establishment dominated the elected positions in the Legislature. In the latter half of the 1830s, with one exception, all of Niagara's elected representatives were either magistrates, clerks of the peace, or coroners.[22] The magistrates were equally busy as pluralists seeking other public offices. When Bartholomew Tench applied to be the collector of customs at Port Colborne in 1843, a notation on his application described him as 'a general applicant for office.'[23] The same description applied to many of his fellow magistrates.

Magistrates were appointed to all communities in each district, regardless of size, and in theory every inhabitant of the colony should have had reasonable access to a local magistrate. In a number of districts of Upper Canada, this was often not the case. James Aitchison describes the shortage of qualified magistrates across the colony as 'chronic, widespread and appalling.'[24] Niagara was better served than most of Upper Canada, but in the early years even Niagara had trouble finding enough qualified men. Robert Hamilton complained in 1799 of the difficulty he had even in finding men to recommend as magistrates: 'I have recommended as additional magistrates those only whose situation, character and abilities promise service to the public – I have to lament that such characters are but rare in this new country and it is also very unfortunate that the greatest part of the respectable members of our society are confined as yet to the town of Niagara in a corner of the country.'[25] Over time, as the population grew, it became easier to find magistrates throughout the district, but even in the 1840s complaints were made to the government about the lack of magistrates. Some complaints were politically inspired, such as the charge by an MPP, David Thompson, in 1845 that four townships in Haldimand lacked magistrates. 'The consequences are lamentable.

Crime stalks about at noon day ... A few days since in order to obtain a warrant for a felon I had to travel 42 miles. Why should this be so?'[26]

Other difficulties also emerged. By 1833, as described above, only a small fraction of the 117 men listed on the commission of the peace for the Niagara district were active as magistrates.[27] One of the duties of magistrates was to sit as associate justices at the assize courts. In 1838, when the assize court faced a large criminal docket because of the Rebellion, the provincial attorney general had to request additional magistrates for Niagara: 'all the Gentlemen who are named as associates for the Niagara District are either dead, sick or absent without leave.'[28] The prestige of being named a magistrate did not translate in every case into a willingness to fulfil the duties of the office, and the lists rapidly became out of date.

After the Mackenzie Rebellion, the colonial government realized that the Niagara district needed more magistrates. Of those appointed in 1833, 30 per cent had moved out of the district or out of the colony by 1842.[29] Magistrates proved to be just as mobile as other segments of the colonial population. What is particularly interesting is that the system of appointing magistrates had not changed from the earliest days of the colony. The government still sought nominations of respectable and prominent individuals from leading figures in the district. Earlier in the decade, a nod from Chief Justice Robinson had been the quickest way to acquire an appointment. His disapproval was also the surest way to halt a recommendation. By the end of the 1830s, prominent local politicians who were long-serving magistrates themselves had taken over Robinson's role. The key person in the Niagara district was William Hamilton Merritt. Merritt exercised considerable behind-the-scenes influence both in 1838 and in the following decade in forwarding the names of suitable individuals from Niagara to the government.[30] He was also active in opposing nominations of his political opponents and men he felt were unsuitable for other reasons.[31] Merritt detailed the principles on which he based his nominations in 1845: 'having never heard the slightest complaint against the Magistracy of this District as now composed, I would not recommend leaving out any person who has qualified.'[32] This, in fact, had always been the custom. A magistrate whose conduct had raised questions might find himself removed from the next commission of the peace, but in Niagara this was a very rare occurrence.

Following the Act of Union in 1840, the government moved to appoint professional lawyers as district judges to oversee the magistrates. The district court judge, who had to be a trained lawyer, was to serve as chairman of the court of quarter sessions, ensuring continuity and greater professionalism in that court.[33] Previously, chairmen had been chosen annually from among the magistrates present for the sessions, and in Niagara none had possessed formal legal training. The difference in how the court functioned soon became apparent. The district judge, E.C. Campbell, appointed in 1841, had no hesitation in applying the law, especially in appeals from decisions of magistrates who had no legal training. In 1844 a conviction was upheld on appeal, but Campbell wrote that the magistrate's conviction 'was bad in substance. He awards all the money to be paid to himself.'[34] The legally trained district judge could now assert his authority over lay magistrates.

Until the Union of 1840, and even after it, character and social standing in the district had been key criteria in the appointments to the magistracy across Upper Canada. Thus when the lieutenant governor canvassed individuals for their recommendations in 1829, a prominent local magistrate and figure from the Ottawa Valley, Alexander McDonnell, replied that those recommended should be 'all men of education, sound judgement and established character.' The judge from the Western district, L. Mitchell, echoed these sentiments. 'Good principles and character I hold to be indispensable and a certain degree of good sense and education is desirable.' A prospective applicant from Hawkesbury testified to a belief that the magistracy had to be socially respectable: 'let the British Bench be kept clear of paupers and Innkeepers.'[35] John Clark, one of the elected members of the Legislature from Niagara, submitting his list of recommendations to the lieutenant governor in 1833, similarly stressed that all of them were 'respectable and Loyal men.'[36] Chief Justice Robinson maintained the same principles, telling a grand jury in the Western district in 1836 that 'very considerable influence attaches itself to those who possess the advantages of education, and of superior natural intelligence, and of wealth, and of respectable stations in society ...'[37] John Ball wrote to William Hamilton Merritt in 1842 on behalf of William Servos, '... from his standing in society, I think he is entitled to have his name in the commission and leave it to himself to act or not.'[38] Grand jury service was occasionally alluded to in recommendations for magistrates. The Niagara clerk of the peace wrote on behalf of Lachlan Bell, a Niagara merchant, in 1846, 'he is a man of business habits and when on the Grand Jury has invariably been selected as Foreman.'[39] Equally strong negative recommendations came forward. Thomas Hixson complained to Merritt in 1842 that while he had 'nothing against Mr. Paterson – he is a good man, a man that Confidence can be placed in,' the other rumoured appointee for his village of Clinton, Mr McLean, 'is a Scotchman of the most selfish notions and will not suit the people. I am confident however if it is so we must put up with it, knowing he is an old man and [we] won't be troubled with him long.'[40] This fatalism reflected the reality that from the 1820s only death removed a sitting magistrate. Lieutenant Governor Maitland had removed some magistrates from the Niagara list shortly after he arrived in Upper Canada for supporting Robert Gourlay, but from 1828 to the end of the colonial period no Niagara magistrate was removed from his office.[41]

That respectability was an indispensable criterion for appointment to the magistracy is illustrated by the lobbying over the possibility of more appointments in the Grantham area of Niagara in 1830–1. George IV had recently died and rumours of a new commission of the peace were flying around the Niagara district. The existing magistrates in the area took it upon themselves to recommend candidates for new appointments who were also relatives and friends. The recommendation, however, described them solely as 'fit, discreet and Loyal persons.'[42] What was crucial was who recommended them. In forwarding these recommendations to the lieutenant governor, Chief Justice Robinson added his own endorsement: 'I believe the persons recommended are respectable men – the Gentlemen who sign the letter are already known to your Excellency.'[43] Here again the practice was not dissimilar to that found in England, where, according to Norma Landau, 'from at least the fourteenth century, justices had symbolized the influence of interest.'[44]

This attempt in Niagara to consolidate the local power of the Adams and Merritt families through the appointment of sons and sons-in-law did not go unnoticed. Inhabitants of the district asked the lieutenant governor to appoint 'other Gentlemen ... fully equal if not more capable' of being magistrates who were not related to those already entrenched.[45] The serving magistrates wielded the greater influence, however, because they were known by the government to be respectable. Local cries against more nepotism went unheeded. Democracy played no part in the appointment of magistrates in the Niagara district.

The first lieutenant governor of Upper Canada, John Graves Simcoe, believed that one of the main causes of the American Revolution had been the absence of an American aristocracy to balance rapidly emerging democratic tendencies. He was determined to avoid this situation in Upper Canada. Magistrates were to be an essential element of this new, hierarchical society. They were to constitute local elites and wield economic and social influence as well as legal authority. Their power and local prestige, Simcoe believed, would help to cement loyalty to the British connection among the population at large. The magistrates of the Niagara district lived up to Simcoe's hopes in the wealth they amassed, the control they exercised over their local areas, and their loyalty to the British Crown.

Simcoe encouraged the earliest appointments to become significant landholders. The most prominent local figure, Robert Hamilton, exercised control over 130,000 acres of land throughout the colony during his lifetime, using a variety of means. His business partners, the Dickson family, did not equal him in amassing land, but, like Hamilton, these Scottish entrepreneurs regularly acquired land as payment for debt and in land sales, as did other noteworthy Niagara merchant families and magistrates like Samuel Street Sr and Jr, the Clarkes, and the Balls. Even the Nelles family, which supplied more Niagara magistrates than any other district family, and which generally dominated affairs in Grimsby, had accumulated over 4,000 acres of land prior to the War of 1812. The long-serving Anglican priest at Niagara, Robert Addison, became one of the largest landholders in Upper Canada by the 1820s. Holdings in excess of 31,000 acres provided sufficient wealth to justify his appointment as a magistrate.[46] (Land speculation went hand in hand with the magistracy from the earliest days of the colony.) In England, clergy were appointed in increasing numbers as justices of the peace in the late eighteenth and nineteenth centuries.[47] In Niagara, however, appointments of clergy like Addison to the magistracy were the exception rather than the rule.

Despite occasional complaints, nepotism was taken for granted throughout the Niagara district, especially by those already holding magistrates' positions. The Nelles family of Grimsby were tireless in their efforts to procure appointments for fellow family members and friends. In 1828 Warner Nelles tried to have his son appointed a coroner, arguing that Warner Jr had been trained for the job because his father allowed him to write the reports for the inquests he had presided over. A year later he recommended his son as a second magistrate for the local area. This time the geography of the region was the justification. Warner Sr had been unable to attend a court at the mouth of the Grand River because of high water caused by the dam. Appointing his son would alleviate this inconvenience. Two years later Abraham Nelles wrote to Chief Justice Robinson recommending his son, his nephew, and the son of a longstanding friend as good candidates for magistrates' appointments. He hoped that Robinson would pass these names on to the lieutenant governor with a favourable word.[48] By 1833, no less than five members of the Nelles family were listed on the commission of the peace for Niagara.

As servants of the Crown, the loyalty of the magistrates to Britain was assumed. Twenty-six of the magistrates of Niagara had fought as officers to preserve Upper Canada from the United States during the War of 1812, and some had fled the United States earlier as United Empire Loyalists.[49] In spite of their background, the magistrates of Niagara believed it was necessary in 1819 to reaffirm their loyalty publicly and collectively. The magistrates were convinced that some public demonstration of their loyalty was required to refute any rumours about collaboration with the suspected radical Robert Gourlay, and to protect their positions. The tone of the address to the newly appointed lieutenant governor in January 1819, which was signed by fifty-five magistrates and other leading figures in the district, reflected the urgency of the situation. As the magistrates described it, 'This Loyal District has been calumniated from the wicked and insidious diffusion of the writing of a very few discontented, virulent and malignant characters,' leaving the false impression that Niagara was a hotbed of 'folly and the focus of Sedition and Disloyalty.' Instead, the magistrates assured Maitland, the district's inhabitants were marked by their 'gratitude, loyalty and peaceable demeanour.'

A grand jury address forwarded at the same time reiterated the loyal attachment of Niagara people to their monarch and constitution, 'which we consider quite sufficient to protect our Persons and Property against the hand of Power or the Machinations of Designing Individuals ...'[50] No one could accuse the Niagara elite of backwardness or hesitation in their expressions of devotion to Britain or its constitution. If anything, Niagara magistrates in the 1820s and 1830s displayed excessive zeal in defending the British constitution against perceived enemies. Some had no hesitation in being as partisan as their opponents. William Lyon Mackenzie, the perpetual thorn in the side of the government, complained to the lieutenant governor in 1829 that Niagara magistrate John Crooks, who was also the proprietor of the *Niagara Herald*, and thus a journalistic competitor of Mackenzie, had called him a traitor. Crooks's position as a magistrate, Mackenzie claimed, gave additional authority to his accusation: the allegation was 'without a shadow of truth, altho' stated *on the authority of a British Magistrate.'* Mackenzie reiterated that it was 'the station he bears as a British Magistrate' that gave credibility to Crooks's political charges and demanded a public retraction.[51] This did not happen, but Mackenzie's view of the political power and sway of local magistrates in the Niagara district was widely shared.

Even petty disputes such as one over a road survey in Niagara revealed the expectations of proper conduct for magistrates held by the larger community. They were expected to uphold the 'honor and prosperity of the Government whose Servants they are,' and they were not to advance 'the interests of themselves or their friends or the gratification of party feelings.' The same petition from aggrieved Niagara freeholders to the lieutenant governor employed the overblown rhetoric of the age: 'nothing tends more to wean the affections of a people from its Government or produce contempt, than when they find that those appointed by it to administer the laws, either from ignorance of those laws or from a want of impartiality, convert the courts of Justice into hotbeds of oppression, rendering that stream which should be pure and undefiled into a muddy sink of ignorance or injustice and which instead of being a Government Glory is its disgrace and ultimately its ruin.'[52] In Niagara, the pure stream of justice appeared to have been defiled by partiality on a number of occasions.

Because magistrates could neither separate their judicial roles from their municipal ones nor disregard their obvious personal interest in the outcomes of many of these issues, their decisions were often controversial. Road survey decisions in Niagara were also the subject of a press campaign against the Niagara magistrates, who had allegedly overridden the decisions of three juries and an order issued by the Court of King's Bench. Such arbitrary action was 'diametrically opposite to that most glorious principle of our unexampled constitution – that our Judges should administer Justice without fear, favour or *affection.'*[53] This colonial mixture of law, municipal government, and personal interest seemed to produce incessant and open conflict, if the Niagara experience is any guide.

Competing perceptions of loyalty to the Crown could also surface as political issues when magistrates were attacked for their private land dealings. Edward Evans served as a Niagara magistrate in the townships of Rainham and Walpole from 1821. Ten years later, when some of his opponents petitioned the lieutenant governor seeking his removal, 126 of his supporters countered with a petition of their own, citing Evans's military service and the fact that he had carried out his duties 'justly and strictly to our satisfaction.' The key argument made in Evans's defence, however, was that a number of his opponents were 'disaffected inhabitants and Deserters from the United States forces.'[54] Evans made the same point in his own petition to the governor. He argued that the townships of Rainham and Walpole 'were as disaffected as any other part' during the War of 1812. Acknowledging that he had purchased a large amount of property that had been confiscated, Evans defended himself against charges of extortion and exacting illegal fees by branding his accusers as relatives of the runaways and traitors. Evans categorized himself as an independent 'Gentleman Farmer' who functioned as an 'Impartial Magistrate and a true British Subject.'[55] In other words, the lieutenant governor should pay no attention to complaints about land transactions made by American immigrants against a magistrate who symbolized the British connection, stood for social order, and was captain of the local militia. Character, apparent local satisfaction with their magistrate, and the unwillingness of the lieutenant governor to overturn the actions of one of his appointed magistrates carried the day.

The traditions of the Niagara magistracy were laid down by the merchants who gained ascendancy during the 1780s. Merchants received a surprisingly large number of the early appointments, beating the Loyalist officers who might naturally have expected to garner these prestigious signs of government favour.[56] As Bruce Wilson has shown, these early merchant magistrates had self-interested reasons to maintain British justice and ensure social order. Their frontier society had undergone revolutionary war and there was a new settlement of Iroquois on the Grand River, close to the mercantile networks that provided these traders' main source of wealth. Fears of potential disorder made the merchants early and ardent converts to the need to maintain order, and the appointment of four merchants among the first eleven magistrates named gave them a unique opportunity to shape British justice in Niagara in ways which advanced their own interests.[57] A commitment to social order did not diminish over time. When political agitation seemed to threaten the stability of the colony early in the nineteenth century, Robert Hamilton warned that it could 'break the Bonds of respect from the People to the Magistrates.' This in turn would precipitate 'an end to all order and all well being.'[58]

As the men commissioned to maintain law and order in the Niagara district and to oversee local government, the Niagara magistrates were called upon by the lieutenant governor to assume a variety of special functions. In times of war, emergency, or feared rebellion, the government came to rely on the magistrates. During the War of 1812, eight Niagara magistrates were appointed in February 1812 to serve as commissioners to implement an Act against seditious conduct. In November 1812, during a truce, any two Niagara magistrates could constitute a board appointed to examine anyone claiming exemption from military service as U.S. citizens. They had the authority to permit Americans to cross the border in order to avoid service on the British side, although this authority only lasted until hostilities resumed in December.[59] Abraham Nelles and William Crooks received a government commission to examine treasonous activity in the Niagara district in 1817.[60] In 1838, when rebellion and possible invasion again threatened the Niagara region, the magistrates were called upon to act once more. Daniel McDougal, a town of Niagara magistrate, expressed confidence in a letter to William Hamilton Merritt that in such an emergency 'our magistracy will stand as fair as any others in the province.'[61]

Not all emergencies related to war or rebellion. One threat, which initially appeared to the government to be very serious indeed, was the appearance of cholera throughout the colony in 1832. The magistrates in each district were ordered to act promptly to create boards of health to oversee strict quarantine conditions and any medical care that might be required. The urgency was underlined in a special letter from the clerk of the peace to the magistrates requesting them 'to be punctual in their attendance' at a special session of the court of quarter sessions to discuss the crisis. The clerk added a personal plea in a note asking Alexander Hamilton to come to Niagara for the meeting.[62] Twelve magistrates, including Hamilton, met in a special sessions on 25 June 1832 and decided to create a general board of health in the town of Niagara plus branch boards at a number of places in the district. The minutes of their meeting were printed for the information of all inhabitants of the district.[63] Magistrates were placed on all the boards in order to direct the local battle against cholera.

The worst hit part of the Niagara district was the Welland Canal region, where poverty added to the misery of cholera. By the middle of July, James Clarke, who was in charge of the branch health board in St Catharines, appealed for funds to help preserve 'the lives of many hundreds of paupers' being cared for by the health board.[64] There was near panic among the canal workers and fear on the part of the local magistrates that the canal work might have to be abandoned. By July there were an estimated 100 cases of the disease along the canal, and twenty people died. When the crisis overran the capacity of the local board, 'the sick all flocked to St. Catharines.' James Clarke visited the sick in St Catharines and found 'such a scene of human misery as is beyond description.' He had nothing but praise for the magistrate and fellow member of the Board of Health, Bartholomew Tench, who had come from the canal and 'not only administered medicine to the sick, but assisted me in raising money for their support.' These local magistrates were reduced to raising money privately to dispense charity and medicine. Another magistrate on the canal reported early in August that he had found '40 sick and destitute of any means except that furnished by the cold hand of charity.'[65]

Fortunately for the district as well as for the colony as a whole, the cholera epidemic did not strike with full force and was largely over by the end of the summer. A Niagara grand jury at the fall quarter sessions placed its own moral interpretation on the pattern of infection. 'Its attacks have in most instances been confined to the intemperate and dissolute,' and affected taverns and 'the idle and vicious' who inhabited them.[66] Local magistrates in the hardest hit communities, however, did their best to care for the sick and to provide much-needed relief with totally inadequate resources. Their reports do not convey the feelings of moral superiority expressed in the grand jury presentment.

The magistrates of Upper Canada were enjoined by their oath of office to do 'equal right to the poor and to the rich, after your cunning, wit and power, and after the laws and customs of the province of Upper Canada, and statutes thereof made.'[67] Within the colonial criminal justice system, the magistrates were not only to try offences that came before them but also to conduct the preliminary stages of criminal proceedings. They could act alone or in pairs and collectively as the court of quarter sessions. Contemporary documents make clear that the magistrates played other roles as well. In the absence of local coroners they were called upon to officiate at coroners' inquests. These could prove long and unpleasant. James Cummings related how at an inquest in Chippewa in the summer of 1840, 'the body was in such a state of decomposition, I could scarcely get a person to touch it and it was 11 o'clock at night before we got it into the coffin.' He and the coffin maker had to perform this grisly task themselves and it took them until early morning to complete it.[68] Dr James Muirhead, who originally came out to Upper Canada as an army surgeon and son-in-law to Colonel Butler of Butler's Rangers, which entitled him to substantial land grants in the 1790s, was chairman of Niagara's court of quarter sessions in 1832. He tried criminals, sentenced them to jail, ministered to their medical needs, and when one, Isaac Ducket, died in jail, he performed the autopsy. His involvement in the life cycle of Niagara crime was complete.[69] Although personally arresting suspects did not form part of a magistrate's duties, arrests could give rise to proud boasts. One unnamed Niagara magistrate entertained Anna Jameson with 'a fearful description' of how 'on a dark, stormy night in the preceding winter, he had surprised and arrested a gang of forgers and coiners.'[70]

Magistrates had considerable leeway in how they enforced the law. In the small communities they presided over, many cases, especially minor ones, were resolved through the magistrate's mediation. We do not have evidence of exactly how many times this occurred, but several cases from the files of Alexander Hamilton's tenure as a magistrate in Queenston (1818–33) carry the concluding remark, 'compromised,' meaning that the parties had settled their differences out of court or with the magistrate's assistance. Some include formal arbitration bonds or legal documents setting out the settlement. Occasionally, this mediation occurred after the trial had begun, as in the case of the King vs Edward Walker at the fall quarter sessions in Niagara, 1829. After the testimony of all the witnesses had been heard, the prosecutor requested that the charges be dropped. 'It has been thought better to do so, as being most for the benefit of the community at large and all others concerned.'[71] A sense of what was best for the community was obviously a factor here and in other cases throughout the district. From the approval given by the magistrates it is quite likely that they took the initiative in reaching this solution, believing, as they did, that they knew what was best for the community.

Another 'compromised' case from the fall quarter sessions in 1829 again suggests that the magistrates together, or Alexander Hamilton acting on his own, had intervened after hearing the details. This was a case of assault and battery. A fifteen-year-old youth, Dwight Coft, had passed the house of Luther Dunn, a cabinet maker. Dunn asked Coft where he was going and the youth replied that it was none of Dunn's business. Dunn then said, 'if you answer me that way again, I will kick your damned arse.' Coft repeated it was none of Dunn's business, whereupon the cabinet maker punched him, knocked him down, and then kicked and cuffed him. Dunn acknowledged the assault and paid Coft fifteen shillings and costs. Coft then dropped the prosecution with the approval of one or more of the magistrates.[72]

Similar resolutions were reached even when the assault had been a severe one. Thomas Foster, a labourer on the Welland Canal, had pursued Robert Buchanan early in June 1831, bitten 'a large piece' out of Buchanan's left cheek, and broken his shoulder in two places. The case was quickly dealt with following the advice of the local magistrate, David Thompson, who wrote to the clerk of the peace that the two had since 'made friends' and wanted the papers withdrawn. Thompson's recommendation was based on the fact that before this incident both parties were considered to be 'honest and decent men.'[73] Thompson's intervention effectively halted the trial and allowed the case to be settled quickly. Foster pleaded guilty and received a token fine of one shilling plus court costs.

Another example of the leeway magistrates exercised in enforcing the law comes from a private complaint in the case of a debt owed to a Niagara magistrate in 1830. The complaint was referred to the chairman of the court of quarter sessions, Dr James Muirhead. When Muirhead investigated he found that a cow belonging to the plaintiff was about to be sold to pay the debt. Muirhead reported that, 'from motives of humanity,' the sale had been delayed 'that the poor man might have time to raise the money, as the milk was essential to his children.'[74] With the help of friends, the plaintiff raised the money to pay the debt.

When questions arose as to how much discretion was available to the local magistrates, the attorney general, Henry Boulton, replied in 1830 'that Magistrates may exercise their discretion in allowing persons to compromise trifling misdemeanours where the interests of the public do not require an example to be made.' He continued, by 'discouraging the prosecution of petty offences not affecting the public, I conceive they will best discharge their duty and serve the public interests.'[75] Niagara magistrates exercised discretion in a wide variety of petty offences, settling them in order to stay formal prosecutions.

Installed to uphold the King's peace and to conduct all aspects of local government through the courts of quarter sessions, magistrates served a variety of important roles. While servants of the Crown and accountable to the lieutenant governor, they exercised considerable autonomy in carrying out their tasks. In the process of conducting official business, moreover, most Niagara magistrates advanced their own economic interests successfully. Not everyone, however, succeeded in improving his reputation or his financial prospects through the magistracy. One disgruntled ex-magistrate informed the lieutenant governor that he had 'incurred the hatred of all opposed to the due administration of the Laws, a serious injury to professional prospects and a positive loss of property and money.'[76]

Whatever their opponents may have thought or said, the Niagara magistrates were not passive agents, blindly implementing a government agenda. They were fully capable of representing their own or their community's interests when it was in their interest to do so. Their local power, however, derived in large part from their distance from the colony's capital, which enabled them to act with a great deal of independence. Officials in the colonial government, from the lieutenant governor down, followed a practice of not interfering with decisions of the local magistracy even when petitioned to do so. At the same time, the actions of the Niagara magistrates repeatedly demonstrated sensitivity to the needs of the colonial government. They were prepared to act quickly in its support when the government called on their services, especially in times of emergency.

NIAGARA SHERIFFS

The office of sheriff was a lucrative prize, eagerly sought after in the early colonial period of Upper Canada. Each district of the colony had only one sheriff, although deputies could be appointed to assist the sheriff to carry out his various functions. Where in nineteenth-century England sheriffs were appointed for periods of a year, sheriffs in Upper Canada were appointed at the pleasure of the Crown. Longevity of tenure helped to make the sheriff in Upper Canada a much more important figure than his English counterpart. In England the office of sheriff had declined in both power and social prestige since the Middle Ages.[77] Even as late as 1836, the Legislative Council of Upper Canada argued that because sheriffs were appointed for life in Upper Canada they were more 'responsible' than English sheriffs. The sheriff in Upper Canada was 'more amenable to public opinion and censure, and has stronger reasons for acting correctly.'[78]

In Upper Canada, as he had been in the thirteen colonies, the sheriff 'was a familiar figure.'[79] Sheriffs played a key political role in Upper

Canada, although it was a different one than that played by American counterparts. The political importance of the sheriff was clearly understood by the lieutenant governor and his officials in the colony's capital, York (later Toronto). The lieutenant governors of Upper Canada jealously guarded their right to appoint their own sheriffs. We must be careful not to accept all the implications of William Lyon Mackenzie's criticisms of the sheriffs as 'mere dependents on the Government,' holding offices that were 'mere sinecures.'[80]

As a powerful local servant of the Crown, responsible for the maintenance of law and order in his district, the sheriff had to be utterly loyal to established authority and willing to act, even in unorthodox ways, during times of crisis. Far from being politically impartial, sheriffs could and did act to ensure that other local officials remained true to the government's position. In ordinary cases where political considerations did not come into play, which made up the bulk of legal business, sheriffs may well have demonstrated considerable political impartiality. Nevertheless, a sheriff who failed to prove his own loyalty to the satisfaction of the lieutenant governor could find himself abruptly dismissed from office. In Niagara partisanship was a necessary requirement for the successful aspirant to the office of sheriff, and the most successful incumbents continued to be just as partisan after obtaining the office.

The income earned by sheriffs derived mainly from the fees they charged. In the large Home district, Sheriff Jarvis could expect over £500 pounds sterling annually, and possibly double that or more. In 1833 the sheriff of the Newcastle district earned nearly £1,200 in fee revenue.[81] The lucrative fees which made the sheriff's office so desirable to colonials in search of secure, well-paying government positions might not be apparent from the brief description of their jobs provided by J.K. Johnson: 'They sold land for non-payment of taxes, made arrests, kept the jails and conducted hangings as required.'[82] Sheriffs were also given the responsibility for summoning jurors, administering writs of the courts, and executing sentences passed, including capital ones. The Niagara sheriff could count on a revenue comparable to those of his counterparts in the other districts of Upper Canada. His annual salary was a deceptively low £50, but he also collected a large fee revenue from sales of land for unpaid taxes or debt.[83]

Four men served as sheriffs of the Niagara district in the period 1800–39, illustrating the continuity in office of these key servants of the Crown. The first sheriff was appointed in 1800 when the district was officially created. Prior to that date, the sheriff of the Home district had appointed a deputy, Thomas Page, to look after the Niagara region. James Clark, a barracks master, held office for only three years, giving way to Thomas Merritt in 1803. Merritt had served with Simcoe's Queen's Rangers during the American War of Revolution and then migrated to Upper Canada as a United Empire Loyalist. Better known in Canadian history as the father of William Hamilton Merritt, he received land as his reward for serving with Simcoe and settled at Twelve Mile Creek (later St Catharines) in 1794. He fought in the War of 1812 and was taken prisoner. Merritt was a pallbearer at the funeral of Sir Isaac Brock. In his capacity as sheriff, he had to oversee the executions of the traitors ordered by the 'Bloody Assize' in July 1813. This brief biography underlines that he possessed impeccable credentials to hold public office and makes the events of 1820 even more remarkable. For what was most notable about Merritt's long tenure as sheriff was his abrupt dismissal in 1820 for allegedly aiding the Scottish radical, Robert Gourlay, during the latter's sojourn in the Niagara jail.[84] Merritt's dismissal drove home the message that there was no room in Upper Canada for sheriffs who assisted radicals in their political designs. Sheriffs had to be solidly on the side of the British colonial government, maintaining order and avoiding any action that might undermine the established social and political structure of the colony.

There is some evidence, however, that Merritt's dismissal in 1820 had its roots in the circumstances of his original appointment and the anger of an embittered rival. Thomas Otway Page, the original undersheriff for the Niagara region, was forced to resign when Merritt received the sheriff's position in 1803. Seventeen years later he had neither forgotten the circumstances nor forgiven Merritt. It was Page who informed the lieutenant governor that Merritt had permitted Gourlay to publish seditious articles from the Niagara jail, when as sheriff he should have prevented this. Although Page promised to produce written testimony to prove his charges, he was unable to persuade anyone to testify against Merritt. He attributed this reluctance to Merritt's local influence. Page told the lieutenant governor's secretary that 'it was by intrigue that Merritt got the Sheriff's Office. His friends got it for him under false pretences after they knew that I had the promise of the office.'[85]

Lieutenant Governor Maitland had arrived in Upper Canada in 1818 and immediately suspected that the radical Gourlay was pushing the colony towards revolution. Having come from England, where the threat of radicalism in the aftermath of the Napoleonic Wars had the establishment thoroughly frightened, Maitland was especially sensitive to a possible recurrence in Upper Canada. He described Gourlay in a despatch as 'half Cobbett and half Hunt,' a reference to the two leading British radicals of the time. Their influence in England was obviously in his mind, even if the apparent connection between English radicalism and a revolutionary plot in Upper Canada was imaginary.[86] Maitland undoubtedly wanted to prevent a colonial repetition of the mass riot at Spa Field in London in December 1816, or the much worse Peterloo massacre of August 1819. The danger seemed greatest in the Niagara area. Although Merritt was described by the lieutenant governor as 'an old Servant of the Crown,' his conduct towards the imprisoned Gourlay, according to Maitland, 'was so notoriously improper as to be the subject of general remark and Public discussion.' What Merritt was alleged to have done was to permit Gourlay to publish his attacks on the government, in one case reading 'the libel in Manuscript in the Gaol' and then delivering it himself to the printer. This was so far from what the lieutenant governor considered the proper 'support to the Constitution' owed by a servant of the Crown that he quickly dismissed the sheriff as part of his drastic action to prevent potential revolution.[87] Maitland did not mention how he had received his information about Merritt in his despatch to the colonial secretary explaining why he had dismissed the Niagara sheriff, but the British government was unlikely to question the action of a newly appointed lieutenant governor, especially one who could claim to have suppressed an incipient rebellion.

The sheriff had to be as much a political agent of the government as a legal one. Merritt's successor as sheriff of Niagara, Richard Leonard, soon demonstrated that his political skills were more in tune with the thinking of the new lieutenant governor. After earlier war service against Napoleon in the siege of Alexandria, Leonard had fought in the battles of Sackett's Harbour, Lundy's Lane, and the assault on Fort Erie during the War of 1812. Following the war, he settled at Lundy's Lane and was appointed lieutenant colonel of the 1st Lincoln Militia.[88] Given his background, Leonard must have seemed an ideal choice for sheriff. Maitland could count on Leonard to root out any radicalism remaining in the Niagara peninsula after Gourlay had been deported.

Richard Leonard performed the desired political role with the same zeal that he performed his legal duties. He worked assiduously to cultivate support for the colonial government and to discredit the government's political opponents. He remained in regular communication with the lieutenant governor's secretary, reporting on political currents in the Niagara district. At the end of February 1827, Leonard complained that the Niagara MPPs were making 'the most gross misrepresentations' on the Naturalization Bill, a controversial piece of legislation then before the Legislature. In his view, they were nothing but 'rascals' in league with the government's detested adversary, William Lyon Mackenzie, who were causing great uneasiness 'among the poor simple Inhabitants of the District.'[89] Leonard advocated more government patronage for newspapers that supported the government as an effective way of combatting political opponents. He suggested more business be given to the editor of the *St. Catharines Farmer's Journal*: 'I am sure he will be useful.' Leonard encouraged the lieutenant government's secretary to 'give [the editor] a helping hand by recommending him to your friends,' adding a soothing reassurance early in the spring of 1827, 'that the tranquillity of this part of the country is perfectly restored.'[90] Such was Leonard's political influence that near the end of his term Chief Justice Robinson consulted him about proposed new appointments to the list of magistrates for Niagara. Leonard responded quickly with his own recommendations. Among others, he recommended David Thorburn of Queenston, who 'will, I am convinced, make a useful and zealous Magistrate; a little energy is wanting in that quarter.'[91]

Niagara's sheriff did not hesitate to tell the colony's chief justice that more zealous magistrates were needed in the Niagara district. Nor was Leonard above direct political intimidation of the district's officeholders and magistrates. While walking to church on a Sunday with the postmaster and magistrate at Fort Erie, James Kerby, in late April, 1827, Leonard warned him that he was under suspicion for letting William Mackenzie insert Kerby's name in his paper as his agent. Kerby was so upset that he immediately wrote to the lieutenant governor with a full confession, pleading loyalty and denying any link to Mackenzie or to his politics. 'If, therefore, I have erred in my judgement in this instance, it was not done with a view to cause my friends to alter their opinion of me, As a *true natural born Subject*.'[92]

The sheriff was in charge of the jail and of the prisoners in it, and his duties included arranging the executions of any condemned to death. Few executions occurred at Niagara in times of peace – only one between 1820 and 1836 – so the sheriff was rarely called upon to officiate at actual executions. In 1829, however, Richard Leonard participated in a cruel and elaborate farce designed to intimidate a horse thief and deter horse theft across the Upper Canadian-United States border. The convict, Michael Mason, as Leonard later wrote, 'was led out as he supposed for execution on the day named in his sentence,' but on the sheriff's orders, 'no preparations were made for the occasion,' probably meaning that no executioner had been hired. As was usual for public executions, a large crowd had assembled and a local militia troop was on duty. Leonard described what he had done in a letter to the lieutenant governor, in which he acknowledged that he was aware prior to the execution day that Mason was to be spared but colluded in the farce in order to make the prisoner 'feel as much as possible for the crime he had committed.' Not until the prisoner was brought out for execution did he learn that the lieutenant governor had commuted his sentence.[93]

Leonard's actions may well have reflected local feeling about the crime of horse theft. At the time of Mason's trial the St Catharines paper reprinted a commentary from Niagara on Mason's criminality: 'Horse-stealing is one of the greatest evils that exists in the Province, especially on the frontiers – besides, there was something so daring in the manner in which the theft was committed, and his behaviour afterwards, that it created an impression that it was not the first time he had committed such a crime.'[94] Even after the death sentence had been officially commuted, terror was used to try to frighten Mason out of his criminal ways. Sheriff Leonard was a willing participant in this process.

One other man had been sentenced to death at the Niagara assizes in 1828, Daniel Ellsworth, for the crime of bestiality. The leading magistrates of the district and Sheriff Leonard quickly organized a petition to the lieutenant governor, asking that Ellsworth's life be spared. Although he had committed 'the horrible crime of Bestiality,' Ellsworth had 'a Wife and three young children altogether dependent upon him for sustenance and support.'[95] Community public opinion united behind this petition. With 216 signatures, it was one of the largest petitions in a Niagara criminal case to reach the lieutenant governor in this period. Further petitions on Ellsworth's behalf were forwarded early in 1830 by the local MPP, William Woodruff. Woodruff accounted for the extraordinary public response to Ellsworth's conviction and sentence with the suggestion that a great injustice might have occurred. 'I beg to state the opinion almost universally prevails of his innocence ...'[96] *The Niagara Gleaner* supported clemency on the grounds of his connections: 'We believe that almost every person present at the trial was anxious that he should receive a pardon, chiefly in consequence of the interest excited for his wife and three children, and for the sake of his respectable connexions.'[97] Colborne responded to these humanitarian pleas by commuting Ellsworth's sentence. Sheriff Leonard's role in each of these cases illustrates his personal involvement in the legal duties of his office.

Leonard's successor, Alexander Hamilton, was the son of one of the most powerful figures in the Niagara district. Alexander's father, Robert Hamilton, had risen quickly to become the dominant economic figure of the region. He combined economic status with an equally powerful political base: Robert Hamilton was appointed a magistrate in 1786 and lieutenant of the county in 1796, and he served as a judge of the Court of Common Pleas from 1788 to 1795. Bruce Wilson, in his biography of Robert Hamilton, reveals that 'a series of commercial links, strengthened by family ties, was a major determinant in the distribution of place and power in early Upper Canada.'[98] Robert Hamilton was the centre of these links in his time.

Alexander Hamilton, who held the office of sheriff of the Niagara district from 1833 until his death in 1839, did not succeed in maintaining his father's fortune, but he certainly used his family connections to amass an equally large number of government offices. His biographer claims that 'he systematically applied for major posts in the Niagara district as they became vacant,' demonstrating the same entrepreneurial skills in patronage that his father had exhibited in commerce.[99] Hamilton was named a justice of the peace in 1817; he also served as deputy postmaster and deputy collector of customs, as well as judge of the Surrogate Court at Queenston during the 1820s. His long campaign to obtain the office of sheriff and the fact that he was willing to resign as a magistrate in order to become sheriff might suggest a hierarchy of prestige in these public offices, with the position of sheriff at the top. Alexander Hamilton, however, was probably motivated by his knowledge that the position of sheriff was more lucrative.

Hamilton owed his appointment as sheriff to the patronage of George H. Markland, the inspector-general of Upper Canada, who had the ear of the lieutenant governor, Sir John Colborne. It was Markland who informed Hamilton that Leonard had resigned the position and Markland spoke to Colborne on Hamilton's behalf. The appointment was by no means a foregone conclusion: the previous deputy sheriff,

Kidd, had submitted a petition asking for the position which had been signed 'by almost all the principal persons in the District.' Markland told Hamilton that the lieutenant governor had all but promised the job to him, but the petition and the amount of support Kidd had garnered had 'staggered him; besides some persons who should have been your most strenuous friends have acted otherwise.'[100] Hamilton lost no time in putting his own application before the lieutenant governor. After another long interview with Colborne, Markland was able to report that he had secured the job for Hamilton and persuaded the lieutenant governor to let him keep his other posts as well.[101]

Multiple office holding was too well rooted in the tradition of the Upper Canadian elite to be eliminated in the case of the son of Robert Hamilton. While the sheriff's office was a lucrative prize, Hamilton's financial needs were such that he needed to retain his other offices, especially his jobs as postmaster and customs collector. Considerations of conflict of interest did limit some colonial appointments. For example, no one could be appointed attorney general and judge at the same time, nor could sheriffs serve as magistrates. But no ethical considerations stood in Hamilton's way. His excesses, however, were sufficient to attract criticism from local newspapers.[102]

After obtaining the office Hamilton demonstrated little interest in the day-to-day sheriff's business. He was certainly not prepared to move from his home in Queenston to Niagara to carry out his new duties. This may have been because he was in the midst of constructing an imposing mansion, 'Willow Bank' in Queenston, reputedly 'one of the best examples of colonial architecture left on the continent. For severe and stately magnificence combined nevertheless with an air of generous hospitality and welcome, it would be hard to surpass.'[103] Instead, Hamilton tried to move the sheriff's office to his Queenston house. The attempt aroused the anger of Niagara district inhabitants, who expressed their discontent vigorously in a grand jury presentment sent to the lieutenant governor at the March quarter sessions in 1834. The jurors said that such a move would hurt creditors trying to collect debts and seriously affect the administration of justice. They asked the lieutenant governor to compel the sheriff to carry out his business from the county town.[104]

When the lieutenant governor informed Hamilton that it would not be possible to move the office to Queenston, Hamilton hired a deputy to live in Niagara and carry on the business of the office for him. The man he employed, Alexander McLeod, later attested that he had been given 'the entire control of the Sheriff's office.' According to McLeod, Hamilton never spent 'one hour in the Sheriff's office during the four and a half years that I was his deputy.'[105] McLeod's grievance was that Hamilton continued with his duties as postmaster but also received upwards of £ 400 sterling a year as his share of the revenues from the sheriff's office. If McLeod's later testimony is accurate, the revenues from the sheriff's duties in Niagara made it financially worthwhile for the son of the richest and most powerful man in the district to forsake his magistracy for the sheriff's position. He could afford to hire a deputy to do the work, as long as the lion's share of the revenue went to him. Hamilton was certainly not known for his generosity: a prisoner who wrote to him in 1834, saying that he found himself in jail with 'no shoes nor stockings to wear and no money to by [sic] any,' and requesting Hamilton to let him have 'a pear [sic] if shoes and stockings,' received a curt rejection.[106] Nor did the financial disputes which had characterized Hamilton's life end with his death. His deputy, Alexander McLeod, and Hamilton's estate subsequently engaged in a lengthy legal battle over the fees owing to the sheriff's office.

Although McLeod dismissed Hamilton's interest in the business of the sheriff's office, during the crisis of the 1837 Mackenzie Rebellion Hamilton was very active on the frontier, monitoring possible raids across the border and keeping the government informed about any potential threats from the United States. He also acted as an unofficial diplomat, meeting representatives of American communities across the Niagara river to maintain peace along the troubled border. When he was unable to meet with a deputation from Lewiston at the end of December 1837, he wrote to the man who headed the Town's Committee of Vigilance, agreeing with their determination to suppress any potential insurgent expedition and to protect property on both sides of the river. Hamilton reiterated that the Upper Canadians had no desire to attack their American neighbours. For his part, he was happy to maintain communication with this American group until 'the present excitement shall cease.'[107]

During periods of political tension, the sheriff and the local magistrates became even more indispensable local agents of the colonial government. In the Mackenzie Rebellion period the government took advantage of Sheriff Hamilton's plural office holdings. Because he was also the postmaster of Queenston, Hamilton was secretly ordered by the government in June 1838 to forward all letters 'that are Suspected of containing treasonable Matter, or that are anyway of a Suspicious character.'[108] As both the sheriff and the local postmaster Hamilton functioned as the eyes and ears of the government on the border during this precarious time, when Britain feared that events in Upper Canada might lead to another war with the United States. He was also requested to employ a paid spy to operate on the U.S. side of the frontier and to file reports on any military equipment, the number of boats, and the movements of the suspected rebels. Hamilton gathered intelligence on the movements of suspicious persons and on the activities of secret societies throughout the district at the express command of the lieutenant governor.[109] And when no other executioner could be found, Hamilton himself had to execute one of the prisoners, James Morreau, following the Rebellion of 1837. The lieutenant governor approved of 'the cool and firm manner in which [the execution] was performed.'[110]

The office of sheriff has steadily declined in political importance since the early nineteenth century, but during the colonial period sheriffs were key players in the districts of Upper Canada, ensuring political stability, maintaining law and order, and implementing the political wishes of the lieutenant governor and his chosen government ministers. In a frontier district like Niagara, the sheriff proved to be an indispensable servant of the Crown. But neither the sheriff nor the magistrates acted alone in the administration of the criminal justice system. They turned to local constables to carry out the practicalities of law enforcement and the system itself depended heavily upon juries for findings of fact. The next chapter examines the part played by Niagara juries and constables in the operation of a system of justice that was heavily reliant upon local men.

3

Servants of the Court

The transplantation of the English criminal law system to British North American colonies ensured that the jury trial would play the same central role in colonial justice as it did within England. The second Act passed by the Upper Canadian Legislature in 1792 established trial by jury throughout the new colony and proclaimed jury trials as 'one of the chief benefits to be attained by a free Constitution.'[1] Two years later the Legislature passed another Act to impose fines upon any clerk of the peace who did not turn over to sheriffs a list of men from the assessment roles who were eligible to be called for jury duty and any sheriff who did not impanel jurors for court duty. Those summoned for jury duty could also be fined for not serving. The clerk of the peace in each district prepared each year a list of 'inhabitant householders' for the sheriff, who used it to summon the required number of jurors. Jurors could not be asked to serve two years in succession and they were to be selected from different parts of the various districts.[2]

In the mid-1830s, by which time the system had been in place for almost fifty years, the method of selecting juries became the subject both of debate and considerable political partisanship. The Legislative Council argued that jury selection in Upper Canada had been modelled as closely as possible upon the system found England. No Upper Canadian law governed the selection of grand juries for the assize courts: 'their qualifications, their powers, the mode in which they are summoned, their duties and manner of performing them, are all taken from the law of England. Nor has usage here varied in any one respect from the Law and practice prevailing in the Mother Country.'[3] The sheriff was entrusted with selecting twenty-four men from those 'of the greatest intelligence, most considerable property and established character in his District.' It was expected that most of the grand jurors for the assizes would be magistrates, although 'Merchants and respectable Farmers are also returned.' In transplanting the grand jury to Upper Canada, the British government tried also to import the hierarchical underpinnings of the rural British gentry. Grand jurors for the quarter sessions, however, were chosen from householders on the assessment rolls. The social and economic conditions of the new colony meant that quarter sessions grand jurors represented a broader selection of the colonial population than did their counterparts in England. The key criteria had always been 'the general standing and repute' of those selected, 'which depends upon a combined consideration of their property, character, intelligence and occupation in life.'[4]

The sheriff was also charged with selecting the petit or trial jurors. Anyone listed on an assessment roll as an 'inhabitant householder' qualified for this service, with men over sixty exempt. Here the 1794 Act actually broadened the qualifications for jury duty considerably from what they were in England. By embracing the idea that all 'inhabitant householders' were eligible, Upper Canada extended the right and obligation of jury duty to nearly all adult men with property. The sheriff's role in selecting jurors was indispensable, as far as the colony's elite was concerned, as it ensured that 'men of reputable habits and possessing a reasonable degree of intelligence to direct their judgement' were chosen. If the selection were left to elected township officials, as the reformers of Upper Canada demanded, the Legislative Council foresaw that the colony's jurors would be 'men of grossly immoral and intemperate habits, reprobates in their lives and conversations, notorious gamblers or swindlers ... men of the weakest intellect, and most perverted understandings – open scoffers at religion, men whom no one that respected his own character could think of selecting.' With the sheriffs in charge of selecting jurors, 'we are in the constant habit of seeing honest, intelligent, respectable yeomen, and intelligent and upright merchants and tradesmen impanelled.'

The Legislative Council repeated views that had been aired publicly in Niagara on previous occasions when the Legislature had tried to change the way in which juries were selected. In 1828, in a letter to the *St. Catharines Farmers' Journal*, Dr J.J. Lefferty, a moderate reformer and MPP who would later become a magistrate (1833), defended the selection of jurors by sheriffs, stating that those summoned in Niagara 'were generally men of intelligence and talent, and where talent existed, honesty was generally its accompaniment.'[5] The Legislative Council insisted that no experiment to change the selection of jurors should be contemplated. In 1836 Upper Canada's legislative councillors still viewed the jury as 'the cornerstone of freedom – the best security for order – and the distinguishing boast of Englishmen and their descendants.'[6]

Not until 1850 did a reform government place the responsibility for selecting jurors in the hands of elected township officials. In 1840, however, the lieutenant governor requested that his executive council review the method by which assize grand juries were appointed. Because magistrates dominated the appointments to these juries, many citizens believed that they were excluded 'to prevent them being made acquainted with the intentions of the Government; it is thus supposed to be essential to keep up a degree of Mystery.'[7] To dispel some of these misconceptions the lieutenant governor wanted a wider process of selection, although the sheriffs were still to exercise their power 'with the requisite prudence and discretion.'

Even a hint of impropriety in the selection of jurors could invite public comment. *The Niagara Gleaner* reported a rumour in 1825 that the panel of assize jurors 'is by no means made up from the most intelligent and independent portion of the inhabitants.' Instead, people 'equally remarkable for ignorance and stupidity have been summoned.' In 1825 the population of the district was still small enough for the character of prospective jurors to be known and subject to criticism, something that changed as postwar immigration swelled the population of the Niagara region. *The Gleaner*, however, did not attach blame to the sheriff, Richard Leonard, 'whose character in the District stands very fair.'[8]

Once summoned, jurors on petit juries acted as tryers of fact in trials at both the court of quarter sessions and the assizes, while grand jurors met privately before each court session to hear evidence about the cases coming for trial and to interview witnesses. If the grand jury found that a case should proceed to trial, it returned a true bill. A true bill required twelve of the twenty-four grand jurors summoned to sign the bill of indictment. The petit jury which tried the case was composed of twelve men. Their verdict had to be unanimous. In Niagara, especially in the very early period, many of the jurors knew the prosecutors and defendants and acted as 'Neighbour-Witnesses,' meaning that they worked from a perspective of personal knowledge of the people involved and the context in which the events occurred.[9]

By the end of the colonial period in the United States, juries, especially grand juries, had become 'an indispensable part of the government in each of the American colonies.'[10] Upper Canada too, like other British colonies, incorporated juries into the practice of local government. In the Maritimes the grand jury has been seen as a key component of colonial government while in colonial America juries have been viewed as making a unique contribution to the development of representative government.[11] John Beattie has portrayed the grand jury in eighteenth-century England as 'the one authentic and legitimate voice of county opinion,'[12] while Norma Landau characterizes the pronouncements of grand juries in England, termed presentments, 'as the voice of the county speaking true.' The constitutional role of the grand jury, Landau argues, was rooted both in English law and in later Stuart political thought.[13] The grand jury in Upper Canada, as in other British colonies, derived from the English tradition of the 'Grand Inquest' in which the grand jury voiced the opinion of the district (in England the county) on any matters of public concern, as well as determining whether the charges brought before it should proceed to trial.[14]

Alexis de Tocqueville, writing in the 1830s, perceived that in the United States the jury had raised 'the people itself, or at least a class of citizens to the bench of judicial authority,' and he characterized the jury as 'above all a political institution.'[15] The Quebec Legislative Assembly in 1830 declared similarly that the rights of citizens to serve on juries and to elect their political representatives 'are equal and cannot exist independently of each other.'[16] The same report described the jury as a significant training ground for civic affairs and a vital means for the dissemination of information. No less than in other parts of British North America, the jury, especially the quarter sessions grand jury, was an integral element of local government in the Niagara district, and it could on occasion serve as a political institution even if it was not a centrepiece of democracy. While in England the tradition of grand jury presentments declined in the early nineteenth century, the practice did not begin to fade in Upper Canada until the latter part of the nineteenth century.

Despite the political and legal importance of the jury in Upper Canada, not everyone was willing at all times to serve on juries. Absenteeism had always been something of a problem. Notes on the list of jurors for the court of quarter sessions in October 1828 indicate that sickness, lameness, and age excused five petit jurors and four grand jurors from service.[17] By the late 1830s it was becoming increasingly difficult for the authorities in Niagara to find men willing to serve as jurors, especially as the likelihood of having to try capital cases increased. Those seeking to escape jury duty often exhibited a good knowledge of the law and culture surrounding jury selection. One A. Gordon wrote to the sheriff in June 1838 stating that he had served as a justice of the peace ten years earlier and therefore did not expect to be called to serve on a quarter sessions grand jury. In case that excuse was not sufficient, he also attached a note from his doctor to excuse him on the grounds of haemorrhoids.[18]

In the aftermath of the Rebellion of 1837 the Niagara region experienced an economic downturn and an outflow of population, which made finding willing jurors even more of a challenge. Deputy Sheriff Alexander McLeod wrote to Sheriff Hamilton at the beginning of July 1836, 'in consequence of a number of the Grand and Petit Jurors having sent to this office apparent good excuses for declining to attend as Jurors at the [quarter] Sessions, I am under the necessity of sending a few tickets for you to choose out of the Assessment Roll five respectable Grand Jurors and six Pettit in your vicinity, say Queenston or St. Davids.' Hamilton wrote to his deputy at the end of August, 'there are cases of the most serious Nature on our Calendar for this Assizes. Every pains should be taken to have juries of the most respectable character and intelligence.'[19]

In this note Hamilton had crossed out the word 'class' and substituted the word 'character,' but there was little doubt the two words were almost synonymous in his mind, and equally little doubt that he reflected the beliefs of the province's government and elite as articulated in the Legislative Council report of 1836. The reformers would have found his words to constitute further evidence of their charges of jury packing. In the eyes of the government, however, Sheriff Hamilton was doing his job exactly as desired.

Other evidence suggests that in some cases even greater effort was made to ensure that appropriate jurors were selected for certain cases. In one instance in 1834, the attorney general's office consulted William Hamilton Merritt about the selection of a special jury in a civil case involving two other magistrates of the Niagara district, John Clark and Samuel Street. Special juries could be asked for in trials at the assizes; jurors for these trials had to possess a minimum £200 of property and they were chosen in a specified manner.[20] The request was a pretty clear invitation to pre-select or pack a special jury for a civil trial, although the reasons in this instance are somewhat ambiguous. It is possible that the government wanted to ensure that the jury did not consist of men with a conflict of interest. 'I trust that it will not occupy too much of your time to run over the list, drawing your pen through those which ought in no case to be received, marking those with the letter "A" who are approved men, and leaving the doubtful without any mark of approbation or disapprobation.'[21] Merritt likely complied with this request, which was prefaced by the flattering but accurate comment that no other person 'so well knows the relation in which each person stands to the parties interested ...'

Rumours of jury packing by Niagara sheriffs had long circulated in the district. The allegation that sheriffs manipulated jury lists to ensure favourable jurors was made in the trial of Robert Gourlay and again in several civil trials where special juries were impanelled.[22] While it is impossible to prove or disprove these allegations in the absence of extant evidence, in politically charged trials and civil cases involving important figures in the districts, it seems highly likely that sheriffs like Richard Leonard or Alexander Hamilton resorted to manipulating jury lists. The extent to which such manipulation affected jury verdicts is harder to assess, because Niagara juries jealously guarded their independence.

Magistrates in Niagara did not have to resort to coercion to find jurors until the Rebellion period. Then, briefly, they were forced into more severe actions. In December 1838, when sufficient grand jurors could not be found to make up a quorum in the quarter sessions, the magistrates fined six men who refused to answer the summons.[23] They also removed a number of jurors' names from the list of petit jurors in 1838 because they were Quakers.[24] Mennonites and Tunkers had been relieved of jury duty by legislation passed in 1809.[25] Until the post-Rebellion period, however, most men of the Niagara district generally responded to a summons to serve on juries with remarkably little protest. Even those who wrote asking to be excused on account of ill health implied their willingness to attend if their health permitted.[26]

Following the Rebellion, population decline and economic downturn may have affected the inclination of individuals, especially those living some distance from Niagara, to serve on juries. Eleven prospective jurors, all living outside the town of Niagara, sent in medical excuses for the March sitting of the court of quarter sessions in 1841.[27] Occasionally a magistrate would intercede on behalf of a prospective juror. James Cummings, the magistrate in Chippewa, wrote to the clerk of the peace in April 1842 on behalf of George Smith, who had been summoned for jury duty: 'Smith is a good, quiet, honest fellow, but never was at Court in his life, knows nothing about being a Jury Man and wishes to get excused.'[28]

The grand juries at the assizes in Niagara, as in the rest of Upper Canada, relied on magistrates for their membership. This tradition too was imported from England. Although in Niagara magistrates were not the only members of assize grand juries, the number of non-magistrates was always very small, never more than four out of twenty-three, and the foreman was consistently a magistrate.[29] The same magistrates could be found on the assize grand juries year after year. In the ten-year period, 1828–37 magistrates Daniel McDougal and James Lockhart served as assize grand jurors six times and Henry Nelles served five times. Several other prominent Niagara magistrates served two, three, or four times, giving a continuity to assize grand juries that did not exist at the court of quarter sessions. Since the average size of assize grand juries in these years was nineteen, the magistrates had a disproportionate influence on their deliberations.[30]

Rather than being pliable and subservient servants of the courts, Niagara jurors in the courts of quarter sessions often exhibited an independence of view and a feisty opposition to attitudes or positions taken by the magistrates. In Niagara, the courts did not always speak with one voice, nor were juries afraid to criticize the magistrates. A Niagara grand jury in 1832 complained to the lieutenant governor about the 'inattention and neglect on the part of the Magistrates of this district to their duties at the Court of Quarter Sessions.' The chairman of the court, along with jurors and witnesses, was often kept waiting from one to two hours for a quorum of magistrates to permit the court to function. The jurors recommended appointing more magistrates, 'able and efficient persons of whom there is no deficiency.'[31] Another grand jury in 1838 put on record their annoyance about being given only half an hour's work over two days. The jurors described themselves as having travelled many miles, neglecting private interests to attend to that of the public, and hence frustrated with the inefficiency of the court.[32]

Niagara jurors notably demonstrated their independence in the Randal case in 1825. Paul Romney has described the acquittal of Robert Randal on a charge of perjury as 'the most prominent case of a politically repressive prosecution in which an Upper Canadian jury returned a verdict against the judge's direction.'[33] The fact that the jury needed only five minutes to reach its verdict of not guilty in a case with such political overtones indicates that Niagara juries were quite capable of reaching their own decisions, even in the face of strong judicial pressure.

The Randal trial garnered extensive publicity because Randal was an elected member of the Legislature and a leading reformer, but Niagara juries exhibited a similar independence of mind in other, less well-known political cases. After an anti-American riot occurred in St Catharines on 4 July 1833, William Hamilton Merritt, by then one of the district's pre-eminent magistrates, returned to St Catharines to find, as he later recounted, 'a general impression prevailing that the riot was countenanced by our Authority.'[34] The riot had been witnessed by a local magistrate and a constable, both of whom told Merritt they did not interfere because of the violence of the mob. Merritt believed corrective action was required and he proceeded to have depositions taken before all the St Catharines's magistrates, who then bound over the suspects to appear at the next quarter sessions in Niagara. Merritt's actions were praised by St Catharines's American residents. One wrote to him that in forcing the matter to be heard before the court, Merritt would prove that English law 'was sufficient to protect all persons within this jurisdiction, and that they do not require the aid of an infuriated mob.'[35] When the case was heard at the Niagara court of quarter sessions, however, a grand jury found 'no bill' and threw it out.[36] Merritt did not disguise his anger at the lack of legal protection for Americans living in St Catharines and complained in open court that 'the affair should not be smuggled over.' The Niagara grand jury then sent a formal presentment criticizing Merritt to the lieutenant governor. Merritt's comments had cast 'a reflection on the Jurors in discharging their duty.' The lieutenant governor forwarded this presentment to Merritt, who agreed not to proceed any further if the parties themselves remained quiet. He apologized to the lieutenant governor for occupying his attention 'with a subject so uninteresting.' In this case the grand jury first defied the wishes of a leading magistrate and then censured his conduct. By forcing the issue, the grand jury caused everyone involved to take a step back and reconsider their actions in an affair that could have escalated further.

Niagara juries did not always succeed in getting their way. In one unusual case the members of both the Niagara grand jury that referred the issue for trial and the petit jury that tried the case subsequently petitioned the lieutenant governor about the punishment accorded to the convict. William Forsyth Jr was found guilty of assault and battery and the magistrates tacked a month in jail on to a hefty fine. The jurors, who obviously knew Forsyth, petitioned against the jail sentence on the grounds that his young family had no other source of support. When this petition was referred to the magistrates they refused to change their sentence, on the grounds that 'a full Bench' had decided the punishment for what 'was considered a very aggravated assault.'[37] Forsyth had seized a servant by the windpipe, severely choking him, at the same time swearing he would kill him.[38] Typically, the lieutenant governor in this case upheld the decision of the Niagara magistrates.

Forsyth's father was the controversial owner of the Pavilion Hotel in Niagara Falls. Given Forsyth Sr's own personal history and the acrimonious disputes he had regularly been involved in, this division between jury and magistrates was not surprising. As Forsyth Sr's biographer notes, 'rumour and innuendo hung over Forsyth like the ever-present mist over the falls.'[39] He had been the victim of government persecution in the so-called Niagara Falls Outrage, a dispute over property rights on the Niagara river.[40]

What is particularly noteworthy about the juries of colonial Niagara is the frequency with which they sent presentments to the lieutenant governor or laid them before the local magistrates, expressing local concerns or requesting redress of apparent injustices. In some instances assize grand juries forwarded presentments to the lieutenant governor on matters of district concern, but the quarter sessions grand juries were more aggressive in presenting local grievances to the governing authorities. Niagara juries clearly functioned as non-elected representatives of the community in raising the voice of the community on a wide range of colonial problems, carrying on the English tradition of the 'Grand Inquest' even after it had withered in England.

One further example illustrates the interaction between the jury and the community petition as a means of forcing the hand of local government in the person of the Niagara magistrates. In the absence of a coroner, when John McIntyre was found dead in the Welland Canal on 9 March 1834 the two local magistrates summoned a coroner's jury to determine the cause of the death. Coroners' inquests had an ancient history in English law, and both the office of the coroner and the law governing it came to Upper Canada and the other British colonies in North America. The finding of a coroners' jury was equivalent to that of a grand jury.[41] After the jury determined that McIntyre had likely fallen into the canal and drowned while intoxicated, members of the jury, along with other local freeholders, petitioned the court of quarter sessions. The petition incorporated the jury's findings, including the fact that McIntyre 'had been violently bruised previous to his decease.'[42] It also makes clear how horrified the members of the jury were to discover what had really happened. McIntyre had gone into the local tavern, owned by a Henry Sloan, on Christmas Eve, 1833. He had been sober when he entered the inn, but subsequently 'became Drunk, noisy and quarrelsome.' Henry Sloan ejected him from the inn. McIntyre had then been seen in a fight with another individual, but was not seen again until his body was found the following March, when spring thawed the ice in the canal. The petitioners used the case to confirm their belief that Sloan 'does not keep a peaceable, sober and quiet house – but on the contrary that it is the resort of the Drunken and the dissolute.' The 'awful and lamentable catastrophe' had been caused by McIntyre's excessive drinking in company with 'the Drunken and dissolute' routinely found in Sloan's tavern. The petitioners as individuals wanted the magistrates to do what they as jurors had been unable to accomplish: revoke Sloan's licence and close his tavern. The two magistrates who had convened the coroner's inquest very likely shared the same opinions as the jury, and may even have encouraged the jurors to petition the court of quarter sessions.

Their petition illustrates that these local inhabitants fully understood the role and power of the jury, including a coroner's jury. They clothed their grievances in a legal language. For these men the law was not some abstract entity with which they occasionally came into contact; it was a living reality and they knew how to use it to try to redress a serious local problem. Frequent jury service gave them a knowledge of law and of the operation of the court of quarter sessions. They also demonstrated that they were not satisfied to function merely as a coroner's jury and report their findings. As individuals, they wanted to reform the legal abuses and gross immorality they had found.

The court of quarter sessions responded to the petition by issuing subpoenas to some of the petitioners to appear at the next court to prosecute Henry Sloan.[43] Following the court order, the chairman of the court of quarter sessions for 1834, William Hamilton Merritt, together with one of the local magistrates who had convened the inquest, David Thompson, visited Henry Sloan personally.[44] The local pressure initiated by the jurymen and reinforced by the magistrates had a quick result. Sloan decided to close his tavern and move out of the district rather than face a prosecution and the possible removal of his tavern licence. Informal justice in this instance proved more effective and faster in producing the results the local community wanted.

Grand juries were equally useful to the magistrates on occasion: by referring contentious and ambiguous issues to grand juries, the magistrates could claim that they had taken appropriate action in response to complaints received. In January 1829 twenty-four residents of Pelham petitioned the Niagara magistrates about attacks said to have been made on Jason Sheppard, a local leader of a small Shaker sect. The petition referred to the violation of the rights of British subjects, in this instance 'a harmless and inoffensive People.' The petitioners were very deferential in begging leave 'to remark (but without the least Intention of declaring to you) that they consider the future Safety of their Persons and Property' at stake. The magistrates quickly referred the petitioners to the grand jury for redress.[45] No prosecution resulted, but it is possible that some informal action took place to discourage future attacks, as no further mention of attacks on Shakers is found in the Niagara records. In another instance the magistrates used the device of a grand jury presentment to alert the lieutenant governor to the negligence of one magistrate in not collecting fines. The clerk of the peace added in a covering letter, 'Had the complaint been considered sufficient to warrant it, an Indictment would have been laid before the grand jury.'[46]

Long before the incorporation of Niagara as a town, grand jury presentments were used as local petitions to try to control local behaviour, or to eliminate 'certain nuisances and abuses which now exist.' The abuses and nuisances referred to in a presentment of 1828 included swine running loose within the city, people indiscriminately shooting muskets, and others driving horses, carriages, wagons, and carts recklessly and, even more alarming, 'so many women of loose habits ... prowling our streets at all hours in the night ...'[47]

Quarter sessions grand juries also provided protection against various forms of abuse to criminals, debtors, and others in the local jail awaiting trial. At every meeting of the court of quarter sessions, grand juries examined the jail and heard from the prisoners. In 1832 a Niagara grand jury made out a formal presentment against the local jailer, Peter Wheeler, and the jury foreman wrote 'true bill' on it to indicate how serious the matter was. The jury found that Wheeler 'had withheld ... a sufficiency of fuel, in extreme cold weather,' and that he had used 'abusive and obscene language' to prisoners' wives, as well as providing food that 'was putrid and unfit for use.'[48] In this instance the campaign against the Niagara jailer had been led by the debtors, who did not regard themselves as criminals and expected more humane treatment. They succeeded in having Wheeler formally rebuked. A committee of magistrates was created to draw up appropriate regulations to prevent Wheeler from continuing to abuse inmates of the jail.

Successive quarter sessions grand juries wrote presentments about the inadequacies of the Niagara jail in an attempt to secure the necessary improvements. By 1839 one grand jury was so infuriated by the fact that 'the presentments made for many years on this subject have *not been attended to by the Magistrates*' that they sent their presentment directly to the lieutenant governor with a covering letter, saying 'nothing has been done' to improve a dreadful situation. The magistrates had claimed the responsibility lay with the sheriff, but the Niagara jurors, tired of lame excuses, wanted the lieutenant governor to remedy the problem. Their presentment characterized the jail as 'in a state not only disgraceful to the District but to a Civilized people.'[49] The near bankruptcy of the district may have contributed to the magistrates' unwillingness to act, and even this presentment did not lead to any immediate or substantial changes. The jurors had done all they could to make the government aware of the problem, but it was not in their power to mandate solutions.

Because of the relatively small population of the district, Niagara juries had ready access to character witnesses for the people prosecuted. Occasionally, as in an assault trial at the fall quarter sessions in 1845, such witnesses could lead to a petit jury changing its mind. Solomon Darney was convicted of assault and battery on 21 November 1845, but after receiving letters from the local magistrate and another inhabitant of Port Dalhousie, where Darney lived, giving Darney a very strong character reference, the petit jury altered its verdict. Their justification was that they had heard 'from respectable persons that the said defendant is a man of remarkably good character,' and therefore unlikely to have committed the assault. The jury went out of its way to justify the original conviction on the evidence explained to them, 'and in their view most correctly,' by the presiding judge, but the new evidence of the defendant's impeccable character had persuaded the jury that his guilt was 'not at all probable.'[50] The conviction was allowed to stand and Darney received a small fine and two weeks in jail.

With the decline of the jury in Canada since the colonial period, historians and others have lost sight of its former importance.[51] Especially at the level of the court of quarter sessions, the jury helped to legitimate legal processes for the local community. At the same time, it acted as a voice for that community. As the experience of the juries in Niagara illustrates, colonial juries did not hesitate to communicate community viewpoints to local government and to the lieutenant governor. The surviving jury presentments from the Niagara district cover a wide range of subjects. While some failed to achieve their objective, many presentments helped to create political change at the district and even colonial levels. Jurors in Niagara not only served the courts, in many instances they also served their own community interests.

NIAGARA CONSTABLES

The enforcement of the law in the Niagara district, as in the rest of Upper Canada, rested in the first instance on constables appointed by the magistrates and paid expenses for the specific services they carried out rather than a salary. These early constables were 'conservators of the peace'; bound to obey a magistrate's warrant, they were also authorized to arrest without warrant all 'traitors, felons and suspicious persons.'[52] In Niagara they remained the primary peace officers until well into the 1840s. In 1846 St Catharines and Niagara, the two leading towns of the district, both appointed Boards of Police to oversee municipal policing. But until then constables throughout the district were appointed on the specific recommendation of magistrates in each town or community, once approved by the court of quarter sessions. They received no formal training until at least the early 1840s, when there is evidence that some new constables received a day's instruction.[53] Nor did they wear a uniform to identify themselves. They were simply local citizens who could be called upon by the magistrates to enforce the law and apprehend suspected criminals. The office of constable was already ancient when it was imported into Upper Canada, another institution inherited directly from England.[54]

Constables in theory represented both royal authority and their local community. The peace they were empowered to conserve was the king's peace, and their local community benefited because if the king's peace prevailed inhabitants could live free from the fear of crime and lawlessness. In practice, constables functioned directly as the right hand of the local magistrate. No foreigners could serve in the office, even if they were naturalized, and 'gentlemen of quality' did not have to serve provided there were others eligible. In Niagara, however, there is no record of a gentleman of quality refusing to serve. In other words, the question of class did not arise in Niagara appointments.

Constables were not required to possess the same wealth, reputation, or local standing as the magistrates, and few did. What was essential was the confidence of the local magistrate. As Judge Gowan later told a grand jury in Simcoe County, 'Men respected in the neighbourhood they are taken from, men of decent means – "the abler sort of men" should be selected.'[55] Those selected were often nominated to serve for subsequent years, giving the constabulary of the district a degree of continuity. Frances Ann Thompson concludes that 28 per cent of Niagara's constables served for two years or more. The majority, however, 72 per cent, served only for one year, ensuring considerable rotation of the office among the district.[56] Thompson also found that most of the constables in the Niagara district were farmers, although the percentage of farmer constables declined from 40 per cent in 1828 to 25 per cent in 1840. As the towns of Niagara grew in population, many constables were shopkeepers, local artisans, millers, and manufacturers rather than farmers. Some thirty-five Niagara constables also held posts as officers in the militia and a significant portion (estimated at 24 per cent) held elected offices at the township level. A small number (eleven) were related to the Niagara magistrates and at least five Niagara constables were later appointed as magistrates.[57] Thompson says of the constables, 'as respected neighbours, relatives and friends, constables who had a wide correspondence with their community formed an acceptable bridge between the authority of the magistracy and the community.'[58]

In 1834 the court of quarter sessions approved the appointment of seventy constables throughout the district, three of whom had been elected at one township meeting.[59] The number of constables appointed grew rapidly in each succeeding year, reaching 184 by 1845, an increase disproportionate to the population growth of the district. The magistrates reserved their right to approve all constables, but in the few townships where the inhabitants had decided in the 1830s to elect their constables, the local magistrate endorsed the election and the court of quarter sessions then approved the individual constables.[60] By no means all of the constables were active in performing their duties.

Only fifteen of the sixty-eight appointed in 1829 submitted accounts for payment within the subsequent six months, a proportion which remained consistent through the 1840s.[61]

Some religious minorities in Niagara were not compelled to serve as constables. A Quaker from Pelham, Hiram Page, signed a declaration in 1844 that it was 'not agreeable to Law' for him to serve as a constable. The local magistrate certified that Page was a Quaker and added, 'that it would be inconsistent ... to require him to be a Constable.'[62] What he meant was that it would be inconsistent with Page's Quaker beliefs, and the Niagara authorities accepted that. In another case in 1843, James Stewart was appointed a constable for Rainham; he indicated he did not want to serve because he was a Tunker who did not swear, but affirmed, rendering him ineligible on religious grounds to carry out the office. He stated he had been solicited to accept office as a magistrate and then as a constable, but he had always turned the offers down. As a Tunker, 'he never meddles himself with public affairs.' Stewart persuaded his local magistrate to write on his behalf, asking that someone else be appointed, 'as there are many who would be glad to serve or have the appointment.'[63] Whether many were glad to serve is debatable, but the Niagara district never had any serious problem filling its annual quota of constables.

Serving as a constable could be arduous and dangerous, and in the early colonial period often involved travelling long distances. The location of the district jail in the town of Niagara, in the northeastern corner of the district, meant that constant travel was the constables' lot. The roads they travelled on were often impassable, as contemporary complaints reiterated, especially in spring when thaws caused flooding, often reducing the roads to muddy seas. Frances Ann Thompson has calculated that the average distance Niagara constables travelled per individual journey was twenty-three miles, requiring two or three days, and 40 per cent of their journeys were longer than the average.[64] Very few of the prisoners they escorted escaped en route, an estimated eighteen over the thirteen years from 1828 to 1840.

The experience of one Niagara constable, Thomas Wiggins, from the town of Dunnville, in November and December 1843, illustrates what constables could be called upon to do. Wiggins was ordered to arrest one Edward Welch on a charge of felony involving the theft of a pair of oxen. To do this, the constable travelled seventy miles, located the oxen, and then arrested Welch. He had to keep Welch overnight and was responsible for the expenses of feeding and lodging his prisoner.

The following day Wiggins travelled with his prisoner the remaining thirty miles to Dunnville, where Welch was examined by the magistrate. Wiggins had also been responsible for bringing the oxen back and they too had been lodged and fed overnight. Following Welch's examination, Wiggins took him to Niagara to the district jail, another journey of over fifty miles. As soon as this journey was completed, he was required to escort another prisoner to the Niagara jail. Because the roads were now impassable, he had to wait for a boat, which meant looking after his prisoner for two nights and three days. Wiggins then had a short break from criminal work until early December, when he was sent on a twenty-mile journey to arrest John Quirk on a charge of murder. He brought Quirk to the Niagara jail, a seventy-mile journey, and delivered him to the Niagara jailer on 4 December 1843. Once the court of quarter sessions had approved the account he submitted, Wiggins was eventually (in January 1844) paid £14, 5s. to cover his costs. Wiggins was an unusually active constable. The previous year he had escorted nine Welland Canal rioters fifty miles to the Niagara jail, as well as arresting one man for theft and another for refusing to do statute labour. He must have spent a great deal of his two-year tenure as constable in constant travel.

While constables charged expenses and fees for their labour, their work was really performed as a genuine public service. Many constables were committed to maintaining law and order in their local community. In 1849, for instance, Andrew Drew, a constable at Wainfleet, travelled a total of 380 miles to Warwick in the Western district to arrest John Elmsley on suspicion of murder and bring him back. He then served thirteen subpoenas on witnesses who lived in different localities, travelling an additional eighty-nine miles. During the week this took, he had to look after his prisoner. That Elmsley was then discharged for lack of sufficient proof was no doubt a frustrating result for Drew, although he was reimbursed for the expenses he had incurred.[65]

Not all constables were so fortunate as to have their accounts approved and immediately paid by the magistrates of the court of quarter sessions. The anger of those whose accounts were rejected is very plain in a letter one constable wrote to the clerk of the peace, asking him to resubmit his account for bringing prisoners to the Niagara jail, 'which our worthy magistrates have been pleased to reject.'[66] The magistrates kept a close watch on the accounts submitted. David Davis's account was rejected in 1842 'because it [did] not appear that the party

was arrested and 40 miles is a distance which is not very often travelled or to be travelled in a Township like Louth to arrest a man.'[67] In
1839 Solomon Soper arrested Hannah Johnson on a felony. He then
looked after her for ten days because she was ill. The magistrates,
however, rejected his claim for expenses because Soper had permitted
Johnson to escape.[68] Deputy Sheriff McLeod queried the sheriff in 1838
about another constable, 'Did you employ that troublesome old fellow, Oliphant or do you know who did? His account is ... preposter-
ously exorbitant ...' McLeod refused to sanction it.[69]

Constables who had their accounts rejected turned to their local
magistrate for assistance and held him responsible. James Cummings,
the magistrate for Chippewa, wrote in 1841 on behalf of two of his
constables who had been unsuccessful in obtaining reimbursement: 'I
have been repeatedly asked for the amount – and the parties attach
blame to me for not attending to get payment for them.'[70] Many constables were forced to subsidize the enforcement of the law out of
their own pockets.

Some of the constables' accounts lay unpaid for lengthy periods of
time, causing them great hardship. John Page, a constable for the village of Gainsborough, wrote a plaintive letter to the magistrates in
October 1836 trying to recover expenses incurred a year earlier in
arresting a local man and taking him to the Niagara jail. As Page said,
he had laid out his money some time ago, and only the magistrates
could authorize reimbursement of the £1 15s.[71] He was eventually paid,
but not until January 1837, well over a year after he had spent the sum
in the service of law enforcement. The reputation of the Niagara magistrates for penny-pinching no doubt contributed to the problems faced
in 1839 by the commander of the Coloured Corps, a unit formed to
defend the frontier in the aftermath of the 1837 Rebellion. When the
commander asked a local constable to take a prisoner to the Niagara
jail, the constable demanded to have his expenses paid in advance.
Another constable from the same town likewise refused to convey the
prisoner and submitted his resignation.[72] Both were replaced, but not
before the commander made one of his sergeants a special constable
to carry out the warrant.

In 1831 thirteen Niagara constables petitioned in vain to have their
fees increased for attending the assizes and courts of quarter sessions.
They had found it 'peculiarly oppressive' to attend the courts on allowances of 2s. 6d. a day when so many lived 'at a distance' from the
town of Niagara.[73] The combination of financial hardship and the trans-

portation problems involved in bringing suspects to the Niagara jail meant that very few constables were active in bringing offenders to justice without a prior warrant issued by a magistrate. W.J. Blacklock, who studied 150 Niagara district case files, found that constables initiated an arrest without a prior warrant in only seven cases.[74]

In peacetime, constables were able to carry out their duties in most parts of the Niagara district unaided except in emergencies. In times of threatened rebellion, invasion, or civil unrest, however, the government turned to the military to reinforce the constabulary. After the Rebellion, when the frontier was still affected by border disturbances, the Coloured Corps continued to function as military reinforcement and in the 1840s the government of the Canadas decided that the Welland Canal required additional force. In 1843 it commissioned a specially organized force of canal police and resurrected the Coloured Corps to provide military back-up. When some of the canal workers lost their jobs in the spring of 1844 a riot ensued and two constables were badly beaten with shovels and axes. The military was called in to arrest the men responsible.[75] One, Terence Riley, was charged with maliciously shooting at Edward Wheeler, the head of the Welland Canal police force. He was found guilty and given the severe sentence of five years at hard labour in the Kingston Penitentiary. Riley's crime was seen as a crime against public order, as Mr Justice Hagerman affirmed in passing sentence: 'the offences taking place on the Canal demand the severest and most exemplary punishment for they are calculated to destroy the whole fabric of civilized society.'[76]

In a lengthy presentment detailing the various problems along the Welland Canal, a grand jury in January 1844 alluded to the difficulty of policing the area because there was reputedly 'an immense quantity of fire-arms amongst the labourers.'[77] These had been smuggled in from the United States. The jury believed that the Niagara court should issue warrants to seize the contraband firearms. The commandant of the military forces along the Niagara frontier, Colonel Elliott, similarly feared that the Welland Canal region in 1844 was in a 'lawless state.' After one alarm over an Orange Day parade Elliott wrote, 'the local Magistracy are not efficient and there are no Police ... The Troops therefore instead of giving aid, are left to be actual conservators of the peace.'[78] As the canal work neared completion in the latter part of the decade, the policing problems diminished. The Coloured Corps and the special canal police force were disbanded after the Welland Canal was declared open for navigation in 1850.

Unemployment was a constant feature of canal labour, especially during winter. Unemployed workers congregated upon the canal banks, providing not only a spectacle of poverty but also a major challenge to the local forces of law and order. Cultural and religious divisions inherited from Ireland contributed to regular skirmishes and riots, transforming the canal zone into an arena of armed conflict. But feuding owed primarily to unemployment and neither the magistrates nor the constables could create jobs. The canal constables were not popular with the labourers and violent confrontations regularly occurred. Ruth Bleasdale has argued that in the 1840s the government of the Canadas 'marshalled the coercive power of the state against labourers on the public works.'[79] Certainly, the Welland Canal region was unique in the Niagara district in the nature and amount of police and military force wielded to maintain law and order. In the canal area the traditional method of local policing was inadequate. Here, following the Mackenzie Rebellion, the local constabulary was not left on its own to conserve the peace. The government, fearing the larger political consequences of lawlessness and wanting the canal completed, decided that it did not possess sufficient force to maintain public order.

Most prosecutions in the Niagara district were initiated by the victim of a crime. Constables made arrests and executed search warrants, or served subpoenas and escorted prisoners to jail. But nearly all of these activities involved acting as agents of magistrates or victims: constables rarely initiated criminal prosecutions on their own.[80] In the Niagara district constables do not appear to have been active in resolving criminal issues before they reached the courts. They were genuinely servants of the court, in that they acted upon orders issued by the magistrates.

Constables then as now risked injury as they tried to arrest violent or potentially violent individuals. When William Wadsworth, a Queenston constable, threatened Barney Woolman with a prosecution while a card game was going on in a local tavern, Woolman punched him in the mouth, loosening a tooth. 'As you are going to take the Law of me,' he said, 'I will give you something to take the Law for.' Woolman pleaded guilty to assault and battery and received a token fine of one shilling and costs.[81] Even when constables had been assaulted in the performance of their duty Niagara juries were often reluctant to convict, and if they did, the penalties, with one or two exceptions, tended to be light. No cases of assaulting an officer were heard at the assizes prior to 1837. From then until 1850, a total of eleven cases involving fifteen people were heard. Only five resulted in convictions.[82] A few less serious cases were tried in the court of quarter sessions.

In one case in 1840 a jury found Samuel Cramer not guilty of assaulting a constable, Edward Honor. Honor had intervened to protect Phyllis Messenger from a sexual assault by Cramer when she cried out to him to assist her. Even in these circumstances the jury did not find sufficient evidence to convict Cramer of assault.[83] Honor's actions, however, were in keeping with his name and illustrated the willingness of Niagara constables to intervene to protect others even at the risk of their own security. Constables themselves could be prosecuted and some were, especially for assault. Chester Wadsworth, also of Queenston and very likely a relative of William, was convicted twice in one quarter of 1836 for assault and battery on different individuals. Both times he was fined £1, 5s. and costs.[84]

Because Niagara was a frontier region, its constables had to cross the border in search of fugitives and had also to be on the lookout for suspicious characters from the United States. The financial account that Donald McDonald, a constable for the town of Niagara, submitted to the court of quarter sessions in October 1836, detailing his services during the previous three months, illustrates both the frontier element of his job and the wide range of duties these early constables were expected to perform. McDonald had been responsible for committing a man found in Buffalo and suspected of murder in Toronto. He had also looked after an orphan child for a night, arrested a woman and four others for 'keeping a house of ill fame', and guarded the Niagara jail for four nights prior to an execution.[85] McDonald's activities were typical of the busier constables located in the towns along the Niagara river and in St Catharines.

Most of the arrests (43 per cent) made by the constables involved property crimes. Fewer, 33 per cent, involved crimes against persons, including more serious crimes, and almost 13 per cent involved morals offences.[86] Frances Ann Thompson also worked out that of nearly 2,400 orders given to the Niagara constables by the magistrates or other legal officers in this period, only six constables refused to carry out the order or otherwise failed to act appropriately, a quite remarkable indication of compliance.[87] These statistics are convincing proof of the effectiveness of the Niagara constabulary in carrying out their duties, and they are matched by the relative infrequency of recorded complaints from magistrates or citizens about their local constables. In the few recorded instances when constables failed in their duty, the magistrates quickly applied the force of the law. When John Stewart, a constable for the village of Gainsborough in 1831, permitted his prisoner, James Fields, to escape, apparently in return for a share of his proceeds in a theft, the magistrate, William Anthony, sought advice from the attorney general and issued a warrant for Stewart's arrest.[88]

More common, however, was a magistrate's glowing endorsement of the actions of Constable Samuel Smith of Thorold in October 1835. The magistrate, Jacob Keefer, had sent Smith out 'in the worst weather' to apprehend suspects, 'on account of the greater probability of finding them about their houses.' The men in question had returned to the district after being banished from Upper Canada for a serious felony. Smith captured both of them, but one escaped with the help of an accomplice. Smith was sent out again to capture the accomplice, 'whom they arrested somewhere in the Black Swamp near Niagara.' Keefer wrote, 'the Service was one requiring judgement and energy and was faithfully performed in the midst of Stormy and disagreeable weather ...'[89]

In the Niagara district the ancient English institution of the constable remained the basis of policing until the incorporation of towns led to the creation of municipal police forces, beginning in 1846. Upper Canada followed Britain in this change. The 1830s was the last decade in which parish constables were solely responsible for law enforcement in rural England.[90] For over fifty years in Niagara, the constables appointed annually by the magistrates at the court of quarter sessions served as the primary agents of law enforcement, a citizen constabulary carrying out a wide range of functions at the behest of the local magistrates. Judge Gowan proudly contrasted Upper Canada's constabulary with the system of policing found in the United States: 'Thank God *we* require no organized semi-military force, with deadly weapons in their hands, to uphold the dominion of law – but Peace Officers may not be dispensed with.'[91] This boast was not entirely true, as the Welland Canal experience proved, but Niagara did rely primarily on the village or town constable. The constables' dedicated work in many instances ensured that the colonial legal system in Niagara, as in other parts of Upper Canada, functioned with reasonable effectiveness. Suspects were arrested and escorted to the district jail, and subpoenas were issued for witnesses to appear at trials. Constables performed a wide variety of functions within the judicial system, and without their commitment, the system would not have been able to operate at all. With a few rare exceptions, the Niagara constables established a highly creditable record in serving the court and the magistrates who ran it.

PART TWO

Morality

When Upper Canada was created as a separate colony, John Graves Simcoe, its first lieutenant governor, had emphasized that piety and morality were the foundation of a lawful society, just as Christianity was the unquestioned basis of morality within the English system of law that Upper Canada inherited. The handbook of law W.C. Keele compiled in 1835 for the use of the magistrates in Upper Canada stated, 'the Christian religion, according to high authority, is part and parcel of the law of England. To reproach or blaspheme it, therefore, is to speak in subversion of the law.'[1] In this sense Upper Canada was no different from the American colonies prior to the American Revolution where, as David Flaherty observed, 'sin and crime, divine law and secular law, the moral law and the criminal law were all closely intertwined.'[2] Flaherty goes on to suggest that a gradual process of secularization occurred from the latter half of the seventeenth century and continued steadily through the American Revolution. The process of secularization can be detected in Britain and in its colonies as well, but if Puritan fervour was absent by the time Upper Canada was created, the link between Christianity and the law had not vanished, nor had the role of law in enforcing Christian moral standards.

Flaherty concludes that in the American colonies 'the attempt to use criminal law to uphold the moral law was a failure.'[3] Was this also true of Upper Canada? For the early British governors of Upper Canada, and for the Loyalist immigrants who rapidly became the elite of the new colony, the moral order was in theory as unbreakable as the cherished British connection. As the nineteenth century progressed, conceptions of morality in Upper Canadian society changed, but the law continued to be the vehicle for codifying and expressing it. Carolyn Strange and Tina Loo point out in their study of law and moral regulation in Canada after 1867 that 'morality is ... difficult to define because it is an abstract concept' and that 'it is no less contestable than law.'[4] The cases cited in the following chapters illustrate just how contestable court-enforced morality could be in the Niagara district in the first half of the nineteenth century.

John Beattie has written that in Upper Canada in the 1830s 'moral order was the indispensable foundation and guarantor of a stable society, that is a society resting on harmonious social relationships, on a respectable working population and, at least by implication, on the natural authority of men of wealth and standing.'[5] He goes on to argue that if immorality led to crime, the very foundations of the moral order might be under threat. But in the daily practice of justice, did the enforcement of law and the punishment of crime encourage morality? Was a Christian concept of morality ever-present in the courts? What was the real relationship between law enforcement and morality in early-nineteenth-century Upper Canada? The following three chapters explore the connections between Christian morality and the legal system in the early nineteenth century by examining sabbath breaking, the treatment of the insane, and conceptions of public charity in the Niagara district. The fate of a prisoner judged to be criminally insane, the subject of chapter 5, may not seem to pose questions of morality to modern legal scholars. But to both officials and Niagara society in the 1830s treatment of the insane was indeed a moral issue. How should the insane be treated in a Christian society? The local jail was the only facility available for housing those labelled insane, or to use the terminology of the time, 'lunatic.' Within the local jails no treatment or cure was possible and, as the officials soon discovered, the costs of long-term incarceration were very high. In attempting to live up to a Christian definition of morality the Niagara district magistrates found themselves in a legal quagmire, especially when they dealt with issues of charity and insanity, as defined in early-nineteenth-century terms.

4

Enforcing a Christian Moral Order

Niagara district magistrate Bartholomew Tench was strolling along
the bank of the Welland Canal early in the afternoon of Sunday, 14
November 1833, heading towards Gravelly Bay (Port Colborne) when,
as he later recalled, he observed several men, five at least, employed
in shingling a home belonging to a person named Smith. At roughly
the same moment his attention was called to the men at work by one
Jenner, a miller. The subsequent exchange was recorded in a deposition made by the magistrate.

'Have you not seen the King's Proclamation to prevent such work on the
Sabbath?' To which deponent [Tench] replied that he would immediately
put a stop to it ... deponent crossed the Canal and went towards the
frame and recognised Joel Skinner, Dan'l Waterhouse, Robert Cram &
others, whose names deponent does not know ... deponent addressed
himself particularly to Skinner and said that it was improper to be at
such work on Sunday. Skinner replied, 'Is it Sunday? It would be a
dam'd deal better for you to be at home minding your own business' ...
deponent replied that he had a right to walk where he pleased and
therefore having seen the offence committed he was obliged to notice it,
... deponent then desired the men to come down ... deponent thinks the
men descended the ladder, ... Skinner continued working and said as he
was to be fined he would work his day out, at the same time using the
most abusive and insulting language, repeatedly desiring deponent to go

to Hell and that he did not value or fear deponent more than another
'Little Counter Jumper.'

After further and equally futile exchanges with Skinner, Tench decided to leave 'with the expectation that the men would have time to
reflect on the impropriety of their conduct and quit the work.' The
magistrate then went to the nearest store to buy himself some snuff
after his unpleasant adventure, only to be goaded by the local innkeeper into another attempt to enforce the law. The second effort was
no more successful than the first, and exposed Tench to even more
humiliation. He tried to get two others working with Skinner to stop
their work and assist him in arresting Skinner. But they walked away
'without paying any attention.' Left on his own, Tench mounted the
ladder Skinner was on and told Skinner he was a prisoner in His
Majesty's name. Skinner eventually came down, but instead of behav-
ing like a prisoner he too walked away. When Tench 'laid hold of him
by the coat' and told him he must accompany the magistrate Skinner
collared Tench, 'tried to drag him in the direction of the grocery where
a number of persons were assembled,' and repeatedly made 'most
violent and threatening gestures with his shut hand' in Tench's face.
Skinner continued abusing the magistrate, 'swearing that he would
not let any dam'd Irish rascal take him.' (As Tench was an Irish Roman Catholic magistrate and Skinner a Protestant United Empire Loyalist, there are undertones of religious and ethnic rivalry here.) Finally, Tench procured an arrest warrant charging Skinner with setting
'the law at defiance ... and his resuming the work with others after the
deponent's departure, to the scandal and evil example of others and
bringing the law into contempt.'[1] But there is no evidence that any
prosecution ensued. The magistrates at the next quarter sessions may
have decided it was not worth the expense of a trial. Skinner was
required to post a bond for £50 to keep the peace with Tench for a
year, but this must have been little compensation for the public ridi-
cule Tench had endured.[2]

Joel Skinner's contempt for established authority and determination
to live his own life, even if this meant flouting established convention,
and his utter disregard for the prevailing orthodoxy of the sabbath,
were by no means unusual. Tench, a well-meaning if ineffective justice of the peace, faced a moral and legal dilemma common to his
fellow members of the magistracy.[3] When an inhabitant of his small
village, whose population was less than 700, pointed to a blatant vio-

lation of the law, he was expected to apprehend the violator and to ensure that justice was done. Failure to do so would undermine respect for the law, to say nothing of his own standing as the local magistrate. On his own and unable to command support from Skinner's family or friends, who instead assisted Skinner in defying the magistrate, Tench apparently had no choice but to retreat ignominiously. Six years later, someone would try to murder him. The culprit in that instance was convicted of shooting to kill and sentenced to seven years' transportation after serving five years at Kingston Penitentiary.[4]

Niagara magistrates were subject to conflicting pressures in the colonial period, as they tried to enforce a Christian moral order in a district where some inhabitants were not shy in demanding that they do just that while others were equally determined to lead their own lives, free of unwelcome judicial interference. It is worth emphasizing that the law the miller insisted Tench enforce was not statute law but the King's proclamation against violations of the sabbath. This was most likely the proclamation issued by William IV in 1830.[5] At the beginning of William's reign, subjects throughout the Empire were reminded of their Christian duties by their newly crowned monarch. As described in the introduction (p. 4), the proclamation was to be read out in every parish church or chapel at least four times a year as well as at the opening of every court of quarter sessions and assizes. It would have been very familiar to Jenner and other members of his community.

The title of the proclamation, 'For the Encouragement of Piety and Virtue, and for the preventing and punishing of Vice; Profaneness and Immorality' places sabbath breaking among a wider set of vices 'highly displeasing to God' that might bring Divine wrath upon the monarch and his subjects. The monarch commanded all his officials 'to be very vigilant and strict in the discovery and effectual prosecution and punishment' of anyone guilty of 'dissolute, immoral, or disorderly practices' including 'profanation of the Lord's Day.' Having the proclamation read in church and at the opening of court sessions was intended to encourage 'Piety and Virtue, and the avoiding of all Immorality and Profaneness.'[6]

The enforcement of a strict Christian moral code had a long royal pedigree in Upper Canada, as it did in Britain. Ever since the conquest of Quebec, the King had instructed the men who governed the Canadas to 'cause all Laws already made against Blasphemy, Profaneness, Adultery, Fornication, Polygamy, Incest, Profanation of the Lord's Day, Swearing and Drunkenness, to be vigorously put in Execution in every part of your Government; And ... [to] take due care for the Punishment of these, and every other Vice and Immorality ...'[7]

In Britain during the latter part of the eighteenth century there had been a renewed enthusiasm for the enforcement of the sabbath laws. The Methodists, led by John Wesley, had lobbied successfully for a vigorous campaign against sabbath breaking and in the 1780s London grand juries had called for stricter enforcement of sabbath laws. These efforts had led to the royal proclamation to encourage piety and virtue and to prevent vice, profaneness, and immorality, which was subsequently issued at the beginning of each new reign. The Anglican evangelical and slave trade reformer, William Wilberforce, argued that 'the institution of Sunday was essential for the preservation of social, political and moral order.'[8] In England, however, the number of prosecutions for sabbath breaking had fallen sharply by 1825.[9]

Across the Atlantic, the Christian fervour of late-eighteenth-century England continued into the nineteenth century among key members of the Upper Canadian elite. When John Beverley Robinson became chief justice of Upper Canada in 1829, his Christian morality soon revealed itself in his expectations of the local magistracy. Magistrates were exhorted to suppress minor social disorders 'which lay the foundations for greater outrages – Gambling, the frequenting of disorderly houses, drunkenness, fighting and the profanation of the sabbath lead speedily and certainly to the destruction of security and happiness in any community which tolerates them.'[10] Robinson's charges to Upper Canadian grand juries echoed and re-echoed the need for vigilant local law enforcement to keep serious criminality in check. The higher the standards of morality in individual communities and the stricter the administration of justice, the better chance society had of escaping crime's worst ravages.[11]

For Robinson and his fellow conservatives, the justice system, in order to function properly, flowed down from the monarch, not up from the people, and it rested upon the control exercised through the monarch's appointed officials. Robinson's teacher, John Strachan, had written in 1810 that the monarch presented to his people 'a pattern of the purest morals' and 'active piety' which embodied an ideal life for his subjects to emulate.[12] Strachan's utopian vision of justice and pure morals emanating from a beneficent sovereign was also a picture of a hierarchical society in which the gradations echoed those of Britain itself. It was, however, so filled with what Robert Fraser has termed 'adulatory pap' that not even Robinson thought it was effective.[13]

One of Strachan's principal premises was the importance of the purest morality, founded on devout Christian belief, as the foundation of society. Or, as a modern commentator has phrased it, the 'Upper Canadian spiritual, governmental and social order were regarded as indissociable.'[14] But flesh-and-blood British sovereigns did not live up to Strachan's ideal and strains in Upper Canadian society were fraying the social fabric and challenging the Christian moral order. Observers regularly noted how far the inhabitants of the Niagara district had strayed from the prescribed moral code, especially the observance of the sabbath, although in this the Niagara inhabitants were no different than colonists anywhere else in Upper Canada. John Howison, who visited the Niagara district in 1819, blamed the state of 'moral degradation' he found there on the lack of regular worship. The settlers regarded Sunday as little different from any other day, except for the absence of work. 'They spend the day in idleness and amusement, either strolling among the woods, and shooting game, or wandering between their neighbours' houses.' Howison believed 'a due observance of the Sabbath' was essential, especially for those whom he termed 'the lower classes,' and the lack of it in the Niagara district caused him to castigate what he labelled 'the Canadian peasantry,' who, 'feeling no religious restraint, are profligate, unamiable and dishonest.'[15] Little apparently had changed by the 1830s, when a newly arrived Scottish presybterian minister lamented, 'The Sabbath at present I am sorry to say it is a Day of Drunkenness.'[16] John Weaver has noted that in this period, 'the secular Sabbath was a recreational institution' that posed constant problems for magistrates.[17]

On the eve of the Rebellion in 1837 Anna Jameson reaffirmed what earlier travellers and immigrants had discovered. She encountered an old landlady in a Beamsville inn who, from a perspective of forty years in the area, gave Jameson 'a horrid picture of the prevalence of drunkenness, the vice and curse of this country.'[18] The Niagara magistrates, assembled in quarter sessions in January 1832, had published a list of rules and regulations for tavern keepers which included a strict prohibition of the sale of alcohol on Sundays to anyone except boarders or travellers. However, as Anna Jameson and other observers confirmed, few tavern owners paid any attention to the regulations if, in fact, they were even aware of them.[19] Similarly, while rules and regulations published for the canal workers on the Welland Canal prohibited profane language and sabbath breaking, canal workers paid little attention to these rules of behaviour.[20]

Not everyone was prepared to accept the innkeepers' open disregard of laws and regulations. Women, who were often the victims of excessive drinking, did not always remain silent. Lavinia Ferguson, a widow who lived in the township of Crowland, went to the trouble of filing a deposition in October 1833 complaining of the conduct of a local tavern keeper named Robert Doan. Doan kept 'a Tippling house where many of the people in the neighbourhood having Families and also the young men of the place, are in the habit of assembling, particularly on the Sabbath, and there get drunk, sometimes commencing on a Saturday and continue on Sunday evening, and as she is informed, on Monday mornings. This is done to the great injury of the families of the married men who frequent the said Inn, and also to the mothers of the Young Men to whom they look for support. The Deponent makes the complaint for the good of the Neighbourhood in which she resides and has been solicited so to do by many who have families, they seeing the evil effects of want and ruin staring them in the face, if Tavern Keepers are allowed to keep Tippling houses and induce the Neighbours to drink and remain away from their families, which is not the intention of the Legislature, in granting Licences to Innkeepers.' Lavinia had visited the tavern herself in search of her brother and found him 'quite intoxicated, so much so that he could not move.'[21] She had to leave without him, but her deposition was based on first-hand observation.

For Lavinia Ferguson, going to the magistrate was clearly a last attempt to resolve a difficult family problem. Her resort to the law provides an example of rural female reaction to the excesses of alcohol, the open violation of sabbath laws, and the flagrant disregard of laws and regulations meant to confine drinking in the Niagara district. Ultimately, her efforts to ensure that the moral code embodied in the law was enforced failed. The magistrate ordered Robert Doan to appear at the quarter sessions court to answer the complaint, but the issue went no further. Such failure had severe consequences for families and for the prestige of the law.

The linkage between religion, morality, and the law was not confined to the Niagara district nor to any one ethnic group. Heinrich Peterson, a Lutheran lay preacher and journalist in Berlin (now Kitchener), articulated an equally strong moral code to his readers shortly after he was appointed a justice of the peace in August 1837. He advised his mainly Mennonite readership of the German paper, the *Canada Museum und Allegemeine Zeitung* to avoid being a 'Sabbath breaker, Swearer, Drunkard or other Disturber of the Peace.'[22] Peterson, in company with other Upper Canadian magistrates of the period, believed that moral and religious offences were just as much disturbances of the peace as offences against the person or property. This belief was solidly entrenched in the law they were sworn to enforce.

There are no extant records of sabbath-breaking cases being brought before the Niagara magistrates sitting collectively at quarter sessions courts prior to 1834. Justices of the peace may have dealt with such cases on an individual basis, but the absence of records makes this impossible to determine. Complaints of moral offences almost never went to the highest courts, the assizes, although Isaac Vanfleet was convicted in 1831 for keeping a disorderly house. The conviction was probably based on the fact that his tavern 'was more boisterous on Sundays than on weekdays.'[23] The expansion of summary justice which began in 1834 encouraged a more efficient disposition of minor offences and gave much more latitude and power to the local magistrate.[24] From 1834 JPs tried to enforce the Christian moral code contained in the laws with greater rigour. Complaints like sabbath breaking, which might never have been brought to the quarter sessions or would have lapsed because of the absence of prosecutor or witnesses, could now be dealt with quickly by the magistrate. Convictions began to be registered for a variety of breaches of the sabbath, giving historians some insight into the contradictions inherent in the prevailing moral order. What was hidden below the legal horizon in the Niagara district prior to 1834, or lost with the destruction of records, comes into view through the magistrates' schedules of convictions from 1835, although an historical microscope is required to bring the picture into full focus.

Historians have long been aware that the practice of Christianity in Upper Canada during the colonial period was far from homogeneous, but we might have assumed that religious services were sacrosanct. How are we then to interpret the conviction of David Flemming, a Grantham labourer, for disturbing the peace, using profane language, and rude and indecent behaviour when he interrupted a service of Canadian Wesleyan Methodists held in Silas Cleveland's house in Thorold on 2 June 1835? Flemming had 'by profane language – by rude and indecent behaviour ... and by mocking and scoffing at the singing and Preaching,' disturbed 'the order and solemnity of the meeting.'[25] Since the service was held on a Monday the offence does not constitute sabbath breaking, but it may be a sign of religious rivalry spilling over legal boundaries. The magistrate, Jacob Keefer, imposed a stiff fine of £2, 10s. and costs. Four more similar convictions were recorded at the fall quarter sessions in 1835 for that part of the Niagara district.[26]

Services held on Sundays were not immune from disturbances and local magistrates often censured disruptive behaviour. In 1836 John Mewburn, the Stamford justice of the peace, fined George Ness, a farm labourer, fifteen shillings and costs for disturbing the worship at St John's Church, Stamford, 'by talking aloud and whistling during the time of divine service.'[27] Jacob Ducher, who misbehaved during a religious service in the Union Chapel at Gainsborough in 1845 by 'talking, Laughing and, by making noises, to the great annoyance of those assembled for Religious Worship,' had to pay five shillings and costs.[28] Miscreants who interfered with religious services in the Niagara district were fined as a matter of course, but William Johnston and John Ferrin had to spend twenty-four hours in the local jail in addition to their fines, for shooting their guns close enough to St Andrews Church to annoy the parishioners during a service in 1840.[29] Magistrates were often familiar with the parties involved, especially in cases brought before them for summary justice. The reputation of the individuals, including their piety or lack of it, and whether the alleged offences had occurred on Sunday could influence the outcome of the hearing. John Mewburn made two labourers involved in a case of alleged assault split the court costs between them 'as a small punishment for breaking the Sabbath.' Reporting the case, he made no efforts to disguise his personal feelings. 'The Parties, Evitts and Berryman, are two of the most drunken reprobates in the Township, the latter neglecting his family and setting an evil example, never attending a place of worship nor sending his family there.'[30]

As mentioned above, the magistrates, sitting collectively at the general quarter sessions, also had the responsibility of issuing or revoking tavern licences. Because of the obvious link between alcohol and crime, the local reputation of the licensee could play a key role in these decisions. In 1835 Edward Kiseley, a magistrate from Bertie, could not attend the quarter sessions, but he joined two other magistrates in signing a petition and wrote separately to the clerk of the peace opposing the renewal of a tavern licence for Alexander Wintermute, formerly a local constable. Kiseley had recommended Wintermute the previous year, but was 'sorry to say that he has since become very intemperate and abusive, and keeps a very disorderly House, which has been a haunt for drunkards and tipplers of the neighbourhood particularly on the Sabbath.'[31]

Inns adjacent to the Welland Canal were particularly notorious not only for serving liquor on Sundays but for encouraging intemperate and violent behaviour. Many complaints never resulted in a formal prosecution, in part because local magistrates tried to find other means of resolving them. On 16 April 1841, John Willims, a Crowland farmer, filed a complaint before two magistrates about an incident that had occurred on the last Sunday in March at a tavern at the junction of the Welland Canal owned by one A. Radcliffe. Willims had witnessed drunken behaviour and a violent assault. When he remonstrated with Radcliffe for 'allowing such conduct on the Sabath,' the innkeeper replied 'that he could not help it, that men wold drink and that he had a Licence to Sell and wold Sell, that none of the Innkeepers on the Canal lived up to their Regulations.' Willims also accused Radcliffe of being too intoxicated himself to do business. The magistrates' solution was to order all the offenders, including the innkeeper, to post peace bonds of £10 for a year, thus avoiding the uncertainty and expense of a trial.[32]

Prosecutions for breach of the sabbath could and did become sharp-edged weapons in neighbourhood quarrels as well as religious disputes. John Lemon of Willoughby successfully prosecuted seven of his neighbours for breaching the sabbath in the summer and fall of 1838. One of them, James Morris, was so angry at being prosecuted for desecrating the sabbath by mowing and hauling his hay that he slammed the door in the constable's face and refused to answer the summons.[33] Lemon may have been an anabaptist and, if so, his piety may have driven him to act against his neighbours. Regardless of his motives, Lemon found the law to be an effective instrument. Other prosecutions appear to have been provoked by business rivalries. This was likely the reason for Thorold miller John Davis's successful prosecution of another miller, John Darling, for 'profaning the Lord's Day by working his mill and grinding wheat' in October 1837.[34]

Successful prosecutions for morals offences at the district quarter sessions were infrequent, no doubt because of the problems involved in ensuring that the prosecutor and witnesses were available for the trial and then convincing a jury that the alleged offence had occurred. Violations of the sabbath could be both the cause of the prosecution and the reason for its success. When three Niagara farmers brought a charge of keeping a disorderly house against Sarah Campbell in December 1836, their deposition claimed that she kept 'a disorderly house where whoring, drunkenness, gambling, fiddling and dancing on the Lord's Day are carried on; where gamblers, drunkards, whoremongers generally resort by day and night.' The court subpoenaed eight witnesses, including the fiddler. Sarah Campbell was found guilty and sentenced to two weeks in the district jail.[35]

Prosecutions for disturbing religious worship or breaching the sabbath were sometimes brought to the magistrates by members of minority populations. Joseph Thompson, along with other members of St Catharines' African Canadian community, brought a formal complaint in 1842 against four presumably white males and secured their conviction for disturbing religious worship. The four had stoned an African Canadian meeting house during a religious service. The magistrate fined each of them ten shillings apiece, plus costs, double the usual amount, perhaps trying to avert further racial incidents.[36] A similar prosecution occurred three years later, an indication that the racial persecution continued.[37] Appealing to the sabbath laws and appearing before the local magistrate offered an avenue of redress that avoided overt questions of race and enabled the magistrates to enforce the prevailing code of morality. African Canadians could be reasonably confident of obtaining convictions on what were seen as minor offences, and were apparently not reluctant to bring charges when all that was involved was an appearance before the local magistrate.

Until 1845, prosecutions for violations of the sabbath in the Niagara district and throughout Upper Canada were brought under the English criminal law the new colony had adopted in 1792. Magistrates clearly found no difficulty returning convictions under the English law, and no convictions in the Niagara district for breach of the sabbath were appealed. Some attempts had been made to pass an Upper Canadian Lord's Day statute. One was led by Niagara MPP Dr John Lefferty, who in 1830 brought in a bill to grant magistrates more authority to enforce sabbath observance. Lefferty personally opposed shooting and skating on Sundays, but his bill was designed to legislate an improved Christian morality. He stated, 'It was a common thing ... for persons to leave their work, and assemble at grog shops on Saturday night and drink and carouse until the next night.' As Lefferty observed, this was 'an injury, not only to the morals, but also to the industry of the country.'[38] He helped to ensure the ultimate defeat of his bill by advocating compulsory Sunday worship, but his unsuccessful effort illustrates a belief that a stricter adherence to a Christian moral code would also be good for business.

In 1845 the Legislature of the Canadas finally passed its own Act to 'prevent the Profanation of the Lord's Day,' making it illegal to 'tipple' on Sundays or permit 'tippling' in any inn or tavern; to be drunk, to brawl, or to use profane language in the streets; to hold or attend political meetings; to play skittles, football, ball, 'or any other noisy game'; to gamble; to run races; to hunt or shoot; or to bathe publicly in any city or town.[39] The undesirable activities engaged in throughout the colony on Sundays were specified and prohibited in Upper Canada's first homegrown Lord's Day Act.

Upper Canada was not the only British North American colony to tighten the regulations against breaches of the sabbath. New Brunswick had passed a Lord's Day Act in 1786, linking profanation of the sabbath with other forms of immorality.[40] This statute was found insufficient and in 1831 it was repealed and replaced by a stronger Act that prohibited specified activities such as shooting, gaming, sporting, playing, hunting, or 'frequenting tippling houses' on Sundays.[41] Lower Canada had possessed specific sabbatarian legislation since 1805, when selling goods, including alcohol, was prohibited on Sundays, and in 1817 regulations were issued to keep order in churches on Sundays.[42] Upper Canada succeeded in passing sabbatarian legislation following the union of 1840, when the climate changed to favour such legislation. William Westfall refers to sabbath observance as one of the two great crusades (the other being temperance) carried on by religious institutions in the province during the middle of the nineteenth century 'to provide Victorians with a moral pathway through the hazards of a materialistic world.'[43]

The legislators who introduced the Upper Canadian Act in 1845 evinced no new concerns about a materialistic world or any sense of a renewed need for moral pathways. Nor did they mention any link to previous royal proclamations on the subject. Colonel John Prince, representing Essex, who piloted the bill through the Assembly and claimed that he had the support of all Upper Canadian members for it, argued that Upper Canada had no statute of its own to prevent people working on Sunday. He then quoted from Blackstone's *Commentaries* to convince any doubters.[44] There was no sense of urgency or unusual importance in the debates on the bill. It was not debated at any length. What the debates convey is a feeling of tidying up a loose end; the introduction of a homegrown statute to legislate something taken for granted both in Upper Canada and in Britain, a Lord's Day Act. If anything, the Act represented an Upper Canadian reaffirmation of the religious and moral values inherited from Britain. These values had been reinforced by Loyalist and later immigrants who moved to Upper Canada following the American Revolution, as well as by British immigrants who arrived after the Napoleonic Wars. In retrospect, what is new is the transfer of this Christian moral responsibility from the monarch to the Legislative Assembly. Apparently beginning with Victoria, regular reminders about the sabbath in the form of royal proclamations ceased, leaving the enforcement of the Christian moral code in the hands of the colonial government or, more specifically, to laws passed by its elected officials.

There were two surprises in the debate. First, not everyone supported the bill. Protests emanating from Lower Canada, which may have reflected feelings in Upper Canada as well, signalled doubts about the ability of any legislation to govern peoples' habits of worship or their activities on Sundays. Here perhaps, was something novel, even modern, a questioning of the role of the state in enforcing the Christian moral order. The other surprise was that the bill was clearly Protestant. Prince had been forced to withdraw his first bill, which applied to both Canada East and Canada West, because of opposition from French Canadian Roman Catholics. The bill had to be limited to Canada West in order to get it through the Legislature.

Peter Oliver links the 1845 Act to 'a mounting concern about social disorder' in the colony, a concern which was also reflected in the rapid spread of temperance societies, a tightening of control over local licensing of taverns, and a desire to see more efficient local policing, especially on public works sites.[45] To legislators like Colonel Prince there certainly seemed to be more challenges to the Christian social order in the 1840s, and these challenges provided ample justification for the colony to equip itself with modern legislative weapons to preserve that order. This was, after all, a time of large-scale immigration, with many transients moving through the colony, and also a period when the emerging Canadian state was assuming new powers.[46] What is uncertain from the debate and the publicity it generated is whether the traditional moral order of Upper Canadian society was under threat.

Did the new Act make any difference in the prosecution of sabbath breaking in Upper Canada? The number of prosecutions for this offence had always been small in the Niagara district. From 1834, when magistrates were given the authority to levy summary convictions, they amounted to less than 5 per cent of the total in nearly every schedule of convictions registered quarterly by the clerk of the peace. One exception was the last register before the passage of the new Act, when an all-time high of fourteen convictions for sabbath breaking were registered, 12 per cent of the total convictions for the summer and fall of 1844. The increase was perhaps a sign that the publicity given to the issue by the Legislature had prompted the magistrates to act more forcefully.[47]

The increase in convictions was not the only indication that some magistrates, at least, were determined to act against sabbath breakers and welcomed the prospect of the new law. Three of the five convictions filed by Jacob Misener at Gainsborough at the April 1844 quarter sessions were for sabbath breaking. In one case, James Gillam of Gainsborough could not pay the usual fine of five shillings after being caught spear-fishing on a Sunday. He was sentenced to two hours in the stocks as a public example. This may have been one of the last times the stocks were used in the Niagara district, and the magistrates' resort to them may have been another attempt to warn the residents of Gainsborough that they had better abide by the sabbath legislation. Misener also convicted a possible relative, Alver Misener, for improper behaviour in a Presbyterian church. His offence was to sell ball tickets during a service 'and other wise Indecently misbehave himself.'[48]

The number of convictions for sabbath breaking in the district increased noticeably in the year following the passage of the law. Magistrates found the Lord's Day Act a handy tool because of the wide range of offences encompassed in the legislation. Six of the eleven convictions recorded by Owen Fares in the village of Humberstone from August to November 1845 were for sabbath breaking.[49] The descriptions of the offences, however, reveal clearly that all the culprits were convicted for being drunk and disorderly. Not working on Sunday gave labourers, especially those working on the Welland Canal, time to drink. Convictions ensued when excessive drinking led to fighting or to public nuisance. The new law was especially useful to diligent constables like Edward Wheeler, the canal constable, who obtained six convictions for sabbath breaking in the spring of 1845 out of a total of eighteen recorded for Humberstone.[50]

While the absolute number of convictions for sabbath breaking and related offences such as disturbing religious services rose in the year after the introduction of the new legislation, there was little immediate change in the relative percentage of convictions recorded in the Niagara district. These convictions accounted for 6 per cent of the total recorded for the April quarter sessions 1845, 7 per cent for the July sessions, and 9 per cent for the April sessions of 1846.[51] By 1848, however, the percentage of sabbath-breaking cases had risen to nearly 24 per cent, or twenty-eight cases out of the total of 119 recorded at the fall court of quarter sessions, an indication of how useful the Niagara magistrates found the new law.[52]

The Lord's Day Act turned out to be a highly flexible instrument for prosecutors and magistrates attempting to impose a moral order on an increasingly unruly Canadian society. When Alfred Talbot, a St Catharines barber, was convicted of sabbath breaking in August 1846, he had actually had been brawling and using profane language in the streets, 'creating annoyance to Her Majesty's peaceable Subjects.'[53] The victims of the fight may have decided to prosecute Talbot on this relatively minor charge rather than assault, believing they had a greater chance of obtaining a conviction.

A determined magistrate like Jacob Misener of Wainfleet could now try anew to stamp out impious and illegal Sunday practices. He convicted one farmer for 'drawing wheat with his team,' another for taking a load of shingles on the highway, and two more for hunting on Sundays during the summer and fall of 1846.[54] These sabbath-breaking convictions were the only ones he registered during this quarter. Jacob Misener's relative, Leonard, the Wainfleet magistrate, continued the family tradition of registering convictions for sabbath breaking in 1850. Some form of private quarrel clearly lay behind this case, which involved an informant. Eusebius Chambers prosecuted Peter Far for sabbath breaking – Peter had entered Chambers's workshop on a Sunday morning to retrieve his violin. Misener found Far guilty and fined him ten shillings and costs. Half of the fine went to the informer, presumably to make informing worthwhile and to provide an incentive for other potential informers.[55] The Lord's Day Act even provided opportunities for sinners beset with their guilt to turn to magistrates instead of to their ministers: in one unusual case, Luke Gibbons turned himself in to the Thorold magistrate for profaning the Sabbath. He received the usual five shilling fine.[56]

With the increasing incorporation of municipalities across Upper Canada, the battle for a Christian moral society gradually shifted to elected councils and municipal police forces. Far from giving up the struggle, they gave it new life. Nicholas Rogers describes the Toronto police of the later nineteenth century as 'domestic missionaries' in the cause, adopting moral reform as their 'particular vocation.'[57]

The increase in the number of convictions for sabbath breaking and related offences recorded in the Niagara district in the mid-1840s says more about the utility of the Lord's Day statute and the willingness of magistrates to levy small fines for these offences than it does about the effectiveness of the law in altering peoples' behaviour. Inhabitants of the Niagara district were quick to point out how little moral improvement had occurred. Thirty-four men from Bertie petitioned the magistrates sitting in the court of quarter sessions in December 1845 to extend their authority 'as conservators of the Peace and Guardians of the Morals of the community' by reducing the number of licensed taverns in their village. They had observed drinking, quarrelling, and swearing on Sundays, 'in total disregard to the provisions of a recent Act of the Legislature made for the better observance of the Sabbath Day.' People 'of good morals and exemplary Christian deportment' were not involved and were unaware of what was happening. Those who frequented the taverns were the last to complain: 'Few indeed are found who are willing to enter formal complaint to the Magistrate.'[58]

The Bertie men were by no means alone in viewing their magistrates as guardians of the community's Christian moral code. But signs of discontent with the rigidity of the law's Christian morality were easy to find, even if open rebellion against it was highly unlikely. Enforcement was uneven, as illustrated by the prosecutions for sabbath breaking. Committed constables and magistrates prosecuted every offence brought to their attention; others made little or no attempt to search out offenders. The hapless Bartholomew Tench was surely not alone in his ineffective efforts to enforce the law. Many prosecutions were the outcome of private disputes that had little to do with the enforcement of a Christian moral order, but for which the sabbath laws were convenient weapons. The law became the vehicle of enforcement when immorality became blatant or caused offence. How and when this occurred in the Niagara district, as in other parts of the colony, was never entirely predictable.

5

Intruders Upon the Precincts
of Crime

When he spoke at the ceremony to lay the cornerstone for the Provincial Lunatic Asylum in 1846, Chief Justice Robinson emphasized the need for this new state facility, which would remove 'the mere helpless and unwelcome intruders upon the precincts of crime' from the district jails and permit them to be treated medically, perhaps in some cases with the hope of a cure.[1] Who were these intruders and how had they ended up in the local jails, 'the precincts of crime,' in nineteenth-century Upper Canada? There is no simple answer to this question. But in the minds of contemporary legal officials many of the people found in the colony's jails did not belong there. The three most common categories of 'intruders' were debtors, paupers, and lunatics, to use the language of the period. This chapter focuses on the moral, legal, and financial challenges posed by the insane to the criminal justice system, while chapter 6 discusses poor relief and paupers.[2] Because the district jail was a catch-all institution from the very beginning of the colony, it performed what we might term today a social welfare function, although this concept would have meant little to contemporary magistrates.

The early colony of Upper Canada quickly found itself wrestling with complex social questions. The local justice system lacked facilities other than the district jail in which to confine the insane, and it was evident to many that the criminal justice system was not properly equipped to deal with the mentally ill. For a long time officials were unable to separate the unwelcome intruders from the criminals themselves. And some of the intruders succeeded in tying the system in judicial knots without consciously setting out to do so.

The case of Patrick Donnelly provides one example of the problems faced in the Niagara district. We know little of Donnelly's biography except that he was an Irish immigrant brought to the Niagara jail on 6 September 1832, charged with the murder of his wife. His arrest suggests an ordinary if tragic tale of a domestic crime, but what happened to Donnelly and his subsequent history mark him out as unique, someone whose history deserves to be better known. While Peter Oliver alludes to this strange case in 'Terror to Evil-Doers,' Donnelly's story has never been fully recounted.[3] Oliver states that Donnelly might have remained in jail indefinitely had not a Niagara grand jury 'jogged Robinson's memory.' In fact, Donnelly remained in the Niagara jail until his death. Chief Justice Robinson who was responsible for putting him there in the first place, took no action to release Donnelly or to find any other solution even after his memory was jogged. Nor would anyone else interfere. Donnelly, labelled a lunatic in 1832, was left to languish in the Niagara jail until he died in 1840.

Patrick Donnelly (the spelling is occasionally given as Donnally) was never convicted of a crime and no trial was held on the charge of murder. While he served longer in the Niagara jail than any other prisoner in the district, his entire time was on remand. Both Chief Justice Robinson, who presided at the Niagara assizes in September 1832, and a petit jury judged Donnelly to be insane and incapable of standing trial for the murder of his wife. How this judgment was made and the fate of Donnelly cast a long shadow in the history of the Canadian colonial justice system. The Donnelly case illuminates the inability of colonial judicial officials to cope with the issues presented by insanity and their helplessness in dealing with those labelled insane. It also helped to propel the changes which led to the creation of the Provincial Asylum.

Donnelly had been brought to the Niagara jail just prior to the September assizes and arraigned on 10 September 1832. Robinson recorded in his bench book notes of the assize cases that Donnelly was 'acting strangely'[4] and he requested the petit jury to determine whether Donnelly was 'of sound mind and understanding or not.' A number of witnesses were called to assist the jury in this task. Who they were and what they said casts an eery light on the legal ramifications of criminal insanity in nineteenth-century Upper Canada.

Robinson was acting within the accepted English legal tradition in having the jury determine Donnell's sanity and in calling witnesses, especially medical doctors, to testify to assist them in reaching their verdict. In England the passage of the Criminal Lunatics Act in 1800 made lunatics 'a formal species' defined in law.[5] It also formalized a procedure for dealing with them and if during a criminal trial a jury found the defendant to be insane, the court could order him to be kept in custody although no verdict had been reached on the criminal charge. This post-1792 English law did not apply in Upper Canada, but it was well known to judges like Robinson. One of its key legal principles was that if the defendant was insane and could not understand his rights within a trial, he was not fit to plead. These rights included challenges to the jury impanelled. The real concern of the law was with the question of intent. In the words of Joel Eigen, 'only intentional behaviour was punishable by law: the perpetrator who failed to understand the wrongfulness of an action could not be said to have acted with criminal intent.'[6] The doctors asked to testify on Donnelly's behalf relied, as did other witnesses, on impressions gained during one or more interviews, a process that mirrored prevailing practices in England.[7] No clear definition of what constituted insanity in criminal law existed either in England or in Upper Canada. It was left to the jury to make the final decision.

The first witness was a neighbour, the constable who had brought Donnelly to the Niagara jail. Abraham Austin told the court that when he had brought him to Niagara, Donnelly 'had acted as if he was out of his head or was mad. He did not give reasonable answers to questions put to him.' Another neighbour, Mary Meaghan, thought Donnelly had 'run out of his mind after he has been so sick about a week before his wife's death.' Then the deputy sheriff, Kidd, and the jailer, Wheeler, were called to testify. Kidd, who had visited Donnelly three times a day from his arrival, suspected him of feigning madness, although he also told the court of Donnelly's tendency towards violence. The jailer reported that Donnelly sometimes 'talks quite rationally and at other times as he is now.' He was unable to say whether Donnelly's insanity was real or faked.

The next two witnesses called were doctors. Dr Telfer, a Niagara physician, admitted that he did not have 'much experience of insane persons.' He, too, had visited Donnelly in jail, and when he had talked with him Telfer had thought Donnelly was sane. But the doctor had also noticed something strange about the way Donnelly acted in court.

He summed up his assessment by stating his belief that Donnelly possessed sufficient reason to know what was happening and to understand the evidence. As an afterthought, Telfer observed that one of Donnelly's eyes had contracted and the other had dilated. He offered no conclusion on what interpretation might be drawn from the medical evidence. The second physician, John Bridges, testified that Donnelly was perfectly conscious of what was happening: 'he understands the subject.'

The next witness was another prisoner, George Smith, who was in the Niagara jail as a debtor. He had accompanied the deputy sheriff in his visits to Donnelly, possibly because Kidd was afraid to visit him on his own. Smith told the court that Donnelly 'answered very regularly and properly as to inquiries.' Smith was sure Donnelly was perfectly sane. 'He looked then as now – looked rather ferocious than wild.' After another doctor had added further details, stating that Donnelly now looked tired, the petit jury examined him and retired to consider whether he was mentally fit to stand trial. When the jury found that he was not, the chief justice remanded Donnelly to the Niagara jail.

The deputy sheriff, the jailer, and a fellow prisoner clearly suspected that Donnelly might be feigning madness to avoid being tried for murder, condemned, and executed. Their testimony was designed to alert the jury to this possibility. The absence of any clear criteria for determining insanity is also obvious. The medical evidence could not have been very helpful to the jury and the notes of the chief justice are silent on any instructions he may have provided. The only clue as to what Donnelly may have thought comes in later testimony from Dr Telfer who reported that Donnelly believed that he had been tried and acquitted in his first appearance before the court. Since he was then remanded to the Niagara jail, Donnelly was either confused, completely ignorant of legal proceedings, or, conceivably, both.

The chief justice did not let the matter of Donnelly's competence rest after he had remanded him. Just before the assizes terminated Donnelly was brought back to court, and again the petit jury was asked to decide whether he was sane and capable of being tried for murder. Again, witnesses were brought forward and asked to testify as to his sanity. Their testimony reveals how hard Robinson had pressed behind the scenes to get the available experts – doctors, the sheriff, magistrates – to visit Donnelly and determine his state of mind. Dr Porter was the first physician called. In the intervening period he had visited Donnelly three times in prison, and each time had conversed with him for half an hour. Like the other doctors who testified, Porter made no mention of carrying out a medical examination. Conversation was the only method used to assess sanity or insanity. Dr Porter believed Donnelly was insane 'as regards the murder of his wife and in some measure so on religious matters' although he told the court that Donnelly 'conversed rationally' on other matters. Porter was convinced that Donnelly was not feigning insanity. How Donnelly could be partially insane on religious matters was not explained, but it begs the question of what actually was discussed and how Porter arrived at this conclusion. One clue as to the subject of their conversation comes from the British traveller, Anna Jameson, who visited Niagara in 1837 and talked to one of the physicians who had testified at Donnelly's trial. Jameson reports the doctor as saying that although he believed Donnelly was insane, he could not prove it. Donnelly 'appeared rational on every subject.' Jameson continued: 'at length, after his condemnation, the physician, holding his wrist, repeated the religious Orange toast – something about the Pope and the devil; and instantly as he expressed it, the man's pulse bounded like a shot under his fingers, and he was seized with a fit of frenzy. He said that his wife had been possessed by the seven deadly sins, and he had merely given her seven kicks to exorcise her – and thus he murdered the poor woman.' By 1837 Donnelly had been in jail for more than four years. Described as a 'wretched maniac' and confined in chains, he appeared to the physician as 'now more, more furious, than when first confined.'[8]

After Porter had given evidence Dr Telfer was recalled to testify. He too had visited Donnelly several times since his previous testimony and he agreed with Porter that Donnelly was not feigning insanity. All Telfer could add was that although Donnelly now seemed to understand he was to be tried for the murder of his wife, he did not understand the consequences. There was a hint in Telfer's testimony that Donnelly thought his wife's death had been ordained by Providence. Another doctor, Raymond, had visited Donnelly the morning of his second appearance in company with two magistrates. He confirmed that Donnelly had answered rationally all the questions put to him except those having to do with the death of his wife. One of the magistrates, Bartholomew Tench, similarly reported that Donnelly had answered questions rationally except those on the death of his wife and on religion. After two more witnesses reiterated the same points, the jury was charged to determine whether Donnelly was now sane.

Their response was the same: Donnelly was not sane and could not stand trial. Chief Justice Robinson, as he later wrote to the lieutenant governor, 'was compelled therefore to remand him & to leave him in custody – untried, at the termination of the Assizes.'[9]

Donnelly now found himself a prisoner of the state, confined in the Niagara jail on remand without having been tried or convicted on the charge of murder. He took no action himself to try and win his freedom, most likely because he was unable to. The local Niagara district authorities who had to pay for his captivity and look after him, however, were not nearly as passive. Two years after Donnelly had been confined as insane a grand jury, after inspecting the jail, asked the Niagara clerk of the peace, Charles Richardson, to forward a presentment to the lieutenant governor. They petitioned to have Donnelly, 'an insane person,' removed from the jail 'and placed in the Penitentiary or some other place where he may be confined in safety.'[10] The Kingston Penitentiary was nearly finished – it opened in 1835 – and the Niagara jurors saw it as offering the solution to the problems presented by Donnelly.

The lieutenant governor's secretary referred the petition to Chief Justice Robinson. Robinson recounted what had happened in 1832 and added 'I have heard nothing of him [Donnelly] since, but I observe the Grand Jury speak of him unhesitatingly as still insane. He cannot be discharged. The Penitentiary is clearly not a place in which he will be received, and I can point out no other to which he can properly be removed, as I am not aware of any public provision being made for the care of [such individuals?] whether they are charged as offenders or not.'[11] The chief justice identified the three salient issues. He interpreted the grand jury's use of the term 'insane' as another jury's finding of fact on Donnelly's state of mind; he confirmed that the penitentiary would not receive any 'intruders upon the precincts of crime', and he highlighted the lack of any legislative provisions for the care of people like Donnelly. Since Robinson had stated definitely that Donnelly could not be discharged, he was not. The Kingston Penitentiary did eventually receive the criminally insane, but not until the following decade were they transferred there in any numbers.

The Niagara grand jury was not the only local body to petition the provincial authorities in an attempt to have Donnelly transferred out of the district. Soon, the campaign to have him removed involved all of the local judicial officials. In March 1835 the chairman of the quarter sessions was ordered to write to the various 'lunatic hospitals' in Lower

Canada to find out on what terms they would agree to receive Donnelly.[12] A month after the grand jury's petition the district sheriff added a personal note to his jail returns, pointing out the problems faced by the Niagara jail because it had become a receptacle for the insane. The jail had not been constructed to allow separation or classification of prisoners. Insane prisoners could either be confined in separate cells, making the overcrowding in the rest of the jail worse, or placed among the criminals and debtors. What was left unsaid was that the other prisoners did everything they could to avoid being placed in the same cells with the insane. The sheriff stated that the lack of proper facilities made it 'almost impracticable to keep proper order or to prevent the almost incessant formation of plots for escape ...' Hamilton asked for the transfer of the insane prisoners to some place 'where they may be properly attended to and give us the rooms now occupied by them for the use of other prisoners.'[13] When nothing had been done and another year had passed, Deputy Sheriff Alexander McLeod added a personal note to the jail returns for 1835: 'From the almost continually crowded state of our Gaol and limited accommodation as well as for the sake of Humanity to the above distressed Object [Donnelly] it would be extremely desireable if his removal could be Effected to some place where there would at least be some chance of his recovery, which in his present place of abode, I fear, is hopeless.'[14] Even McLeod found it repugnant to deny someone who was obviously insane a remote chance of recovery.

The belief that in not providing some separate facility for the mentally insane the colonists of Upper Canada were acting in an unChristian and inhumane manner was widely shared. Peter Oliver cites J.N. Gamble, the chairman of the district sessions of the Home district, writing in 1840 to support a proposal for a provincial asylum, as saying that if one were established, 'the stain upon our character as a Christian community, for our barbarous treatment of the afflicted, may at last be effaced.'[15] When Dr Duncombe wrote his report for the Upper Canadian Assembly in 1836 on the possibility of creating a provincial asylum, he pointed out that the colony was alone in North America by that time in continuing to use jails to house the insane.[16]

The next we hear of Patrick Donnelly is a brief entry under the jail records of the Niagara district in November 1837 authorizing a special ration for him of one pound of meat and two pounds of bread per day.[17] It is not clear whether the magistrates believed that with a more generous food allotment Donnelly might be cured, or whether this is another example of penny-pinching Niagara magistrates insisting on approving every detail of criminal expenses for the district, right down to the daily food allowance for the only long-term prisoner held in the district jail.

In the aftermath of the Upper Canadian Rebellion economic conditions worsened in the Niagara district, and grand jurors complained even more about having to pay local taxes to look after those referred to as 'afflicted persons' in the district jail. In a presentment to the lieutenant governor, crying out for the establishment of a provincial asylum in March 1838 the Niagara grand jurors referred specifically to the case of Patrick Donnelly. Their examination of the jail had revealed that 'an Insane person ... has now been confined there nearly Seven years during which period no Amelioration of his Calamity has taken place, but who we have no doubt might have ere this to a certain extent been enabled to exercise his reasonable faculties had he had the benefit of proper treatment in such an Assylum as alluded to ...'[18] The jurors cited the support of the jail physician for their belief that a cure or at least some improvement in Donnelly's condition might be possible in an asylum, whereas in the local jail nothing could be done for him. They also requested that the clerk of the peace send a statement of the annual cost to the district of caring for Patrick Donnelly to the lieutenant governor with their presentment, and they urged that the Legislature act on their petition in the next legislative session, treating it as a matter of great urgency.

The cost to the district taxpayers of caring for Donnelly was, of course, the key issue and it had become a much more acute one in the post-Rebellion economically distressed district of Niagara. Costs and humanitarian feelings seemed to alternate in the Niagara grand juries' annual presentments to the lieutenant governor, requesting better facilities for the insane. In 1839 they conjured up the horrors of an eighteenth-century Newgate: 'the raving Maniac is confined in the same Ward with the other Prisoners – their ravings and howlings adding (if it be possible to add) to the horrors endured by the prisoners, many of whom are found to be innocent, and many only unfortunate Debtors.'[19]

As discussed below, the Legislature approved an asylum bill in May 1839,[20] but the new Provincial Asylum was not open to admit patients until 1846. Before the new asylum was ready, Upper Canada converted the old district jail in Toronto into a temporary asylum, thus continuing to incarcerate those labelled insane but attempting to isolate these 'intruders' in their own precinct of crime.

Donnelly died in the Niagara jail on 20 November 1840, six years before the provincial insane asylum opened. The jail surgeon, Henry Rolls, submitted an autopsy report to the district magistrates which revealed that Donnelly was epileptic and died from the consequences of an epileptic seizure. The doctor found what he described as 'an irregularly formed bony concretion about three quarters of an inch in diameter and a quarter thick adhering to the dura mater (the membrane lining [the] cranium) and pressing on the brain in the immediate vicinity of which the brain was disorganized and indeed the whole of its substance very much softened which satisfactorily accounts for his insanity and the disease which ultimately terminated his existance [sic].'[21] Donnelly had served eight years in the Niagara jail because he was epileptic.

Patrick Donnelly was not the only person confined in the Niagara jail during this period on grounds of insanity. The magistrates, however, found alternative means of caring for the other insane individuals, usually by paying someone to look after them outside the jail. They had greater flexibility in the other cases because unlike Donnelly these individuals had not been found insane by a jury and remanded by the colony's chief justice. In the summer of 1836, Dr Porter, the Niagara jail doctor, reported to the magistrates that 'a Person of the name of John Campbell has been committed in an insane State, who is a great annoyance to the other Prisoners from the almost incessant noise which he makes. The unfortunate man is now in a State of perfect nudity.'[22] The grand jury supported Porter's conclusion and recommended that 'means be taken to remove [Campbell] to some other place.' The magistrates, pressured to act, took the only action open to them. They authorized someone outside the jail to look after Campbell and paid the costs of his maintenance.[23]

The determination of the Niagara magistrates to evade financial liability for looking after the insane is even more evident in the case of Hiram Vinica. Twenty-six residents of the township of Walpole petitioned the court in April 1836 for financial assistance to look after Vinica, who had for five weeks been 'in a state of Insanity wholly unable and incapable of taking Care of himself ...' The grand jury that received this petition recommended compensation of ten shillings per week to the family who had looked after him and that he be incarcerated in the local jail. Two days later, when it discovered that Vinica was in fact an American, the grand jury forwarded a new recommendation, urging that Vinica be taken immediately to the United States, where presumably the Americans would pay for his care and support.[24] Two constables were hired to escort Vinica to Buffalo at a cost of over five and a half pounds. While native-born lunatics had to be looked after and paid for in the district, American lunatics from the United States were quickly repatriated.

Local magistrates were able to find a temporary solution for John Campbell and remove him from the jail, even if the district still had to pay the costs of his care, and Hiram Vinica could be sent back to the United States. Donnelly's situation, however, was completely different and prompted the district officials to participate actively in a campaign to establish a provincial asylum. In their desire to solve what had become a completely intractable problem they were certainly not alone. Pressure had been building steadily throughout the 1830s for the creation of a provincial asylum. Much of it, and in the end the most influential pressure, had come from districts like Niagara and towns like York, where officials had been forced to accommodate insane people in the local jail. As early as 1830, a Home district grand jury had called upon the Legislature to create an asylum to relieve the district jails of the necessity of housing lunatics. In the same year a legislative committee chaired by William Lyon Mackenzie had highlighted the plight of the insane incarcerated in the local jails.[25] The doctor in charge of York hospital wrote in his annual report in 1831 that 'the District Jail is still the only refuge of the destitute Maniac where he becomes a nuisance of the most revolting nature, and where neither Medical or Moral treatment can be successfully applied for his relief.'[26] In May 1831 the lieutenant governor referred the problem to the York magistrates and the trustees of the York hospital, saying 'within the last ten days, my attention has been called to the wretched condition of social families, and although it may be thought imprudent or absurd to create an Institution at York that may attract the destitute and idle to this part of the Province, I am persuaded that greater evils will result from persons of this description being allowed to enter the Town, without notice, than from searching them out and bringing them to a well regulated establishment supported by the exertions of a few active individuals and public collections.'[27]

The trustees of the York hospital were dependent on public funds and the local magistrates responded that they had no funds available to build an asylum. They were willing to offer £75 to remove the 'distressing nuisance' of the insane confined within the local jail, which is what they estimated it cost to maintain them in the York jail for the remainder of the year.[28] With this impasse, the problem remained unresolved.

The confinement of lunatics in public jails rapidly became a larger problem in York than it was in Niagara, but Niagara officials ensured that neither the governor nor the Legislature forgot about Patrick Donnelly. In 1835 the magistrates themselves, in their role as an assize grand jury, petitioned the lieutenant governor and the Legislature to remove Donnelly from their care.[29] The Niagara district could count on strong support from other districts in its opposition to housing the insane in local jails and in its resentment at having to bear the financial cost of looking after them. Among the districts of Upper Canada, Niagara was one of the most persistent in pursuing remedies for this social ill.

There were also signs of a deeper unease in Upper Canadian society during the 1830s, fears that the moral order on which society rested was being undermined. Accelerating change fuelled by the industrial revolution in Britain and swelling emigration to Upper Canada accentuated this insecurity, especially among the elite. C.J. Taylor suggests that 'aberrations in normal behaviour, crime, lunacy and sickness, were seen as manifestations of disorder, indications that the universe at large was not in harmony. Individual deviancy threatened the social order.' Institutions, in contrast, were perceived as 'obvious bulwarks against disorder.'[30] The biggest and most important of these new institutions was the Kingston Penitentiary, from whose 'moral architecture' emanated a reassuring image of security to reinforce the social order. A provincial asylum would perform a similar function, removing another diseased arm of society and guarding it behind the protective walls of an institution. The perceived need for a provincial asylum was also a recognition that solutions could no longer be found at the local level. In the 1830s not even the sheriffs argued that the insane represented a real threat to Upper Canadian society. The campaign for the provincial asylum was an amalgam of the desire to remove the insane from the local jails and the hope that within an asylum more effective treatment leading to cures would occur.

By the mid-1830s a bipartisan movement embracing both Tories and Reformers was gathering steam and pushing for the creation of a provincial asylum. One of the Tories in the forefront of these efforts was Charles Richardson. Richardson was one of the young men who received lucrative rewards following his involvement in the types riot of 1826. In company with other young, well-connected members of the provincial elite, he had helped to destroy William Lyon Mackenzie's printing office at York.[31] He was appointed clerk of the peace for the Niagara district in 1828 and held the office until his death twenty years later. In 1834 he was elected to the Upper Canadian Legislature to represent the town of Niagara. Richardson served until the union of 1840 and was one of the legislators whose steady pressure led in 1839 to the passage of a bill to create a provincial asylum. Richardson was familiar with the Donnelly case, since he was also the clerk of the peace for the Niagara district. At the very least he had read, if he did not inspire, the regular grand jury presentments on the need to find an alternative solution for Donnelly.

As Niagara's clerk of the peace and someone closely tied to the Niagara magistracy, Richardson was both knowledgeable about the problems presented by housing the insane in local jails and committed to finding a solution that would free the Niagara district of this un-wanted burden. He first gave notice of an asylum bill in 1835, but this proposal went no further. Instead, a three-man committee led by the reformer Dr Charles Duncombe was struck to examine methods for creating and managing an asylum. Duncombe toured American insti-tutions, as an earlier legislative committee had done prior to the con-struction of the Kingston Penitentiary, and submitted a report to the Legislature in February 1836.

Duncombe's report marks a turning point in the recognition of in-sanity as a public problem in Upper Canada. By popularizing the concept of 'moral treatment' then current in leading American asy-lums such as the one built in Worcester, Massachusetts, in 1833, it helped to transform Upper Canadian perceptions of insanity from 'a crime subjecting the unfortunate subject of it to imprisonment, pun-ishment and chains' to 'a disease of the organ of the mind' capable of cure.[32] Duncombe's report heightened optimism about the potential impact of a provincial asylum. On the basis of what Duncombe had seen in the United States, the complete eradication of insanity seemed possible.

Shortly after Duncombe's report was tabled in the Legislature Charles Richardson brought in another bill to create a provincial asylum, this time proposing to finance it with a 5 per cent tax on the colony's banks. This bill also failed, and early in 1837 Richardson introduced a third bill, which later became law, to continue the former system of local district relief payments for the destitute insane until an asylum could be constructed.[33]

Anna Jameson, who was in close contact with the governing elite of Upper Canada in 1837, expressed her regret that the Legislative Assembly had not managed to pass an Act authorizing the construction of a provincial asylum that year: 'The fate of those confined in the prisons is not better; the malady is prolonged and aggravated by the horrid species of confinement to which in such places, these wretched beings are necessarily subjected ... in the meantime this dreadful evil continues – must continue for two or three years longer; and think what an amount of individual suffering may be crowded into this period! When I was at Niagara there was a maniac [Donnelly] in the jail there, who had been chained up for four years. Here was misery of the most pitiable kind suffering all the pains and penalties of crime – nay, far more, for the worst criminals had a certain degree of liberty.' The image of Donnelly confined in chains in the Niagara jail left a lasting impression upon Jameson, and doubtless upon both her readers and those among the Upper Canadian elite to whom she related the tale.[34]

One interesting offshoot of the campaign for a provincial asylum was the effort to collect more accurate statistics on the number of insane, deaf, and dumb in each district of Upper Canada. Instructions were sent out to include these figures in the districts' annual census returns beginning in 1835. Charles Richardson, now both a legislator and Niagara clerk of the peace, had a vested interest in making sure the returns for Niagara were as complete as possible, as he believed they would assist him to buttress his case for a provincial asylum. Other than those for 1836, which have not survived, the figures for the Niagara district reproduced in the following tables were the most complete in the province.[35]

The Niagara district returns in the years 1835–41 raise more questions than they answer. Niagara's combined figures for the insane, deaf, and dumb in 1835, a total of 99 out of a population of 28,636, represent the largest number of any of the districts that bothered to send in returns. But how do we explain the sudden drop in the average total to 59 by 1837, when the district population had risen by nearly 4,000? Either the insane, deaf, and dumb were a highly mobile proportion of Niagara's population, which is unlikely, or the definitions for each category, especially the insane, were loose and shifting. If the statistics represent only the cases that came to the official attention of district officers, that might account for the significant annual variation while highlighting the unreliability of the statistics themselves. It is also possible that Richardson and the district magistrates

Table 5.1
Number of insane, Niagara district, 1835–41

Year	Males under 16	Females under 16	Males over 16	Females over 16	Total
1835	10	14	23	17	64
1836	—	—	—	—	—
1837	1	6	10	4	21
1838	7	2	10	9	28
1839	1	3	15	17	36
1840	5	3	9	15	32
1841	3	3	17	14	37

Table 5.2
Number of deaf, Niagara district, 1835–41

Year	Males under 16	Females under 16	Males over 16	Females over 16	Total
1835	11	6	6	2	25
1836	—	—	—	—	—
1837	5	3	5	8	21
1838	0	2	4	3	9
1839	0	2	6	2	10
1840	5	0	4	4	13
1841	1	2	4	0	7

Table 5.3
Number of dumb, Niagara district, 1835–41

Year	Males under 16	Females under 16	Males over 16	Females over 16	Total
1835	1	4	2	3	10
1836	—	—	—	—	—
1837	8	3	3	3	17
1838	3	0	2	4	9
1839	3	4	1	8	16
1840	0	3	7	4	14
1841	2	1	4	5	12

exercised their influence in 1835 so that as many 'insane' persons as possible were included to reinforce the argument for a provincial asylum.

Whatever the explanation, once the statistics became public they provided further ammunition for grand juries, magistrates, and Richardson to use in the campaign for a provincial asylum. In March 1838 a Niagara grand jury filed a presentment, which Richardson carefully copied and sent to the lieutenant governor, using the census figures to reinforce their other arguments. The jury pointed out 'That by the official returns of the Deaf, Dumb and Insane in this Province there appears a larger number of that class of persons in this District than any other in the Province ... That of these there are a great number supported out of the funds of the District as authorized by law. Necessity as well as humanity loudly call for the establishment of an assylum for these afflicted persons.'[36]

Without distinguishing among the insane, deaf, and dumb – the jurors, like their compatriots, envisaged the asylum as a receptacle for people with various disabilities – the grand jury advanced a nicely blended mix of financial and humanitarian reasons why the province should build an asylum. The humanitarian justification revealed the influence of the moral treatment theory popularized by the Duncombe report, which had apparently lost none of its appeal in the aftermath of the Rebellion:

> We believe that the expence incident on the erecting and maintaining a Lunatic Assylum would be but little more than the sums now paid by the several Districts for the support of such persons, but even allowing it to be attended with greater expence, the benefit arising from it would more than counterbalance that expence, as there is no doubt under proper treatment many of those persons might be restored to a degree of Reason which would enable them to act their part in civilized Society, which cannot be expected under the present mode of maintaining them, and indeed there is no assurance under the present system that the sums so granted are really and properly applied for the benefit of those individuals.[37]

In December 1838, another Niagara grand jury gladly responded to a call from the clerk of the peace of the Midland district to join in a petition requesting the immediate passage of a bill to create a provincial asylum.[38] Pressure from district courts was instrumental in persuading the Legislature to give speedy approval to an asylum bill in May 1839.[39] Court pressure had likewise been a key factor in the creation of an asylum in New Brunswick.[40] The motives of the district officials were certainly mixed, as the Niagara grand jury presentments confirm, but no one questioned the received wisdom of the day that an asylum would cure the insane and relieve the district courts of their financial burdens.

Chief Justice Robinson, opening the new provincial asylum in 1846, confidently believed that the province had taken a major step forward by removing the insane from the precincts of crime. He may even have had Patrick Donnelly in mind when he wondered 'what desolate years of misery must they in some cases have endured, and what wretched discomfort must their presence have occasioned others.'[41] Robinson represented the unanimous voice of contemporary court officials. The new system would replace general confinement in jails with more 'humane and scientific specific confinement of the gaol, the penitentiary and the asylum to permit the rehabilitation of the criminal on the one hand and the supervision of the lunatic on the other.'[42] This optimism proved unfounded. Insane individuals continued to be placed in district jails, as Peter Oliver has confirmed, and few of those sent to the provincial asylum experienced any improvement in their condition.[43] Local courts had great difficulty in trying to separate the administrative problems presented to them by the insane and the destitute poor, while a great deal of court time, especially that of the grand jurors, was spent in grappling with the complex social and moral questions posed by these groups. The insane continued to constitute unwanted intruders on the criminal justice system.

Prior to 1840, and for a long time afterward, local officials confronted the combined problems of the insane and the destitute poor. Not even the intervention of the state at the provincial level in the 1840s solved the problems posed by the criminally insane. For local court officials the solution was first to separate the insane from other prisoners and then to remove them from the district. Local officials took every opportunity to transfer their criminally insane prisoners to the Kingston Penitentiary, and by 1850 the penitentiary faced the same crisis the local jails had experienced earlier, because of what James E. Moran describes as a 'perceived epidemic of criminal insanity.'[44] This crisis was in turn temporarily resolved by moving the criminally insane to the Toronto Asylum, but the asylum's superintendent strongly criticized the introduction of what he called 'moral monsters' into the population of medically insane people. The superintendent's response was to ship them back to the penitentiary as soon as he was able to assert that they had recovered their sanity. Not until 1855 was the

Rockwood Criminal Lunatic Asylum established in Kingston. With the creation of Rockwood criminal insanity received official recognition in Canada, and in theory at least it became possible to treat the criminally insane institutionally according to scientific principles.

Such institutional remedies were not available to the courts of Upper Canada in the earlier period. The local magistracy and other officials came to realize during the 1830s how ill equipped they were to resolve the problems presented by the insane. In Niagara, as in other districts of Upper Canada, rather than trying to find local solutions, officials lobbied instead to have the state remove the insane from the care of local authorities and place them in larger provincial institutions. Where state institutions did not yet exist, pressure was exerted to build them. The locality's primary interest was not finding cures for the afflicted, but transferring expensive and undesirable human and social problems to a higher level of government. In the long run, this transfer did not provide either a cheaper or a better solution, but it did mean that no more men like Patrick Donnelly would languish for years in local jails without opportunity for treatment.

6

The Cold Hand of Charity

'The Canadians,' wrote Susannah Moodie in *Roughing it in the Bush*, 'are a truly charitable people; no person in distress is driven with harsh and cruel language from their doors.'[1] As individuals, the inhabitants of Upper Canada undoubtedly deserved this accolade. Voluntary charity was a virtual necessity for community existence among the Upper Canadian pioneers, even if many were so poor they could offer little in the way of practical help. But did individual charity extend to public charity in a colony which had consciously rejected the English poor law in 1792?

New Brunswick was the last of the British North American colonies to emulate the English system of poor relief. New Brunswick's Poor Law of 1786 was modelled on the system transplanted to the New England colonies, under which each town or parish assumed the responsibility for the relief of its own poor.[2] We do not know precisely why Governor Simcoe excluded the poor law from the English laws adopted by the newly formed Upper Canadian Legislature. The rejection may have been due to administrative concerns including the absence of clearly defined parishes, the difficulties inherent in levying a poor rate, and the fear of creating a pauper class.[3] Upper Canada was the first British colony to reject outright a legislated poor law (in Quebec it was taken for granted that the poor laws of England were never formally received) but historians are still uncertain of the reasons for this formal rejection.[4] Criticism of the poor law and poor rates was endemic in England at the end of the eighteenth century, although not all critics went so far as to endorse Edmund Burke's precepts for the poor: 'Patience, labour, sobriety, frugality, and religion should be recommended to them; all the rest is downright *fraud*.'[5]

Whatever the explanation, the absence of clear legislative directions for poor relief in Upper Canada created an ambiguity that lasted well into the nineteenth century. Richard Splane points out in his study, *Social Welfare in Ontario, 1791–1893*, that the exclusion of the English poor law 'cannot justifiably be regarded as the outright rejection of the principle of public support for the maintenance of those in acute need.'[6] But neither was there a clear acceptance of public responsibility. Stephen Speisman argues that in Toronto prior to 1900, 'the dispensing of "charity" was considered a purely religious function.'[7] A complex patchwork of voluntary, institutional, and public forms of relief emerged in Upper Canada, none adequate in itself, as Upper Canadians wrestled with the moral issues of how to look after the growing number of poor and disadvantaged.

The ambiguity became more pronounced in the years after 1815, as large-scale emigration swelled the population of Upper Canada. Many in Britain were only too happy to encourage local parishes to solve their problems of poor relief by assisting the poor to emigrate. What happened to them in Upper Canada was left for the colony to resolve with its own funds. Upper Canadian leaders, too, strongly advocated emigration to Upper Canada as a means of alleviating Britain's burden of poor relief. One of the earliest proponents of emigration was the radical Scot, Robert Gourlay;[8] he was followed in the 1820s by leading Upper Canadian figures such as Henry Boulton and John Strachan. Each saw emigration as a safety valve for Britain and each assumed that emigrant paupers would soon be able to fend for themselves in the colonies.[9]

In the absence of provincial legislation, the local districts had to devise their own solutions when it came to caring for the poor. The Midland district magistrates resolved in 1819 that no more district funds would be appropriated for poor relief, trying to transfer the burden to the counties, townships, and volunteer societies.[10] Other districts retained control at a district level. In his analysis of the transformation of poor relief in Upper Canada between 1817 and 1837 Rainer Bachre acknowledges that 'historians know little' about poor relief practices prior to 1840.[11] He shows that the provision of poor relief changed structurally, particularly in York, from voluntarism, expressed

either through individuals or voluntary societies, to institutionalization, culminating in the Emigrant Asylum and the House of Industry.[12] This change paralleled the huge inflow of pauper emigrants in
the years 1828–36 that contributed to a doubling of Upper Canada's
population. What happened, however, in those parts of Upper Canada
in which no such institutions existed?

As we have seen, the courts of quarter sessions had been given
responsibility for local government, which over time embraced poor
relief. The magistrates in quarter sessions were the only body, apart
from the provincial legislature, authorized to levy and spend tax dollars for local needs. Poor relief gradually entwined itself with local
government in the districts, and the legal process determined who
received public support. Supplicants wanting welfare either approached
the courts in person or sent a petition, which was usually supported
by neighbours and sometimes written on their behalf. Given the court's
distance from the outlying areas of the district, many of the requests
for support came as petitions. These requests were then turned over to
quarter sessions grand juries, who would examine the petition and, if
possible, the petitioner. The jury reported on the facts of the case and
made a recommendation in a formal presentment, the same legal document used to determine whether or not a person charged with a crime
should be formally indicted for trial. On the basis of the recommendation, the magistrates either granted relief or rejected it. There was no
appeal for the hapless petitioner in case of rejection. By subsuming
poor relief under the criminal process, Upper Canadians helped to
reinforce the image of the pauper as little different from the criminal.
The legal treatment meted out to suspected criminals and to paupers
supposedly rested on a clearly defined body of law. This was true in
the case of people charged with crimes, for British and Upper Canadian legislation specified the crimes with which a person could be
charged. Until the 1830s, however, Upper Canadian legislation was
silent on what should happen to paupers.

The Niagara magistrates in the April sessions, 1828, approved a
pauper list of twenty-one people, all of whom received public support
from district funds. Seven received 3s. 9d. per week. This represents a
dollar a week, whereas contemporary wages paid to workers on the
Welland Canal ranged from ten to thirteen dollars per month. The
remainder were granted either five shillings a week or ten shillings
per month. Four on the pauper list were children, two identified as
orphans and one as a foundling. Ten were aged and infirm. The others

were apparently mainly victims of illness. None was identified as a lunatic, a complete reverse of the pattern found a decade later.[13]

Once someone was placed on the pauper list, support from the district continued from one quarter sessions to the next, unless the individual died or moved out of the district. The magistrates reviewed the list at each quarter sessions, removing those who had died or moved away, adding new names, or imposing special conditions. In July 1828 the Niagara magistrates eliminated five names and approved two new cases, in one granting a single payment of £2 10s. for 'a Sick Man going to Kingston.'[14] One of those removed from the list, Henry Chipman, had been under a doctor's care in Chippewa for a 'disease of the eyes' and unable to work.[15] By July he had recovered and left the country. In another case the magistrates were not sure whether the woman pensioner was still alive; before authorizing a continuation of support, they requested verification by a magistrate. Another received her weekly allowance on the condition that she live out of town. Although the quarterly reviews regularly culled the pauper list, the magistrates found it easier administratively to approve extensions of support for the list as a whole, as a court order of April 1829 illustrates: 'Ordered that the pauper list of October last, continued until January be still continued until next July sessions with the addition of John Ellis at three shillings and ninepence per week.'[16]

For people in need, getting on the pauper list was the major hurdle to be overcome. In 1828 no one could predict the outcome of any one application, although in the 1820s the magistrates seemed disposed to assist the elderly, allocating meagre pensions to a few applicants. Thirty-eight residents of Thorold and Stamford, including constables and a town warden, supported the claim of Christopher Burt, 'an aged man of 83 and unable to support himself.'[17] He received 3s. 9d. per week. Mary Palmer, a Willoughby widow, petitioned that she could no longer support Barbara Brown, a widow of a soldier who had served in the Queen's Rangers and later in the York Militia. 'The aforesaid widow has been nearly forty seven years in the Province, and is nearly ninety years of age; and is not possessed of any property whatever; but has subsisted above five years entirely on my charity, since her pension has been withheld.'[18] Barbara Brown was added to the pauper list at 3s. 9d. a week.

Illness also could occasion compassion. Silas Vandecar petitioned that he had taken a sick Irish emigrant and her child into his house, the woman's husband having died. He and his wife nursed them throughout the winter of 1828. Two doctors who corroborated the facts told the magistrates, 'Mrs. Vandecar has had repeated attacks of illness requiring Medical assistance, occasioned we presume in a great measure by fatigue in the care of Mrs. Corn and by going into a cold part of the house to lodge that Mrs. Corn might occupy her room.'[19] The magistrates granted a minimum allowance to the Irish woman for four months, after which she was removed from the list. Their personal charity brought no financial benefit to Silas Vandecar and his wife. Ten years later Vandecar was a prisoner in the Niagara jail, unable to pay his debts and dependent on the jail allowance for food and wood to keep him warm.[20]

Mental retardation might or might not incline the magistrates to mercy. At the January sessions in 1828 the grand jurors presented 'that it had been represented to them by Mrs. Frances Fish, Widow, that an Idiot Woman calling herself Susannah Nark came to her house some time in the month of December last in great want and distress since which time the said Mrs. Fish has been obliged to give her the necessary support or inhumanely turn her from the house to want or perish.'[21] The jurors then examined Susannah Nark and reported 'that she appeared to them like a person quite incapable of supporting herself.'[22] This was the crux of all such examinations. Neither magistrates nor jurors sought medical evidence on the nature of the illness; the purpose of the examination was to discover whether the claimant was really incapable of self-support. The jurors recommended that the magistrates provide relief to the widow Fish, but there is no evidence that this recommendation was acted upon.

Three cases reveal something of the diversity of human misfortune that swelled the pauper list. One common element was disease. John Stevenson wrote to Dr James Muirhead, the Niagara doctor and JP who, until his death in 1834, often served as chairman of the district quarter sessions, on behalf of an elderly African Canadian man named King, requesting that he be reinstated on the list. King, who was ill, had returned from York, and was 'destitute as ever, an itinerant Pauper to [the] inconvenience of the Public.'[23] He was given an allowance of fifteen shillings a month. Another petition came from George Russell on behalf of Edmund Green, 'a stranger and destitute of any means of support,' who had arrived at Russell's house early in June 1829, suffering from spinal injuries and broken ribs after a fall. Russell was reimbursed for his medical expenses and Green received an allowance until January 1830.[24] William Ross, his wife, and their five children emigrated to Upper Canada from Ireland in 1828. He fell ill in the summer of 1829 and could not support his family. After Thomas Creen, an Anglican priest at Niagara, wrote on his behalf, testifying to Ross's 'utter poverty and helpless situation' and recommending the family 'as proper objects of public or private charity,' the Ross family was added to the list at 7s. 6d. a week.[25]

In 1829 the Niagara magistrates' attitude towards poor relief noticeably hardened. Why this change of heart occurred is unclear, but the magistrates decided to crack down on poor relief. The chairman of the quarter sessions in this year was Alexander Hamilton, one of the sons of the richest member of the merchant oligarchy which had originally assumed control of political offices in the district and which remained locally powerful.[26] Hamilton, as we saw, later became sheriff of the district. The magistrates placed the general question of poor relief before a quarter sessions grand jury in January 1829, no doubt with appropriate directions. The jurors responded with a presentment stating 'that in 1820 the Pauper List was £200 and now, 1829, is £250, an increase too rapid for the District to afford, which in eight years last past has increased to the sum of £2,000 which is too great a sum for the District to apply and we believe illegally applied.'[27] The jurors' reference to the apparent illegality of poor relief underlined the absence of statutory authority, since the provincial legislature had not passed any Act authorizing the payment of public funds for poor relief. The magistrates promptly rejected all new petitions for relief at the January sessions. Those on the existing list continued to receive support, but they were warned not to expect the funds to continue.[28] In response to doubts over their authority to dispense district funds for poor relief the magistrates sought a legal opinion before the April sessions.

Among those caught in the net of this policy change was Margaret Cantril, a widow with five children. Cantril and her husband had emigrated from Ireland in 1819. They moved to the Niagara district in 1826, and Thomas Cantril had worked on the Welland Canal. He went to Guelph in 1828 to obtain land and died there of fever; Margaret then became ill herself. Even though George Keefer, the local justice of the peace, supported her claim, the magistrates at the January sessions 1829 rejected it.[29]

No record of legal advice on their authority to provide poor relief survives, but at the April sessions, 1829, the magistrates continued the pauper list. They were doubtless influenced by the views of another, less pliant grand jury which claimed that if poor relief were halted the paupers would be 'in a state of misery.' The jurors added, 'and knowing the proportion of Tax to Each Inhabitant to be so very trifling in the present System – Therefore pray Your Worships to continue their support as heretofore.'[30] Twenty-one individuals and families received relief at the April sessions in 1829, a minuscule proportion of the more than 20,000 inhabitants of the district.

The contradictions in the attitudes towards public relief in the Niagara district must be set against a background of relative prosperity and a tradition of private charity. The *Buffalo Republican* commented in 1828 that in Upper Canada 'there are fewer paupers and a lower rate of taxation, than perhaps under any other civil government in the world.'[31] Private charity was not only accepted, a charitable disposition was one of the essential characteristics of a gentleman in Upper Canada. Among the self-described gentry in Niagara, which included the magistrates, charitable subscriptions were as fashionable as they were in the province's capital, York. In 1827 a subscription was taken up to aid the 'wives and families of the distressed Greeks, reduced to a state of the greatest misery and distress in consequence of a protracted war with an oppressive and inhuman foe.'[32] The gentlemen of Niagara who had seen their own district capital burned during the War of 1812 were enthusiastic participants. The membership of the Niagara Chapter for Promoting Christian Knowledge, which first met in 1826, reads like a *Who's Who* of the Niagara magistracy. This society was dedicated to raising an annual subscription to purchase Christian literature for the poor.[33]

Local patriotism in Niagara subsumed 'the benevolent purpose of relieving our distressed countrymen at all times, when they shall really require it,' as one article of the Loyal Canadian Society, established in May 1844 to commemorate the battle of Queenston Heights, proclaimed. The men who created the society consisted of a number of Niagara magistrates, including three of the Nelles family of Grimsby.[34] Private subscription lists were regularly organized for worthy causes, and private charity was welcomed as part of the public duty of an Upper Canadian gentleman, especially when the appeals were cloaked in a Christian context of moral obligation. Failure to subscribe could bring a professional reputation into disrepute. Yet the same magistrates who could respond generously to private solicitations adopted a much narrower view when it came to allocating public funds for poor relief.

In 1833 a group met in Niagara to form a private committee to dispense poor relief to deserving persons, but the name of the society they created, the 'Niagara Society for the Prevention of Vagrancy and Common Begging, and for the Relief of the Sick and Destitute,' suggests that its primary purpose was to prevent a nuisance rather than to provide relief to those in need.[35] Niagara magistrates were prominent among the members of this committee, which resolved that no aid would be given without a visit to inspect the circumstances of the petitioner. But nothing more is heard of this brief attempt to substitute a private system for the legal process that continued to provide the primary means of poor relief in the district.

Niagara magistrates were not alone in their parsimonious views on the expenditure of public funds for poor relief. Magistrates in other parts of Upper Canada also tended to interpret the statutes strictly in relief cases. The Home district magistrates in July 1800, for instance, responded to a petition for relief, 'that the Acts of the Province did not authorize them to make use of the public money, otherwise than as the said Acts precisely allowed.'[36] Yet the very existence of a pauper list in Niagara in the 1820s illustrates the ambiguity in contemporary legal interpretations and undermines the arguments of those who claim that the 1792 statute barring the introduction of the English poor law made it legally impossible for local authorities to use tax revenue for poor relief.[37] In Niagara, public funds did go to poor relief, even if the amounts involved were niggardly and few paupers received assistance. Practice in Niagara, however, may well have contravened the intentions of the provincial law-makers. The Legislature passed an Act in 1830 allocating fine revenues to district treasurers for general purposes, instead of continuing the English custom of paying some at least to church wardens or overseers of the poor for poor relief. This Upper Canadian practice was justified on the grounds of 'there being no Public Provision made for the Support of the Poor in this Province ...'[38]

News of the Niagara magistrates' apparent determination to do away with the pauper list became public in 1829. The Reverend Robert Addison, who had served as an Anglican missionary and priest in Niagara for nearly forty years, an eminent figure in the district and a former magistrate himself, led the public chorus of disapproval. In one of his last acts before his death Addison wrote to the magistrates: 'I am sorry to understand that notice has been given that the allowance to Paupers is to be discontinued. Many of them I fear will be reduced to Extreme distress, for Bread is very dear, and most of these miserable human beings are utterly incapable of helping themselves.'[39] Addison's successor, Thomas Creen, wrote to the magistrates in July 1830 on behalf of William Ross, who had been supported since 1829. Ross was 'still in a destitute, helpless and suffering condition and without public aid must be subjected to the most abject want and wretchedness.'[40]

The pleas of the clergy went unheeded. The Niagara pauper list as such disappeared in 1830, although one of the magistrates was reimbursed in October 1831 for advances he had made to paupers who had not known they had been removed the previous April.[41] The stand taken by the magistrates remained unpopular in the district. In January 1831 another quarter sessions grand jury complained, 'the determination of the Magistrates to withdraw any succor from the paupers of this District has greatly grieved this Grand Jury and they respectfully state that it is their opinion that the sentiments they feel are generally prevalent among the Inhabitants of the District, who they are confident would still be gratified with rather A further extension than any restriction of the relief which this populous and wealthy District ought of Right to offer to the Extremely small Number of Paupers which the District contains ...'[42] The following October another sessions jury asked the magistrates to reverse their decision and permit relief to paupers who were genuinely in distress from sickness, age, or infirmity.

Neither of these strongly worded presentments succeeded in altering the magistrates' entrenched position.[43] A petition requesting relief for a Mrs Richards, a widow of a United Empire Loyalist who was being cared for by neighbours, and which came with twelve supporting signatures to the January sessions 1832, was summarily rejected. The sessions chairman, Dr James Muirhead, wrote a revealing marginal comment on the petition: 'There is now no provision made for the poor. Every Township must provide for their own poor.'[44] This was certainly what the magistrates wanted, even if their views callously disregarded local public opinion. Transferring responsibility for poor relief to local communities which had neither public funds nor the taxing power to raise them was not a practical possibility.

The magistrates, however, could not prevent grand juries from making presentments on behalf of individuals. At the same January sessions, 1832, the jury pleaded that assistance be given to Elizabeth James and her daughters, Jane and Margaret Harris, who lived in Pelham and 'were well known to several of us.' Elizabeth was over eighty, 'Jane has been blind for many years and Margaret is entirely insane.' The jurors argued that the allowance, if granted, could be turned over to the town wardens of Pelham with instructions that it be 'prudently and faithfully applied.' They beseeched the magistrates 'by every feeling of humanity and pity' to provide relief, but not even this heartfelt and personal plea could melt the flinty hearts of Niagara's justices.[45]

Yet the Niagara magistrates were no more consistent in the application of their new policy than they had been with their previous approach. In the case of Mary and Sally Risinbarrick (or Risenburgh), which occupied the court's attention over a number of years, public pressure succeeded in wringing funds out of a reluctant magistracy. Mary Risinbarrick first came to the attention of the Niagara magistrates at the April sessions, 1828. She was then a widow, over seventy years of age, of Daniel Risinbarrick, a discharged veteran of the Canadian Volunteers, who lived in Pelham with a mentally retarded daughter of twenty-three. In her petition for relief Mary described herself as 'weak in Body and Constitution by her advanced old age ... and without a spot of Ground that she can call her own, her husband having died without leaving her any; or any other means of support than what she might by her own industry procure.' She added that she had 'frequently been under the necessity of stooping to the disagreeable employment of soliciting the cold hand of charity, of begging for that subsistence which an Idiot child and herself required.' She threw herself on the mercy of the magistrates, a desperate individual at the end of her tether. Four neighbours corroborated the facts in her statement and strongly recommended mercy, 'especially on account of the child, she being 23 years of age and totally incapable of providing for or taking care of herself.' Mary was, in her neighbours' eyes, 'a proper object of charity.' The magistrates accepted the evidence and granted Mary Risinbarrick an allowance of 3s. 9d. a week, raised to 5s. at the July sessions.[46] If her husband had actually served in the Canadian Volunteers for the United States during the War of 1812, the magistrates set aside issues of loyalty in granting Mary a district allowance.

Shortly before her death, Mary petitioned for an increase in her allowance, because no one was willing to care for her and her child. Eleven neighbours signed her petition, but it had no effect.[47] Mary Risinbarrick died in December 1829. Her funeral expenses were paid by the district and the allowance she had received was reduced in

January 1830 to 3s. 9d. per week to support her daughter, Sally. In January 1831 David Thompson, one of the justices of the peace in Thorold, wrote on behalf of the daughter, describing her as 'an insane Woman now at the House of David Bonesteel in Thorold,' and requested that she be put on the pauper's list.[48] The magistrates voted 6–1 to pay David Bonesteel a dollar a week for his expenses during 1830.

A year later David Bonesteel again wanted assistance. Bonesteel was illiterate, and someone in Thorold who was well acquainted with the legal system clearly prepared both this and subsequent petitions. Bonesteel claimed he had looked after Mary Risinbarrick and her daughter since 1829 because they had 'no home and no friend on whom they could depend for assistance.' He was 'under low circumstances himself, yet he could not turn a deaf ear to the calls of humanity; and, relying upon provincial aid, he felt willing to become the instrument of his Country's bounty in keeping these miserable objects from want and absolute starvation.' Bonesteel had received a dollar a week (or 3s. 9d.) until the end of 1830, 'since which time with great disappointment and injury Your Petitioner has been informed that Your Worshipful Body could no more allow any of the public money to be appropriated to such purposes.' The death of Mary had left Sally, whom Bonesteel described as 'a defenceless, friendless object of public charity ... who at this moment exhibits the most appalling instance of unfortunate and degraded humanity ... Entirely childish, and frequently perverse; cleanliness is no part of her disposition, and the wife of Your Petitioner has a task of which, delicacy might forbid a recital.' He could not afford to look after Sally without public assistance, but if he quit he knew 'of no person who would be willing to undertake the disagreeable and costly task.' Bonesteel concluded by imploring the magistrates not to 'let any stern point of Court Rules suppress the dictates of humanity.'[49]

Appended to the petition were thirty-four signatures from freeholders living in Thorold and the vicinity, including the local justice of the peace, David Thompson; the surveyor, John Tidey; and at least one member of a previous grand jury who had signed a presentment in favour of using public funds for poor relief. The neighbours corroborated the facts and supported Bonesteel's request. The document was a manifestation of the strong community support in favour of public assistance for deserving cases, and the magistrates gave way before the strength of its well-articulated argument and the forceful expression of local public opinion. They ordered a payment of £15 for David Bonesteel 'for the trouble he has had with a distressed family.'[50] Ostensibly, the grant was a single payment, but it set an important precedent.

Bonesteel renewed his plea for public assistance in 1833, stating that he had looked after Sally for two reasons: 'he knew of no person who would take her off his hands on any consideration; and from the encouragement your Worships were pleased to give to continue to take care of her.' Again, he obtained support from freeholders in Pelham, Wainfleet, and Crowland who concurred that Sally was 'indeed a helpless Idiot, and an orphan requiring the benevolent care of some sympathizing individual.' The magistrates approved another retroactive payment of £13, amounting to an allowance of 5s. a week.[51]

When Bonesteel submitted a nearly identical petition a year later, in March 1834, with the signatures of two local magistrates among the fourteen supporters, the sessions magistrates turned it over to the quarter sessions grand jury. The jury verified the facts in a presentment, saying 'that Sally Risenbarrick an Idiot Girl ... from her youth up and she is now twenty-seven years of Age ... and is now supported by one David Bonesteel at his own Expence.' The jurors recommended public support 'for the time past and to come' at the rate of 6s. 3d. a week, which the magistrates approved.[52]

The legal process for subsequent public assistance, for the process was rooted in the British legal forms customarily used in the Niagara district, had now been established. Petitions or personal appearances before the grand jury at a quarter sessions, followed by a jury presentment corroborating the facts and recommending public support, became prerequisites for judicial approval and payment. There was no guarantee that a grand jury presentment would sway the magistrates, but without one they would not authorize maintenance payments for destitute individuals. Before David Bonesteel signed his 1834 petition he had persuaded David Robins, a Pelham resident, to take over the task of caring for Sally Risinbarrick. Robins agreed to do this in the clear expectation of continuing public support from the district. He bluntly told the magistrates in a petition the following year that he could not afford to keep Sally 'without pecuniary assistance.' The grand jury recommended payment of 8s. 9d. a week for 1834, with a raise to 10s. a week in 1835.[53] Sally Risinbarrick became ill in 1835 and died in May. The district later reimbursed David Robins for the medical and funeral expenses he had incurred on her behalf.[54]

New legislation authorizing district quarter sessions courts to grant relief to pauper lunatics underscored the change in legal process within the Niagara district that effectively gave grand juries the power to recommend who would receive relief. The Legislature, recognizing the hardships of housing the insane in local jails, passed an Act in 1830 authorizing the Home district quarter sessions court to make relief payments for the insane on the recommendation of a grand jury. The jury received authority to call witnesses and examine them under oath. In 1833 this Act was continued and its provisions were extended to all other districts of the province.[55] No medical or legal definition of insanity appeared in any of the legislation passed by the Upper Canadian Legislature during the 1830s. The definition, and thus the eligibility of a person for public support, was left to the locality to decide.

After the passage of the 1833 Act, the Niagara magistrates began to accept grand jury recommendations for relief of the destitute insane, but only after first consulting the attorney general of the colony. A Niagara doctor, Truman Raymond, submitted a claim for looking after 'an Idiot, insane person' named Elizabeth Willson. Attorney General Boulton checked the Act and found no reason why 'the humane conduct' of Dr Raymond should not be rewarded.[56] Raymond received the money which Boulton believed 'he so justly merits.' In Niagara, the definition of insanity was never clarified. Each case was considered independently by the quarter sessions grand jury and the magistrates. Grand juries were inclined to give the broadest possible interpretation in order to assist deserving cases, while the Niagara magistrates interpreted the law narrowly to keep district expenditure on relief as low as possible.

In July 1836 Isabella Evans petitioned the magistrates for relief. She described herself as the widow of Robert Evans, a private in the 82nd Regiment, stationed in Niagara, 'who died Suddenly and ... left your Petitioner with seven children on her hands one of which is Simple and in no way capable of helping herself. Your Petitioner has neither House, nor Home, nor any means of supporting her helpless family and under her deplorable situation she throws herself before Your Respectable Bench in hopes that you will grant me some Relief out of the Publick funds of the District.'[57] The magistrates' first inclination was to reject the petition out of hand on the grounds that no funds existed for poor relief. Instead, they referred it to the grand jury at the July sessions. The jury recommended payment of an allowance of five shillings a week to the widow Evans 'to assist her in supporting an insane Child.'[58] One of the Niagara magistrates was prepared to accept the grand jury recommendation, but he was overruled by the chairman of the quarter sessions.

For successive juries, support for retarded or handicapped children was axiomatic. For the magistrates it clearly was not. Not even township commissioners could pry district funds from the magistrates to support the handicapped. Two Gainsborough township commissioners wrote to the magistrates at the same quarter sessions, desiring assistance for a twenty-seven year-old girl who 'lives yet withoute the use of her limbs and intirely withoute any knowledge atall and has to be taken care of by her Mother or some other Careful person.'[59] They, too, were turned down.

The inconsistency with respect to the definition of insanity and who was eligible to receive support is strikingly illustrated in the case of George Martin, an African Canadian who lost his legs to frostbite. In 1837 Dr T.W. Porter, the physician to the jail of the Niagara district, submitted a claim for expenses to support Martin, described as 'a helpless crippled coloured man.' Two grand jury presentments recommending support were rejected by the magistrates, who argued that they had no statutory power to order payments.[60] In November 1837 the same magistrates ordered that a maintenance allowance of 7s. 6d. per week be paid, after receiving another grand jury recommendation that described Martin as 'Insane from the loss of his legs.'[61] A year later another request for funds to support him, endorsed by a grand jury, was rejected by the magistrates on the grounds that it did not fall within the statute granting relief to the destitute insane.[62] How George Martin survived without public assistance is not known. Presumably he depended on private charity. He was, however, persistent in his efforts, for in 1839 he persuaded someone to write another petition on his behalf. His amputation had forced him 'to walk on his knees and rendered him incapable of contributing in the smallest degree towards his own support,' and he was therefore 'dependent on the cold hand of charity for the means of sustaining life.' Unless he received help Martin foresaw no prospect 'but to die miserably in the streets.'[63] The magistrates were unmoved by his plea and rejected his petition. Martin's fate was exactly what he had prophesied. He lived on as a pauper in Niagara until the winter of 1845. When he died the expenses of his burial, 7s. 6d., were paid by the district.

Questions of when public should replace private charity and whether those who used their own funds to help people in need should be reimbursed by the district continued to provide the Niagara magistrates with difficult moral and political choices. The petitions regularly made to them often had strong local support. There was a clear expectation among petitioners that public funds would fill the need where private resources had been exhausted or the private individual was too poor to bear the burden of assistance alone. If the petitions to the Niagara quarter sessions are a genuine reflection of local public opinion, and there is no reason to think they are not, public charity was seen as a legitimate and necessary extension of individual benevolence. The absence of statutory authority to support this assumption and the magistrates' record of rejecting petitions whenever possible did not appear to deter those in need from applying to the court for assistance. Because there were no institutional alternatives and no voluntary societies operating in the district during the 1830s, the court of quarter sessions remained the last hope for those seeking relief.

A typical case came before the magistrates at the April sessions in 1833. Dwight Smith, a St Catharines baker, petitioned the magistrates to reimburse him for expenses of over £5 incurred in looking after a Robert Rogers, who had arrived from the United States 'poor and destitute of clothes and in want of work.' Smith employed him, and when Rogers contracted smallpox Smith hired two people to look after him. Smith advanced his claim for reimbursement and his justification for it in the context of a Christian moral obligation embracing both the individual and the community: 'The said Rogers was entirely destitute of any means whereby these expences can be reimbursed to Your Petitioner. He has no friends in the country and was a stranger here. Your petitioner is but ill able to bear the expence himself and thinks the District should assist a little towards performing an act of charity to a stranger who may come among us destitute. Your petitioner has attempted to make a collection but people seem unwilling to perform what should be required of them ...'[64] Sixteen freeholders of St Catharines signed the petition in support of Smith, adding, 'we think him entitled to remuneration from the District and that this is a case which calls upon the public at large to dispense the offices of Charity instead of private individuals.'[65] No magistrates from St Catharines attended the April sessions. The remaining district justices used the excuse of their absence to defer any decision, and there is no indication that Smith ever received compensation from the district.

Another case before the court in 1835 raised the question of how far an individual's obligation to support members of his family extended.

Thomas Angleman, a Thorold shoemaker, informed the magistrates that he supported both his father and mother, who were 'old and feeble,' in addition to his own children. He had also to look after a mentally retarded grandson. His daughter had died and her husband had disappeared. Angleman told the jury and the magistrates that he was 'willing to support his parents to the utmost of his ability, but being a Mechanic and depending on his daily labour he feels unable to bear the burden of all three, having a family of his own to support.'[66] Thirteen freeholders of Thorold, including Samuel Street, the local justice of the peace, corroborated his claim and the grand jury recommended an allowance of five shillings a week to assist him in looking after his retarded grandson. Angleman continued to receive support from the district for the remainder of the decade. In his case, mental retardation or idiocy, as it was described then, was subsumed under lunacy for purposes of poor relief.

Even professionals could be caught in the web of poor relief. A medical doctor, J.B. Matthews, newly arrived in Niagara, submitted a claim for £12 to the magistrates at the October sessions, 1835, after treating a labourer who had been severely injured in an accident while working. Dr Matthews attended his patient for a month and a half without any remuneration and without obtaining authorization in advance from the district justices that his expenses would be paid by the district. In his accompanying petition Dr Matthews pleaded his own poverty, but added, 'I could not in common humanity suffer the poor man to perish (as he inevitably would) without assistance.'[67] Without debating whether the district had a responsibility to compensate doctors who ministered to paupers, or even acknowledging Dr Matthews's work, the magistrates dismissed the claim.

Appeals to the court were often made after local inhabitants had dug deep into their own pockets. A number of Drummondville residents contributed to assist an injured Scottish boy who had fallen from the cliff of the Niagara river in the summer in 1835, but their funds were insufficient to see him through to a full recovery. The petition sent on his behalf to the magistrates claimed that 'the public in this vicinity have already been taxed as far as we fear they are willing to bear while his situation still continues to call loudly for the means of relief.'[68] No district funds were forthcoming. In another instance, even a victim of crime was unsuccessful in a plea for charitable redress by the district. The town wardens of Port Colborne petitioned in March 1841 on behalf of Thomas Brown, a town butcher, who had been robbed and was now unable to carry on his business. Brown had 'become an object of charity' and the wardens applied in vain for district funds to assist him until he could support himself again.[69]

The magistrates' uncompromising attitude on the use of public funds for poor relief led to several cruel deceptions. Individuals looked after paupers believing the district would repay them only to discover that they would not be reimbursed. The town wardens of Dunnville in 1840 told James Sweet to look after a pauper on the understanding that his expenses would be paid by the district magistrates. The wardens then certified the account only to have it rejected at the quarter sessions by the magistrates, who had not authorized the arrangement in advance.[70]

The bureaucracy imposed by the legal system added to the potential for cruelty. On 8 May 1840, Charles Richardson, the Niagara clerk of the peace, received a visit from the wife of Elijah Day. She was 'in destitute circumstances' and had walked from Port Colborne to Niagara to obtain payment from the district for expenses she and her husband had incurred in looking after a pauper for three years. She carried with her a letter dated 2 September 1837, signed by two justices of the peace and the Port Colborne health officer, asking her husband 'to receive into your care Mary Petit, a destitute girl, now labouring under a bad fever. Your account at a moderate price will be presented to the Sessions – and there is every probability that it will be allowed.'[71] Her claim was rejected at the June sessions, and although a committee of magistrates re-examined it in September and recommended that the grand jury investigate further, neither Mrs Day nor her husband received compensation for charitable work carried out at the express request of district officials.

An apparent difference in opinion between grand juries and the magistrates meant that the court of quarter sessions remained divided in its response to relief petitions throughout the 1830s. Juries claiming to reflect public opinion used the power given them by provincial laws to recommend relief for deserving cases. The magistrates, for their part, did not feel bound to accept the jurors' views. After 1837 the magistrates tried to confine district relief payments strictly to the destitute insane, as provided in the provincial statutes of 1833 and 1837. A case in 1838 captures the essence of the continuing tug of war between jurymen and magistrates over relief payments. One of the jurors at the December sessions, Smith Meddaugh, had been caring for an infant orphan. His fellow jurors, in a formal presentment, recommended that the district reimburse his expenses of £7 10s.[72] The magistrates refused, because the statute did not permit payments for orphans. Undeterred by this rebuff, the jurors issued a second presentment the next day, in effect challenging the justices: 'The Grand Jurors having understood that the Court are not disposed to allow the presentment in favour of Smith Middough [sic], the Grand Jurors deem it necessary to inform Your Worships that they are perfectly aware that Mr. Middough's case does not come under the Statute, But they respectfully submit to the Court the circumstances sworn to by Mr. Middough which they deem deserving not only of Pecuniary remuneration but the gratitude of the Public generally.'[73] The obdurate magistrates dug their heels in even more and repeated their judgment that the district had no power under existing laws to apply funds 'for such purposes.'[74] The humanitarian impulse of the jurors foundered on their inability to change the magistrates' minds.

Evidence nonetheless exists to prove that the interpretation of the laws was not always as narrow and legalistic as the examples cited above imply. The words 'destitute insane' were, to some extent, a ritual formula applied by juries to individuals known to be suffering from other disabilities. Someone, for instance, substituted the words 'destitute and insane' in an 1842 grand jury presentment for other, more precise, descriptions: 'aged and infirm,' 'a deaf and dumb child,' and 'an aged and blind person.'[75] Throughout this period, relief payments in the Niagara district went to many individuals who were not really insane, and whose poverty was due to other causes, including age, illness, and physical handicaps.

Table 6.1 provides a breakdown of the requests for relief to the Niagara district court among men, women, and children. Because many of the requests were repeated from session to session, the numbers themselves do not represent over two hundred different people. This table, along with the individual petitions, helps to refine the picture of Upper Canadian rural paupers in the colonial period. Many were aged, without pensions or other means of support. In 1829, two-thirds of the people on the pauper list were elderly. A high percentage were female. A number were mentally retarded children or young adults being cared for by relatives or neighbours who were poor themselves. Some were widows, suddenly left on their own with large families to support. Orphans and destitute immigrants are two other identifiable

Table 6.1
Relief requests to the Niagara Court of Quarter Sessions, 1828–40

Adult males	Adult females	Children	Total
64 (28%)	135 (60%)	28 (12%)	227 (100%)

Table 6.2
Numbers receiving Niagara district relief payments, 1828–40

Year	Number	Year	Number
1828	21	1835	8
1829	24	1836	9
1830	22	1837	9
1831	no record	1838	10
1832	no record	1839	14
1833	2	1840	15
1834	2		

categories. The Niagara paupers who petitioned the court for relief were not the 'idle' and 'worthless' vagrants caricatured in contemporary stereotypes, but the deserving poor who in many cases had the support of their neighbours and grand juries.

The number of paupers actually being supported at any given time was less than might be implied from Table 6.1. Table 6.2 attempts to estimate this figure on a yearly basis, using the district accounts. There are no valid records for 1831 and 1832, years when the magistrates made a concerted effort not to dispense any charitable relief. Few individuals were supported by district funds in any given year, and even by 1840, when the numbers were increasing, the district spent no more than £300 a year on charitable relief.

In the latter half of the decade Niagara grand juries began making presentments pointing out the need for more comprehensive remedies for poor relief in the district. Their task of examining the claimants seeking support at each sessions profoundly affected them as individuals and injected an emotional urgency into otherwise formal legal documents. Two remedies, both institutional, were then under discussion at the provincial level. One was a provincial lunatic asylum and the other, which emerged in 1837, was the possibility of establishing a local House of Industry in each district of the colony or in each major town.

The idea of the workhouse, central to the English poor law of 1834, manifested itself in Upper Canada three years later in the House of Industry Act. The decision taken to house the poor in a series of workhouses located across the province where they would, if able, be given work, was obviously similar in theory to the English reform. In Upper Canada, as in other parts of Britain's colonial empire and in Britain itself, moral reform was an inseparable part of the relief of poverty. The Upper Canadian legislation, with a naive and utopian optimism, anticipated the day when the streets would be cleared 'of the Idle and Dissolute,' crime would decline, and proper habits of work would be instilled in the poor.[76] Houses of Industry, according to their proponents, were the cheapest and most effective method of poor relief.[77]

The 1837 Act relied on the existing structure of quarter sessions courts, magistrates, and grand juries. Magistrates were obliged to proceed with the construction of a House of Industry in any district of the province following three successive grand jury presentments in favour of the idea. In reality, although Houses of Industry emerged in Toronto and Kingston, the Act became a dead letter. The 1837 Rebellion deflected the thoughts of the whole province away from poor relief and the fulminations of the reform press showed how unpopular the idea of additional taxation for poor relief had become. Debates about Houses of Industry occurred in Niagara, the Midland, and the Home districts, but only in Niagara did grand juries offer a series of presentments on Houses of Industry. In this, as in other aspects of poor relief, Niagara offers a distinct contrast to the more urban parts of the province such as Toronto, and testifies again to the interplay in the district between grand juries and magistrates.

The Act of 1837 envisaged Houses of Industry receiving 'the Poor and Indigent' and 'the Idle and Dissolute,' lumping together all categories of paupers except the destitute insane. This inability to separate the deserving from the undeserving poor was not confined to Upper Canada. Nor was the conviction that institutionalization was the best way to resolve the problem of poor relief. Examples from both Britain and the United States reinforced the momentum towards institutions and blinded Upper Canadians to alternatives which might have been better suited to local conditions.

The confusion over the very term, 'House of Industry,' extended well beyond the Niagara region. In this era of laissez faire attitudes to poverty, utilitarian institutions sprang up in various urban centres of British America, primarily as seasonal remedies to the aggravations suffered by the poor in winter. They did not fulfil the expectations of those who launched them. Judith Finguard concludes that they 'were no more concerned with industry than were the public poorhouses of Halifax and Saint John; they resembled refuges from winter more than anything else.'[78]

For Niagara grand jurors, however, provincial support for the concept of a House of Industry provided an opportunity to discard a system of local maintenance payments that was becoming increasingly unpopular. Immediately following the passage of the House of Industry Act, a Niagara grand jury recommended one, saying it 'is imperiously called for in this District.'[79] Neither jurors nor politicians were consistent in their approach, because of the clouds of confusion enveloping the debate over poor relief. Another Niagara grand jury grappled with the need for a House of Industry in November 1837 and wrote a passionate diatribe against the concept. They did not want 'to erect a receptacle for the Idle and worthless that are cast upon our shores being the refuse from the Poor houses from the Mother, and Other Countries.'[80] They added, 'we doubt the policy of holding out inducements to the Idle and profligate of becoming paupers, as we are of the opinion, that all that are able to labour in their country, have the power of earning a subsistance if they have the will to labour.' The jurors foresaw a tax rebellion in the district if a House of Industry were built, a prophecy which was not taken lightly in 1837. No doubt reflecting local opinion, they protested 'against the system of taxing the industrious classes to support the Idle and worthless.' Yet even these jurors favoured 'a suitable provision being made for the Aged, the Infirm, the orphan or the Lunatic,' the very people being supported by district relief payments. The magistrates made sure the presentment received wide circulation in the district, a sign of their sympathy for the jurors' viewpoint.[81] It also was published in some key provincial newspapers.[82]

Although in June 1838 another grand jury rejected the idea of a Niagara House of Industry, before the end of the decade some viewed the possibility more favourably.[83] Typical was a jury presentment made in December 1840 after the jurors had examined the petitioners seeking relief. The jury drew the court's attention 'to the deplorable condition of those unfortunate persons, the destitute and the insane,' and recommended the construction of a building as an interim measure until the Provincial Lunatic Asylum was ready.[84] But the financially hard-pressed magistrates had no intention of spending money on a

House of Industry, partly because they shared the jurors' naive faith that a provincial asylum would relieve Niagara of its destitute lunatics.

Well into the 1840s Niagara grand juries continued to urge the local construction of a House of Industry. The reasons varied, but successive presentments reflected more humanitarian concerns than the utilitarian ones that actuated the building of Houses of Industry in other parts of British America.[85] A jury in January 1842 argued that the current method of poor relief was objectionable from many points of view, but chiefly because there was no guarantee that relief payments accomplished 'the object intended, namely the comfort of those unfortunate persons interested.'[86] The same jurors in a separate presentment blamed the many cases of destitution on children being left orphans, occasional lack of employment, and sickness, all of which, in their view, could be ameliorated by a House of Industry.[87]

The Niagara magistrates responded to the jury's request by reapplying to have all the district paupers receiving relief payments shipped to the temporary lunatic asylum in the old Toronto jail, on the grounds that district funds were going towards its upkeep.[88] This request was refused, as an earlier one had been, because asylum officials in Toronto could not accommodate all the provinces' destitute insane, however defined, in a temporary facility. As the magistrates were slowly discovering, institutionalization, whether in the form of a lunatic asylum or a House of Industry, was not going to resolve the complex puzzle of poor relief in their district.

The frustrations of the grand juries concerning their role in administering poor relief finally boiled over into a full-blown legal confrontation with the magistrates. A grand jury in April 1842 summarized the deficiencies in the existing system: 'The Jurors are furnished with no proof as to the sum actually necessary in each case, and they have no guarantee that the sum allowed will be properly expended; moreover, it does not appear to them that any attempts are made to cure the unfortunate patients.'[89] Above all, they wanted a different remedy for poverty and turned again to a House of Industry. Three successive grand juries in Niagara in 1841 and 1842 made formal presentments recommending the creation of a House of Industry in the district.[90] By law, the magistrates were bound to act, but they did nothing. A later grand jury complained about the delay and when by the summer of 1843 still nothing had happened, a new panel castigated the magistrates for treating the issue 'with contempt' and setting 'an evil example ... to the community of trampling upon the laws, by those to whom the enforcement of them devolved.'[91] The jurors petitioned the governor general, but the government decided not to interfere. The creation of district councils early in the 1840s cast some doubts on the powers of magistrates and juries to act, but it was clear that the executive would not step in to enforce compliance.[92] Thus the Niagara House of Industry idea died, leaving both the legal and practical issues of poor relief unresolved in the district.

The inconsistent opinions exhibited by Niagara grand juries between 1837 and 1842 over the need for a local House of Industry were symptomatic of growing uncertainty over the extent of local obligation to provide poor relief. Grand jury presentments had no more impact upon the magistrates in the late 1830s and early 1840s than they had at the beginning of the thirties. No institutions were built in the district and no better means of providing poor relief was adopted. Even the acceptance of public responsibility for poor relief in the laws of the province remained a thing of the future in 1840.

The legal process in the Niagara district had a major impact on poor relief practices during the 1820s and 1830s. Upper Canada did not follow Britain's example in poor relief legislation. It rejected the old Elizabethan poor law and, apart from Toronto and Kingston, it did not implement the House of Industry Act passed by the Legislature in 1837. In the absence of specific Upper Canadian legislation on poor relief conflicting views about the extent to which local districts were liable to provide it emerged. Responsibility for decisions taken remained with the quarter sessions courts.

Next to hearing criminal cases, in the period 1828 to the 1840s the Niagara district court of quarter sessions spent more time examining petitions from individuals seeking poor relief than it did on any other subject. The burden fell most heavily on the shoulders of the grand jurors, who had to scrutinize each case, hear evidence, and determine whether public support was merited. After exercising their judgment, they passed their recommendations to the magistrates, who made the decisions. Neither the men who constituted the local magistracy, who were at all times acutely conscious of their responsibilities as managers of the district finances, nor the grand jurors could reach satisfactory solutions within very narrow legal framework. The ad hoc judgments of the quarter sessions courts were necessarily arbitrary and sometimes reversed by later court decisions. Viewed from a historical perspective, they offer little evidence of a coherent pattern.

The judicial process governing poor relief in fact contained a large discretionary element, in spite of the magistrates' repeated attempts to enforce a harsh consistency. The absence of a clearly defined policy on poor relief or any real alternatives forced the poor of the Niagara district to approach the court of quarter sessions for assistance. The court's authority in the community was reinforced through this process, although not without evident tensions between the magistrates and the grand jurors. The jurors found it much easier to deal with criminals than with the poor. Cases involving supplicants for poor relief were more ambiguous than criminal cases, and the law provided little in the way of guidance.

The magistrates' fears that poor relief would consume a steadily increasing portion of the district budget proved unfounded. In 1829 the Niagara district spent £250 on poor relief, more than 10 per cent of the district expenses. By 1837, the magistrates' strict legality had reduced poor relief expenditures to under £100, or less than 4 per cent of overall district costs.[93] Actual expenditure had begun to rise again by the 1840s, but poor relief remained a very small percentage of overall district expenditures. The magistrates were all too ready to use the absence of legislation authorizing poor relief to enforce their own laissez faire attitudes towards paupers, ignoring the reality of poverty and physical disability.

Successive quarter sessions grand juries appeared to take a more humanitarian approach, trying to adapt inadequate laws to permit relief for deserving cases. Their presentments suggest they believed they were acting in accordance with local public opinion, which viewed public charity as a legitimate extension of private charity. Because the limits of private charity were painfully obvious to the inhabitants of a district lacking either institutions for relief or voluntary societies, the court's role assumed a vital importance for those who had nowhere else to go. For the paupers who petitioned for help, the magistrates' rejection of their claims on legal grounds reinforced the coldness of public charity in the Niagara district and stood in stark contrast to the many acts of private benevolence. Here again, the law proved to be a poor instrument for creating a Christian moral order.

PART THREE

Crime

INTRODUCTION

How much crime was there in the Niagara district during the early colonial period? Was the moral order of society being threatened by criminal activity? These questions preoccupied the colonial population far more immediately than they do legal historians. One interesting way of answering them is to turn to the judges who tried criminal cases. These judges saw only cases in which arrests had been made, indictments returned, and trials had been arranged. Since many criminal offences were never prosecuted, the judges may not be able to provide final answers. Nevertheless, the collective opinion of Upper Canada's three judges of the court of King's Bench provides an interesting starting point for an assessment of the level of crime in the Niagara district. These men were the most senior judges in the colony and regularly toured the various judicial districts, holding assizes and delivering the jails of their prisoners. The lieutenant governor requested their formal opinion in 1832 after receiving a presentment from an assize grand jury from Niagara urging that the assizes be held twice a year on the grounds that the district jail could no longer contain all the prisoners. Behind their request lay the Niagara magistrates' frustration at the cost of providing for prisoners languishing for lengthy periods in the jail, awaiting trial. Chief Justice Robinson, along with his colleagues Macaulay and Sherwood, observed in response, rather tartly, that 'many years ago there were usually more prisoners for trial in the District of Niagara than there have been latterly.'[1] But the judges were certainly not opposed to a second judicial circuit. Attaching a number of self-serving conditions, they endorsed the idea in their report, although the evidence from Niagara had been anything but compelling. This judicial response might lead us to believe that the crime rate in the district was actually falling in the 1830s.

The local magistrates of the district believed just the opposite to be true. When they learned in 1835 that the British government planned to withdraw the troops which had been garrisoning the Niagara frontier, they quickly expressed their dismay and fear in a petition to the lieutenant governor. Apart from the more obvious concerns for defence, a draft of the petition claimed that the district, 'from its proximity to a foreign country is annually filled with a host of criminals.' Withdrawing British troops from 'one of the oldest and most exposed Towns in the Province' would add to the magistrates' sense of imminent peril.[2] This heightened alarm derived from a recent spate of serious crimes, two murders, a case of grand larceny, and a prisoner who had returned from banishment well before the end of his term. The Niagara magistrates clearly perceived a growing threat to public order as well as increased costs to the district from incarcerating prisoners, and they requested the lieutenant governor's support in trying to persuade the British government to change its mind.

British military authorities, however, had concluded in 1835 that there was no longer any military need to retain troops in Niagara and the colonial secretary reiterated that law enforcement 'belongs not to the Military but to the Civil Authorities,' and 'ought to be found in an efficient Local Police.'[3] The despatch had the tone of a lecture censoring colonials suspected of being parasites upon the mother country, but its essence was unambiguous. Maintaining the King's peace was the responsibility of the local authorities, and must be paid for with their own funds. The British army would no longer be present to prevent jailbreaks or to provide a reassuring presence to local inhabitants. The timing of this despatch now seems ironic. British troops were not withdrawn, and their presence seemed vital when rebellion broke out two years later, in 1837. The argument advanced by the colonial secretary foundered. Fear of growing crime in the mid-1830s combined with fear of rebellion and foreign invasion to create a climate of paranoia along the Niagara frontier, especially among those responsible for its security. This background is necessary to an understanding of the way in which the elite of the district viewed the question of crime and criminality through this period. Whether their view corresponded to that of the broader population is much more difficult to determine.

7

Crimes and Punishments

CRIMES AGAINST THE PERSON

Crimes against the person, especially assaults, were the most common crime dealt with by the court of quarter sessions in the Niagara district. The Niagara court of quarter sessions records contain 372 cases of assault (including assault and battery and aggravated assault) from 1828 to 1846. In this period, in contrast to earlier times, more serious cases began to appear before the court of quarter sessions. Reporting business in the court of quarter sessions which sat in January 1823, *The Niagara Gleaner* claimed that many of the cases 'were of a trifling nature.'[1] By the 1830s, that was no longer true.

As Table 7.1 demonstrates, the number of assault cases brought before the court of quarter sessions rose rapidly during the early 1830s, but the legislation of 1834 that gave expanded powers of summary jurisdiction to magistrates had the immediate effect of reducing them. Assault cases and many other minor and regulatory offences were now tried in each locality of the district. Some magistrates would occasionally refer serious personal assault cases to the court of quarter sessions. In 1835, for instance, Grimsby magistrate Warner Nelles sent a particularly brutal assault to the court of quarter sessions, stating, 'assaults are of every day occurrence in this part of the country and unless some severe examples are made we shall find it difficult to have the peace kept at all here.' In this instance, four men were found

Table 7.1
Assault cases prosecuted at Niagara Court
of quarter sessions,1828–46

Year	Number	Year	Number
1828	35	1838	8
1829	30	1839	4
1830	52	1840	6
1831	43	1841	7
1832	39	1842	5
1833	62	1843	10
1834	17	1844	20
1835	12	1845	8
1836	5	1846	1
1837	8	Total	372

guilty and sentenced to pay fines of £5 each, plus court costs, for a beating which, according to a local surgeon, left Edward Armstrong with three wounds on his head and 'marks of external violence visible on several parts of his body.'[2]

Assault cases had to be very severe or seen as posing an imminent threat to public order before they went to the assize courts. Only two assault cases in Niagara were prosecuted at the assizes prior to 1838, and even in the post-Rebellion decade, as shown in Table 7.2, only thirty-three cases of assault reached the level of the assize court. A more likely explanation for the rise in assault prosecutions was the violence associated with the canal labourers in the early 1840s. A peak in assault cases at the court of quarter sessions can be detected in 1843 and 1844, probably for the same reasons. When the canal construction was completed in the latter part of the decade and the number of canal workers declined, there was a corresponding decrease in these cases.

Although Niagara's population was smaller than that of the neighbouring Gore district, the total number of assault cases in Niagara to reach the level of the courts was higher. Most of these cases were dealt with by the court of quarter sessions. Niagara's record of prosecution may testify to a greater willingness to prosecute crimes of violence among Niagara residents than those in other parts of Upper Canada. There may also have been a feeling among the magistrates that regular prosecution was necessary to retain a veneer of public order in a frontier society notorious for personal assaults.[3]

Table 7.2
Assault cases prosecuted at Niagara assizes,
1828–46[4]

Year	Number	Year	Number
1828	0	1838	1
1829	1	1839	6
1830	0	1840	3
1831	0	1841	1
1832	0	1842	5
1833	0	1843	5
1834	1	1844	3
1835	0	1845	5
1836	0	1846	4
1837	0	Total	35

The vast majority of assault cases prosecuted in the Niagara district involved men assaulting other men. A small number involved women assaulting women, and even fewer cases involved men assaulting women. In an unusual case James Smith, a Niagara labourer, was summarily convicted for assaulting Jane Feilds in June 1841. Smith had ordered her out of his house; Feilds responded that she would go, 'but that she was as good a woman as he was a man.' The two went outside and started to fight. After they were separated by witnesses, Jane Feild 'then flew at Smith and they stood up like two men fighting.' When Jane Feilds testified about this affair, she insisted she 'was about to whip him' when the bystanders intervened. Smith was fined ten shillings and costs.[5]

The most serious crime against the person was murder. In the period 1827–46, twenty cases of murder were tried at the Niagara assizes. Less than half the number of people were charged with murder in the neighbouring Gore district in these years.[6] As Table 7.3 illustrates, in seven of the Niagara cases guilty verdicts were recorded, ten cases resulted in not guilty verdicts, two cases were not heard, and in one the defendant was declared insane and not fit to stand trial.[7] Murder trials varied greatly, depending on the nature of the offence and when it occurred. Colonel Norton, for example, was tried for murder in 1823 but found guilty only of manslaughter, fined, and discharged. The killing in question had occurred during a duel and the local paper reported that 'his conduct was truly honourable and he would no doubt have been acquitted altogether, if he had not from

Table 7.3
Murder cases prosecuted at Niagara assizes, 1827–46

Year	Number	Outcome	Year	Number	Outcome
1827	1	guilty	1837	0	—
1828	0	—	1838	0	—
1829	0	—	1839	1	not heard
1830	1	guilty	1840	1	not guilty
1831	0	—	1841	1	not guilty
1832	1	insane	1842	2	both not guilty
1833	1	guilty	1843	1	guilty
1834	0	—	1844	1	guilty
1835	1	guilty	1845	0	—
1836	6	1 guilty	1846	2	both not guilty
		4 not guilty			guilty
		1 not heard			
			Total	20	7 guilty
					10 not guilty
					2 not heard
					1 insane

feelings of delicacy withheld his best defence.'[8] Even in the 1820s deaths in the course of duelling were regarded quite differently from other murders.

The treatment accorded to males and females charged with murder was noticeably different. Two of the males found guilty were executed. Of three women charged with murder, two were acquitted and the third was found guilty of the lesser charge of concealing the birth of a child and given a six-month sentence in the district jail. This woman, Dinah Anguish, was only fifteen in 1844 when the offence occurred. She was the first female to appear before the Niagara courts charged with infanticide since the conviction of Angelique Pilotte in 1817, although other cases of alleged infanticide were referred to in the district press.[9] In one instance the local constable apparently helped the perpetrator to escape, drawing the wrath of the *St. Catharines Farmer's Journal*: 'What have our Magistrates done, in regard to this most horrid transaction?'[10] Magistrates were apparently willing to turn a blind eye to a crime that was often difficult to prove, and which in this case had already been complicated by the escape of the suspect. Compassion in cases of alleged infanticide was not limited to the Niagara district, as Constance Backhouse has illustrated.[11]

The Niagara courts' treatment of the crime of rape, or sexual assault as it is now termed, and those charged with this offence reveals a similar ambiguity. No cases of rape were tried at the court of quarter sessions, as justices of the peace were not empowered to judge capital felonies, and only a small number of rape cases (eight) were heard in Niagara's assize courts during the colonial period. In six of these the accused was acquitted.[12] Niagara's low conviction rate for rape mirrors the rate found in the London district during the 1830s, as well as other jurisdictions, and reflects the state of the law in Upper Canada generally.[13] When legislation permitting convictions for assault with intent to rape was passed in 1842 both the number of prosecutions and the conviction rate rose. Eleven cases came before the Niagara assizes during the remainder of the decade, in ten of which convictions were registered.

One of the more remarkable cases of sexual assault to be heard at the Niagara court of quarter sessions was tried in October 1836. Samuel Farensworth was charged with assault, although his real offence was rape against a seven-year-old girl. By charging him with assault, the magistrates enabled the case to be heard at the court of quarter sessions instead of being held over for the assizes. The charge was brought by the girl's father, who assembled fourteen witnesses, including three doctors, and brought them to Niagara from St Catharines. In total, twenty-nine witnesses and three constables testified in a trial whose cost exceeded £50, a very large sum for this period. Both the number of witnesses and the nature of the medical testimony indicate the gravity of the offence in the eyes of the local community. The fact that the doctors were able to agree on their findings probably assisted the jury to return a guilty verdict. Farensworth received the comparatively light sentence of three months in jail and a fine of £25 and costs.[14] By trying Farensworth at the lower court, the magistrates avoided prosecution on a capital charge and increased the likelihood of a conviction.

Another case of assault with intent to rape that came before the court of quarter sessions in 1843 involved a servant girl, Margaret Beance. Beance alleged that a canal worker, Andrew O'Marra, had assaulted her when she went out to milk a cow in the morning. He had thrown her down twice, trying to 'ravish her,' but when she resisted he left her alone. The local magistrate, James Black, signed a warrant for O'Marra's arrest, but Black could not convince Margaret Beance's employer, Mrs Jackson, to give an affidavit, 'although she knows the truth.' O'Marra was bound over for trial at the January sessions, but Mrs Jackson refused to appear at court, even after receiving a subpoena. The prosecution could not continue and O'Marra was discharged by proclamation.[15] Servant girls like Margaret Beance had difficulty in obtaining justice in cases involving sexual assault.

CRIMES AGAINST PROPERTY

Crimes against property were the most common offences to be tried at the assizes in the Niagara district and convictions carried severe punishments. Ann Alexandra McEwen found that 149 cases of larceny or receiving stolen goods were tried at the Niagara assizes from 1827 to 1846, four times the number of assaults.[16] The statistical record of larceny prosecutions is shown in Table 7.4. In the 1820s, judges often combined jail sentences of six months for grand larceny with public whippings of thirty-nine lashes. Even those sentenced for petty larceny could receive sentences for public whippings in addition to imprisonment. Before the pillory vanished in the mid-1830s, the Niagara magistrates regularly sentenced offenders in minor theft cases to an hour in the pillory before being discharged. Whippings were commonly used in the Niagara district to punish property crimes up to the 1820s, but they disappeared completely in the next decade as imprisonment became the punishment of choice.[17] Complaints about unfortunates being 'flogged in the public streets for trivial crimes' helped lead to amendments in 1833 to what had been termed 'the barbarous criminal code of this Province,' amendments written by Chief Justice Robinson to make the criminal law more effective and more certain in its punishments.[18]

Property crimes accounted for 43 per cent of the arrests made by Niagara constables, an indication of the prevalence of such complaints and of the prompt efforts made by those in the justice system to try to apprehend suspects and recover stolen property.[19] Combining prosecutions for larceny at the level of both the court of quarter sessions and the assizes, larceny cases accounted for more of the court business in Niagara than any other type of crime. In the period covered by the tables, 473 cases of larceny were prosecuted versus 407 cases of assault. There is no clear pattern that would lead to the conclusion that larceny cases increased during depressions and declined in times of prosperity. The number of cases tried at the court of quarter sessions rose distinctly in April and July 1837, but there is no evidence to link this rise to the Rebellion later in the year. Nor is the increase in 1840

Table 7.4
Larceny prosecutions at Niagara assizes,
1827–46

Year	Number	Year	Number
1827	3	1837	6
1828	6	1838	11
1829	2	1839	7
1830	6	1840	5
1831	5	1841	7
1832	3	1842	12
1833	2	1843	10
1834	5	1844	17
1835	8	1845	21
1836	4	1846	9
		Total	149

Table 7.5
Larceny prosecutions at Niagara court of
quarter sessions, 1828–46

Year	Number	Year	Number
1828	6	1838	10
1829	14	1839	16
1830	18	1840	29
1831	16	1841	10
1832	10	1842	19
1833	17	1843	16
1834	15	1844	18
1835	20	1845	21
1836	17	1846	16
1837	36	Total	324

easy to explain, although economic hardship in the district may have been a causal factor. The distinction between grand and petty larceny was abolished in 1837, which should have meant that fewer larceny cases were heard at the assize level and more at the court of quarter sessions, as Judge Campbell, chairman of the Niagara quarter sessions, confirmed in 1843: 'I consider all Larcenies triable at the Sessions ...'[20] Whatever the intentions of legislators and judges, the number of larcenies tried at the assizes did not diminish. In 1838 sixteen people charged with theft appeared in eleven cases at the Niagara assizes. During the previous decade, between two and ten people a year had been tried at the assize level for larceny. The number of cases rose again in the following decade, reaching a high of twenty-one in 1846.[21] Public opinion continued to demand that the constabulary act to prevent larceny. Patrick Finn, a constable, went to Queenston in June 1846 'to arrest a man whose name [is] not known, guilty of committing a good many petty Larcenies through the town.'[22]

By the 1840s longer incarceration, hard labour, and solitary confinement had replaced shorter jail sentences and public whipping as the punishment for those found guilty of larceny. Penitentiary sentences ranging from three years to five years with hard labour were not uncommon for more serious offences. A few criminals were sentenced to one or two months of solitary confinement in the Niagara jail for lesser thefts. In a few cases where servants or apprentices were convicted of theft from their employers the magistrates also ordered that the offenders receive only bread and water for one month of their sentence.

Crimes against property were punished severely because contemporary society viewed them as threats to the social order. One such crime was arson and anyone convicted of arson was liable to capital punishment, although no one was hanged for this crime in the Niagara district. One of the most celebrated arson cases involved the burning of a mill belonging to the magistrate Gilbert McMicking on a Sunday morning in July 1840. John DeWitt was not brought to trial for this offence until 1844, at which time he was found guilty and sentenced to life imprisonment at hard labour in the Kingston Penitentiary. DeWitt's trial took place after Brock's monument had been partially blown up and an Anglican church in Chippewa burned, in the aftermath of the Mackenzie Rebellion. Judge Sherwood, who sentenced DeWitt, alluded to these events when he said that 'no portion of the Province had suffered more' from arson than the Niagara region.[23] De Witt paid a heavy price not only for what he had done, and the fact that he had committed the crime on a Sunday, but because of public alarm over a series of political arson crimes on the Niagara frontier.

Theft of animals was also viewed as a heinous property crime in colonial Niagara. In an agricultural society animal theft was taken very seriously indeed. Thefts of animals were more frequent in the fall than at any other time of the year; the thieves may have been conscious of the approach of winter or thought that because butchering was common in the fall losses of animals might be less noticeable. In the case of animal thefts the border was not an obstacle to bringing culprits to justice: Americans and Canadians had similar interests in capturing the thieves and returning them for trial. Conviction rates were also high. Of the thirty-nine cases brought to the assize level, two did not proceed, but in the remainder twenty-eight resulted in convictions.[24] Convicted horse thieves in particular could expect little mercy.

Other forms of larceny were also dealt with severely, but in a few selected cases public opinion in the Niagara district could affect the outcome of a prosecution. Benjamin Abbott was arrested and tried for larceny in July 1844. His accuser suggested in a deposition that Abbott was a dangerous person who had been 'prowling about at night ... Several horses has [sic] been stolen in the neighbourhood recently, and suspicions has [sic] rested on the prisoner as an aider and abetter in these thefts.' Abbott had been charged not just because of a specific theft of a cotton shirt, to which charge he pleaded guilty, but because of his reputation in the community. Sensing this, a surprisingly large number of local freeholders, fifty-five in all, signed a petition to the magistrates stating they knew Abbott was 'deranged in his mind,' but recommended him to the court as 'an object of pity.'[25] The judges were sensitive to these community representations and sentenced Abbott to two hours in the jail for his crime. Two years later, however, the district had him confined in the temporary asylum for the insane in Toronto.

MORAL ORDER OFFENCES

One category of moral order offences, violations of the sabbath, has already been discussed, but moral order offences could also include vagrancy, keeping disorderly houses, gambling, and in one case in the Niagara district, the crime of blasphemy. Collectively, these offences made up only a small proportion of prosecuted crime. They averaged 12 or 13 per cent of the crimes for which arrests were made in the Niagara district, a rate comparable to that found in the neighbouring Gore district in the same period.[26] The number of cases that actually went to trial was even lower than the arrest figures.

The difficulties inherent in tracking moral order offences in the Niagara district are revealed by the way in which the colonial justice system treated prostitution. No cases of prostitution went to trial at either the assizes or the court of quarter sessions, although charges of keeping a disorderly house, heard at both levels, were often related to prostitution. Niagara magistrates found themselves in a continual quandary when trying to deal with prostitution in their particular towns and villages. A case tried in 1836 illustrates some of the complexities they faced. A magistrate in the town of Niagara, John Alma, responded to the entreaties of several people on behalf of Mary Buggins, who had been found half naked on the town streets, obviously ill and in danger of dying. Alma had her examined by a local doctor and then committed her to the jail as a vagrant. Alma later claimed that there were few people in Niagara who 'did not feel for the unfortunate creature,' even though 'her well known depraved character' and 'her indecent, immoral and truly disgusting appearance' had dissuaded any of them from giving her private shelter. He had put Mary Buggins in the local jail as 'a most notorious prostitute.' The next morning, to Alma's great annoyance, three other Niagara magistrates discharged her, unwilling to have the district bear the cost of looking after her. Alma petitioned the lieutenant governor against what he viewed as an arbitrary overruling of his action. In keeping with a general reluctance to interfere in matters of local justice the lieutenant governor chose not to act, although he or his secretary noted that Alma's action had been 'too humane perhaps.'[27] The attorney general, who reviewed the case, found that both Alma and the other magistrates had acted within their legal powers. Mary Buggins had been incarcerated not for an actual crime, but because incarceration was the only way to provide shelter for a well-known local prostitute who was too ill to look after herself.

Magistrates regularly exercised their powers to incarcerate known prostitutes as vagrants and then to release them. This practice was in line with English justice. In England too prostitutes were generally charged as vagrants, or with being loose, idle and disorderly, offences magistrates could deal with summarily under English statute law. In Niagara prostitutes were released after a night or two in the local jail in the hope that these annoying moral pests would move somewhere else. The women were typically incarcerated following complaints about their behaviour. When Corporal Hugh Byrnes complained that four women 'are constantly conducting themselves in the neighbourhood of the barracks at Fort George in a most indecent and profligate manner,' a Niagara magistrate issued a warrant for their arrest. The women remained in jail until someone provided bail and security for their future good conduct.[28] Occasionally, prostitutes' jail sentences became so lengthy that even the grand jurors took notice. In July 1844 a grand jury wrote a presentment stating that they were 'sorry to find two females of bad fame' incarcerated for thirty-six days and subsisting on a diet of bread and water. The jury recommended that these women 'be discharged forthwith.'[29] Earlier that year the Niagara magistrates had decided to treat so-called vagrants, or prostitutes, more severely than other criminals, presumably to deter them from practising their profession in the district. They issued an order that anyone committed to jail as a vagrant would receive no food other than bread and water.[30] In taking up the cause of the two females who had been confined the grand jurors protested the severity of this policy. Ultimately, the policy had no effect whatever. The summer of 1844 saw more prostitutes arrested as vagrants and sent to the Niagara jail than in any previous year. Prostitutes, although never formally prosecuted, were regularly found in the Niagara jail.

Prostitution was often connected to other moral offences. When the Pelham magistrate Bartholomew Tench assembled the evidence against a local innkeeper, Ebenezer Rice, early in January 1836 he was sure there was enough to convict Rice of bringing prostitutes from Buffalo to his inn. In Tench's opinion Rice could also be indicted for 'Gambling, Keeping a Bawdy house, and a breach of the Tavern regulations.' The deposition supporting this charge came from a local farmer, David McAlpin, who said of the prostitutes, 'that the common report of the neighbourhood was that they were women of *bad character* from Buffalo.' Buffalo's reputation had already spread to Upper Canada! This hearsay report was insufficient to support the charges, although the magistrate claimed Rice had escaped conviction on similar charges once before. The grand jury found 'no Cause of Complaint against Ebenezer Rice.'[31] Rice had previously served as a constable and was presumably familiar with the law.

Gambling was another common moral offence in the Niagara district, but even when it was the cause of a formal indictment, a trial rarely resulted. In one early example a trial did take place. Three men were sentenced at the fall assizes in 1825 to two months each in the local jail and to stand for an hour and a half in the pillory for defrauding a man of a horse through gambling.[32] The combination of public shaming and incarceration was used at that time to send a message to the population at large, but there is little evidence that this punishment led to any diminution in the offence. Gambling throughout the district took various forms. In St Catharines in April 1837 three magistrates took depositions about gambling in the form of horse-racing, as well as roulette, which had typically gone on in connection with a local tavern. The tavern owner, John Kimball, had boasted publicly, 'by God any man that complains of me for running today may make his peace, he may settle his business to leave this Country for by God I will skin him.'[33] Three local men defied Kimball and swore depositions against him, but their attempt to enforce a moral code on the recalcitrant tavern owner did not succeed. The case never proceeded to trial. In another gambling case, the loser at a faro table at the Pavilion Hotel near Niagara Falls in 1837 filed a deposition against the hotel owner and the operator of the table. A grand jury supported this charge in a presentment and the magistrates issued arrest warrants, but again no trial took place, perhaps because the suspects fled across the border.[34]

Only one other moral order offence was tried at the assize level in the period 1825–50, and this involved a tavern keeper: Isaac Vanfleet was convicted for keeping a disorderly house in 1831. In 1850 Susan Gilland was charged with keeping a bawdy house, but the case did not go to trial and the accused was presumably discharged.[35] Charges of keeping disorderly houses were slightly more common at the quarter sessions level, although convictions were hard to obtain. In two cases at the spring court of quarter sessions in 1828, the juries sided with the innkeeper.[36] The only other case of keeping a disorderly house to be heard in the 1820s resulted in a guilty finding in July 1829.[37] Magistrates who wanted to clean up their neighbourhoods could do so by denying tavern licences to notorious offenders. Most found it easier to act administratively than to try to assemble evidence and witnesses for court cases.

In the single case of blasphemy for which the papers were sent to the attorney general, the background suggests that the charge served as a convenient vehicle for Joseph Badgely to seek revenge on John Sweazy in a long-standing quarrel over a tavern licence. The context is also important because the alleged offence occurred in the summer of 1832, when cholera was sweeping through the Niagara district. Many people saw the epidemic as a visitation of God, but John Sweazy apparently did not share the fears of his neighbours. According to Badgely, Sweazy swore, 'God damn God Almighty, I am not afraid of his sending the Cholera to me, by Jesus Christ I haint [sic].'[38] No trial on the charge of blasphemy was ever held and the case remained unresolved. Badgely appeared in court eleven years later on a charge of bestiality, continuing his strange history of involvement with the law in Niagara.[39] A sceptical jury acquitted him.

A common charge such as riot and assault could occasionally disguise a moral order offence. A Niagara merchant and regular grand juryman, Lachlan Bell, brought a complaint of riot and assault against Bernard McGann and Patrick Donnelly for leading a charivari against his house in July 1841. Bell had found his home surrounded by 'a mob of about from twenty to thirty persons, ringing bells, blowing horns and making other noises.' He was unable to convince a Niagara grand jury that this was sufficient cause to bring the men to trial. The jury returned a 'no bill' and Bell was left without further judicial recourse.[40]

REGULATORY OFFENCES

The number of documented convictions for regulatory offences increased noticeably after 1834, when magistrates were empowered to hear and dispose of minor cases summarily in their own communities rather than referring them to the courts of quarter sessions. This authority meant that local differences in the administration of justice became further entrenched. The number of so-called working magistrates increased, extending beyond those who regularly attended the court of quarter sessions. Regulatory offences are almost invisible on the criminal justice horizon in Niagara prior to 1834, but from that date magistrates were required to register their summary convictions every quarter. Regulatory offences then emerge as summary convictions for such things as selling liquor without a licence, refusal to perform statute labour, or unique offences like peddling although not a British subject. Summary convictions also begin to increase significantly in number each quarter, suggesting that the majority of the real business of minor criminal justice occurred at the level of the locality after 1834 rather than at the court of quarter sessions. By the mid-1840s Niagara district magistrates registered 100 convictions on average per quarter, far more than the number of cases heard yearly at the quarter sessions or assizes.

Regulatory offences still constituted a minority of the convictions registered by the magistrates. Of eighty-five summary convictions registered in Niagara at the April quarter sessions, 1844, sixteen, or 19 per cent, were regulatory offences. A year earlier only thirty-four convictions were registered, but nearly all of these were for some manner of

Table 7.6
Summary convictions, Niagara, April 1844

Type of crime	N = 85	%
Crimes against the person	32	38
Trespasses & property offences	29	34
Peace, order, moral offences	8	9
Regulatory offences	16	19
Other	0	0

Source: AO, RG 22, Series 372, 52–26.

Table 7.7
Summary convictions, Niagara, July 1846

Type of crime	N = 111	%
Crimes against the person	59	53
Trespasses & property offences	15	13.5
Peace, order, moral offences	15	13.5
Regulatory offences	22	20
Other	0	0

Source: AO, RG 22, Series 372, 63–30.

assault. Only one regulatory offence was included. Seldom, if ever, did regulatory offences account for more than 20 per cent of the convictions registered at the quarter sessions. Here, as in the courts of quarter sessions, assaults predominated, with property offences following close behind. Niagara magistrates often resorted to the generic term 'trespass' to describe offences which might or might not be property crimes. The statistics sampled in Tables 7.6 and 7.7, based on two summary conviction schedules, illustrate that regulatory convictions follow behind assaults and property offences in the colonial court system. By the 1840s, however, as a category they exceeded offences of peace, order, and morality.

The people of Niagara made regular use of their magistrates and courts to initiate prosecutions, especially for assault and theft. There is little numerical evidence, however, of a society in the grip of a crime wave. Nor can we find utterly convincing evidence to support theories that certain crimes, such as larceny, were prosecuted more forcefully in times of economic depression, as was apparently the case in eighteenth-century England.[41] As John Beattie reminds us, 'prosecutions arose from a complex of interacting forces and from a series of decisions made by a number of men.'[42] This was just as true in Niagara as it was in England. We should therefore exercise caution in applying theories seeking to explain criminality over long historical periods to shorter periods in specific North American jurisdictions such as Niagara or, as Donald Fyson has found, Quebec.[43]

THE MOST SPLENDID BUILDING

John Strachan, the leading Anglican of Upper Canada and a prominent member of the Family Compact, wrote a guide book in 1819 for prospective British immigrants which he published under the name of his brother, James. Strachan wrote of the former capital, Niagara, then recovering after being razed by the American forces during the War of 1812: 'In the town, we saw nothing so remarkable as the contrast between the church and jail: the former entirely out of repair, and most discreditable to the people; the latter, the most splendid building in Upper Canada.'[44] Strachan was not alone in his praise of the jail's architecture. A Scottish botanist, John Goldie, who visited Niagara in the summer of 1819, also commented that the new jail was 'considered the finest building in Canada.'[45] Unlike Strachan, Goldie had no axe to grind about the lack of public support for the church. He was merely a traveller, passing through Niagara on his way to the Falls, and noting down his impressions in a private diary. That both men should agree in their judgments of the jail suggests they were echoing broader public sentiment. The jail had been the first public building to be rebuilt after the end of the war, but for a jail to be described as 'the most splendid building in Upper Canada' was still odd. What did it say about Upper Canadian colonial society that a jail should be its most splendid building?

Another traveller had passed through Niagara the year before. John Duncan, also a Scot, was in some ways a more perceptive observer than either Strachan or Goldie. Duncan reported in detail on North American institutions and society, and both his description of the Niagara jail and his conclusion are revealing, especially since he also visited and reported on penal institutions in Boston, Baltimore, and New York. The building that housed Niagara's courthouse and jail was imposing, even grand, when viewed from the outside, but the jail was backward and primitive when compared to the penitentiaries being constructed in the United States. Duncan described the jail as follows:

> Niagara is possessed of a court house and jail; both under one roof. The jail is on the lower floor. The cells, both for criminals and debtors, surround and open from the hall, which leads to the court-room, and the guilty or unfortunate inmates are exposed to the gaze of everyone whom curiosity or idleness induces to enter. The partitions and doors of the various cells are composed of strong pieces of oak, firmly bolted together; the doors are about nine inches thick, consisting of two thicknesses of wood with sheet-iron between them. Some of the Debtors' apartments have a small window to the outside, but the criminals have no light but from a small semicircular opening in the door. The debtors have fireplaces, but the criminals have only the miserable comfort of looking out at a stove in the middle of the hall, from which no perceptible warmth can reach their dismal abodes. It must be truly dreadful to pass a Canadian winter in such a place. How miserably does this prison contrast with those in the United States.[46]

Duncan's description highlights a number of contrasts between the Upper Canadian penal system and those found in the American states to the south. Until the 1830s, Upper Canada relied solely on local jails to house its prisoners rather than immediately following the Pennsylvania example and creating a state penitentiary. These local jails, like the one in Niagara, often combined courthouse and jail. The combination was expedient and cheap, but it highlighted the contrast between the two arms of the law, majesty and terror, by confining prisoners immediately below the room in which they faced justice.

Niagara's courtroom was at the time the largest in the province. A description purportedly of the trial of the Scottish radical Robert Gourlay in August 1819 has the judge sitting on 'a judicial throne,' complete 'with spacious, cushioned chairs.'[47] The judge reigned upstairs, dispensing the king's justice, while below stairs the jail's inmates froze in the winter or, like Gourlay, nearly suffocated in the summer heat. Their suffering was greater than that of the debtors, who occupied a higher level in the prison hierarchy, enjoying the privilege of 'apartments' equipped with fireplaces and other amenities denied to criminals. The architecture of the reconstructed Niagara jail reinforced the hierarchy of the judicial system and the British values it was seen to represent. It was a Loyalist statement, reaffirming the British connection and the structure of British justice.

The Niagara courthouse and jail completed in 1818 served the Niagara district until 1846. The 1818 building was certainly a considerable architectural advance on its predecessor, a log building designed as a blockhouse. Described as 'a charming, neo-Classic building' of 'Flemish-bonded brick, with graceful arcading' in the ceremonial upper storey that also possessed 'fine Venetian windows,' the new Niagara courthouse was intended to be 'the principal ornament' of the rebuilt former capital.[48] The Royal Arms of George III were prominent in a painting that hung above the judicial bench, and the lion in this painting actually looked out on the courtroom, glowering fiercely, as if he personally embodied the awful might of the law.[49]

Until the Kingston Penitentiary opened in 1835, the Niagara jail was the only place of incarceration for criminals in the district. Within the jail, as travellers had observed, there was a clearly defined social hierarchy among prisoners. Jurors, court officials, and magistrates subscribed equally to this stratification. The basic division was between debtors and felons. The former were confined because of lack of payment of debts, the latter as a punishment. Vagrants of various sorts were also regularly incarcerated. Grand juries, especially in the 1840s, wanted to make the distinctions among prisoners more manifest in a number of ways. When an exercise courtyard was constructed, the grand jurors wanted a separate portion set aside for 'air and exercise' for the debtors, with the felons being required to do profitable employment 'either in cutting stone or some other work' to offset the costs of their incarceration.[50] Another grand jury recommended the purchase of 'substantial but not expensive bedsteads (of oak timber) for debtors, so that those whom misfortune may tear from domestic comforts may not like Criminals be compelled to sleep on the floor.'[51] The same jurors also wanted new stoves purchased for the debtors' apartments. Still another grand jury desired that chairs be bought for the debtors and benches for the prisoners.[52] Even the term 'apartment,' used to describe the rooms for debtors, conveyed a very different impression than the term 'cell,' reserved for criminal prisoners. The lack of a wall separating debtors from criminals meant that when wives and families visited the debtors they had 'to listen to the obscenity and profanity of the criminals.'[53] Sympathy for the debtors and a constant desire to make their incarceration more endurable contrasted with the much harsher approach to the hardened criminals.

Grand jurors also wanted to separate youthful offenders from older, more seasoned criminals. If no segregation of the 'most hardened and atrocious criminals,' occurred, as one grand jury put it, the jail would become 'a school and nursery for infamy and vice.'[54] Grand juries also advocated the establishment of work programs to prevent idleness and the provision of moral education. Jurors regularly petitioned to have ministers of different churches perform services on Sundays for the prisoners. Sanitation was another constant preoccupation. One grand jury found the whole jail infested with vermin. As a solution the jurors proposed that a separate room be set aside to receive prisoners, to prevent illnesses from spreading and to clean up those who arrived 'in a most filthy state.' By the early 1840s, jail reform had become a minor crusade in the Niagara district. One grand jury welcomed the fact that both the new warden of the district and the district council 'are now ardent supporters of such improvements as Justice, Social Policy and humanity require.'[55] The construction of a new jail in 1846 enabled some of the changes recommended to be implemented.

The Niagara jail became in many ways a barometer of the well-being of the district. When dangerous criminals were confined in it, or when serious overcrowding occurred, alarm signals emanated from the jailer, the sheriff, or the magistrates. The lieutenant governor responded to one of these alarms in 1834 by agreeing to provide for a military guard around the jail, 'as long as [the] forgers are in confinement.'[56] Escapes indicated greater peril and as Sheriff Leonard wrote in 1829, the jail's 'solitary situation and vicinity to the American frontier,' made it possible for Americans to cross over, especially in winter, and rescue prisoners.[57] Concern about escapes did not diminish after the Rebellion years. In 1845, the jailer reported that two attempted jail breaks had occurred within a three-week period. The jail housed 'at least ten inmates that are most desperate characters,' and who were trying to escape to avoid being sent to the penitentiary. This report prompted the magistrates to hire extra constables to mount a night guard during the period of the assizes.[58]

Jail overcrowding, while contributing to concerns over security and the health of inmates, meant as well that the district magistrates would have to allocate more funds to cover the costs of housing large numbers of prisoners. W.J. Blacklock examined the jail ration accounts of the Niagara jail and discovered that with the exception of 1831, the number of people incarcerated in the district jail rose steadily from 1828 through the 1830s. The magistrates were certainly aware of this trend and it helps to account for their nearly frantic efforts to persuade the lieutenant governor to hold two assize sessions a year. Between 1828 and 1836 the total number of days served in the jail by prisoners more than doubled. By 1832, on average, prisoners were spending forty-seven days in the jail, either waiting for trial or serving a sentence. A second assize was authorized in 1837, which helped to clear the jail of prisoners, but even by 1838–9, 20 per cent of the district expenditures related to the costs of the jail.[59]

A sense of the jail's vulnerability became acute in times of international crisis, such as the period of the Mackenzie Rebellion. When state political prisoners were confined in the Niagara jail in 1838, fears about a potential lack of security increased and spread to the upper levels of colonial government. One of the military commanders wrote to the Niagara sheriff in July 1838 to warn him about 'the insecure State of the Jail at Niagara.'[60] He had authorized more military guards for the outside of the jail because he did not want to be blamed for the escape of any prisoners. The solicitor general was also on edge, telling Sheriff Hamilton bluntly that 'nothing could be more injurious than that the prisoners should effect their escape.' Draper ordered a much tighter security regime and informed the sheriff peremptorily that 'a visit from yourself now and then would keep alive the attention of your subordinate officers.'[61] The presence of British troops who could be called upon to guard the jail as needed was also seen as essential to the preservation of the established social order in colonial Niagara. The importance of the district jail, however, diminished after the construction of the Kingston Penitentiary and the creation of a provincial asylum, and once the threat posed by the Mackenzie Rebellion had been dealt with. The former bulwark of a frontier society began to fade in importance as Upper Canada constructed new institutions for incarceration, institutions designed to serve the colony as a whole rather than a single district or locality.

8

Criminal Victims

Historians have traditionally been more concerned with the perpetrators of crime than with its victims. In colonial Niagara two groups of people stand out because of the treatment they received at the hands of the law: women who had been subject to spousal abuse and African Canadians subjected to racial persecution within the justice system as well as without. One group was victimized because of gender, and the other because of race. When a woman or a member of the African Canadian community was a victim of crime, she or he faced double jeopardy in seeking justice.

SILENT VICTIMS

Peter Ward has found the ideals of nineteenth-century marriage embodied in the fiction of the time. These ideals established 'a sliding scale of opprobrium for various infractions'[1] that penalized female infractions more severely than male ones. Ward suggests that the ultimate female infraction was bearing a child out of wedlock. Male infractions were not only regarded less seriously, but the more repellent ones were often hidden from public view. In nineteenth-century Upper Canada wife-beating was rarely discussed and even more rarely prosecuted. Nineteenth-century marriages in Upper Canada, as in Britain, were held to be private and disputes, no matter how violent, were to be resolved within the family. Court intervention was a last resort. Family violence could occasion community action through the charivari or, in some instances, intervention by the church.[2] But neither family members nor the courts wanted to make public spectacles of intimate family matters. Magistrates in Upper Canada were loathe to allow spousal abuse cases even to reach the trial stage. Perpetrators thus almost invariably escaped the punishment they so richly deserved.

In 'Beneath the "Sentimental Veil": Families and Family History in Canada,' Cynthia Comacchio observes that there have been very 'few published studies on family violence in Canadian history.' One she cites is Kathyrn Harvey's 'To Love, Honour and Obey: Wife-battering in Working Class Montreal, 1869–79.'[3] Harvey uses a British model, based on studies of domestic violence in working-class London and Liverpool and premised on a family economy model, to explore wife-beating in working-class Montreal. Her sources include newspaper accounts as well as court records, suggesting that by this period family violence in Montreal was publicly acknowledged by both the press and the courts.

A paper given by Katherine McKenna at the 1996 Canadian Historical Association meeting, 'Lower Class Women's Agency in Upper Canada: Prescott's Board of Police Records, 1834–1850,' similarly illuminates the position of women within the colonial justice system. McKenna examined the records of a court she says was not a criminal court, but one which 'merely tried bylaw infractions, however broadly defined.'[4] Of the 139 cases she found between 1843 and 1849 in which women were the prosecutors, she isolated 32 which 'were related to violence against women committed by men, particularly between husbands and wives.'[5] She also found at least one recorded instance 'of a woman successfully charging her own husband with disturbing the public peace by striking her.'[6] Prescott's Police Court was by no means unique in the way it dealt with violence against women. Charges of breach of the peace were often the means by which wife-beaters in the Niagara district were brought to the attention of the justice system.

In the first half of the nineteenth century cases involving wife-beating rarely came before the magistrates at Niagara's quarter sessions and no wife-beating cases were prosecuted before the assize courts prior to 1850. Nor have I discovered reports of any such cases in the press. (Press reports were almost invariably based on the trials themselves.) In the absence of trial reports we might be tempted to conclude that spousal abuse did not occur in the Niagara district. The court records, however, provide tiny but revealing clues testifying to the existence of a problem which evidence from other countries in the same period, especially Britain, indicates was far more prevalent. Among Niagara's court records are a few graphic depositions of the brutality endured by wives at the hands of their husbands. Were these the only examples of domestic violence? And why were the abusers not prosecuted more often? The answers to these questions reveal a great deal about marriage in colonial Niagara, as well as the position of women in the colonial justice system, and reflect a pattern common throughout nineteenth-century Upper Canada and other British North American colonies.

In her study of working women in early-nineteenth-century Canada Elizabeth Jane Errington cites a letter on marriage that appeared in the *Farmer's Journal* in 1828: 'In the fate of a woman, marriage is the most important crisis, it fixes her in a state of all others the most happy or the most wretched.'[7] An unknown number of Upper Canadian women were fixed in the 'most wretched' state. Errington argues that 'for many colonial women of all classes, marriage was an exercise in raw power.' Upper Canadian law institutionalized 'the potential for unhappiness, abuse and marriage breakdown.'[8] Family violence occurred within a legal context where the wife was 'a legal nonentity.' She was the property of her husband in law and, as Lori Chambers argues, 'the powers of physical control' possessed by the husband could encourage him to commit acts of physical violence against his spouse.[9] The wife had little recourse in law. Between 1820 and 1840 at least five Upper Canadian men were convicted of murdering their wives. While the deaths of wives at the hands of their husbands usually revealed a pattern of abuse, few Upper Canadian male juries found accused men guilty of spousal abuse. Courts would convict wife-murderers, who were seen as heinous criminals, but until the abuse reached this final stage the courts preferred not to intervene.

Two murder cases out of twenty in the Niagara district between 1827 and 1846 involved men murdering their wives. In the Donnelly case, as we have seen, the husband was never tried on grounds of insanity. In the other case the murder was the culmination of habitual abuse and committed during a drunken fit of anger. The culprit, Leslie McCall, was a corporal in the 70th Regiment, stationed at the mouth of the Grand River. Ann Alexandra McEwen's account summarizes what happened to his wife Jane in November 1826. After her husband had received his daily grog ration he became violent, as had happened many times previously. 'Jane's ten-year old daughter watched, horrified, as her stepfather thrashed her mother and struck her with his bayonet.'[10] When McCall eventually sobered up, it was too late to rescue his wife. Leslie McCall was the only man convicted for murdering his wife in the Niagara district during this period, and his sentence of death was commuted.

The Niagara experience can be compared with Halifax in the late eighteenth century, where women constituted a quarter of all homicide victims, but few were killed by their spouses.[11] Jim Phillips points out that in eighteenth century Halifax, 'unusually high levels of deadly violence pertained in the city, and women were killed both in unusually high numbers and in unusual ways.'[12] This was not the case in nineteenth-century Niagara, but we should not assume that women in this district escaped male violence.

Anna Clark reminds us in *The Struggle for the Breeches* that 'the root cause of domestic violence ... was that abusive men wanted to dominate their wives and used violence to do so.'[13] She goes on to suggest that historians search for 'specific triggers for violence in a particular era.'[14] In the case of Leslie McCall alcohol abuse and wife abuse were closely connected. Similarly 40 per cent of the Old Bailey cases reported by Anna Clark involved alcohol, and the figure was higher in Glasgow.[15] Kathryn Harvey does not have specific percentages for her Montreal study, but she informs us that, 'in the majority of cases, men were arrested both for being drunk and for striking their wives.' For this small Niagara sample, the 40 per cent figure is probably close to the mark.

The British Parliament did not pass a statute against wife-beating until 1853 and even then the law proved ineffective. As Anna Clark's study of wife-beating reveals, British law treated it 'differently from other assaults, hesitating to interfere in the private relations of man and wife.'[16] In England wives could seek a peace bond from a magistrate, but these were difficult to obtain and often did not provide the desired protection.

Anna Clark informs us that one woman a week appeared before the Middlesex magistrates in the eighteenth century to complain of violence from her husband, and more than four a week made similar complaints during a three-month period in Glasgow in 1824. Can we find parallel numbers in the colony of Upper Canada and, if not, why not?[17] Constance Backhouse describes a harrowing tale of spousal abuse in the Midland district following the marriage of Esther Hawley and George Ham in 1813. In the case of Esther Hawley Ham, heard by Chief Justice Campbell in 1826, Judge Campbell stated that 'a man had a right to chastise his wife *moderately* – and to warrant her leaving her husband, the chastisement must be such as to put her life in jeopardy.'[18] The law, expressed by the province's chief justice, gave no support to wives who fled their husbands alleging mistreatment. Yet an abused woman had little alternative except to seek shelter from family or friends. The option of divorce did not yet exist: marriage was envisaged as an indissoluble life union. The Upper Canadian Legislature did not grant its first divorce petition until 1839 and by Confederation only seven had been heard. There was no provision in ecclesiastical law for annulment due to spousal abuse or any form of mistreatment by a marriage partner. Backhouse sees the case of Esther Hawley Ham as 'setting the stage for a century of Canadian judicial precedent denying women basic protection against ruthless mistreatment. Case after case revealed women brutalized by vicious husbands. They were strangled, beaten with the handles of brooms, scalded with boiling water, threatened with loaded revolvers, kicked, bloodied, bruised, blackened and blistered.'[19] When cases of spousal abuse became extreme and public, the community sometimes tried to intervene, although when and how this intervention occurred varied from case to case.

The Esther Hawley Ham case is also remarkable in that it is one of the few spousal abuse cases to be tried at an assizes anywhere in Upper Canada in the period prior to 1840. No case of wife-beating was tried at the Niagara assizes, so there are no judicial pronouncements to compare with that of Judge Campbell. One case in 1833 reveals some of the reasons why assize trials for wife-beating were non-existent in the Niagara district. Grimsby magistrate Henry Nelles committed Benjamin Anderson to the Niagara jail to await trial in January 1833. Anderson's wife, Rachel, and two other women had made depositions about Anderson's violent behaviour towards Rachel. He had threatened her life and beaten her on numerous occasions. Anderson had also appeared at Mary Hill's place with a pistol and threatened 'to murder her [Rachel] as soon as he could find her.' Nelles wrote to the clerk of the peace of his concern that the women would not appear to give evidence in a trial 'as they are all in very reduced circumstances and cannot get [the] means to take them, and pay their expenses while gone – neither can they furnish sureties for their appearance at Court.'[20] The poverty of these complainants prevented an assize trial, although Benjamin Anderson spent seven months in the Niagara jail awaiting trial.

Upper Canadian courts rarely punished wife-beaters because these criminals almost never appeared in court. The Niagara quarter sessions records, the most complete we have for Upper Canada from 1828 on, do, however, provide a number of examples of early nineteenth century wife-beaters. This small sample of cases, none of which was publicly reported, illuminates the brutality of marriage for colonial wives tied to violent husbands and underlines the inadequacy of available legal remedies. The cases also document the role of community intervention in trying to prevent blatant spousal abuse.

Niagara did not witness community intervention along the lines of action taken in Colborne in 1845. There a house painter named Gilbert roused his neighbours to fury by 'grossly abusing his wife.' Taking the law into their own hands, the neighbours tarred and feathered him and 'then, tying a cord to one of his legs, barbarously dragged him several times over head through the water and along the sand till the poor wretch was well nigh dead from exhaustion and pain.'[21] After he recovered, Gilbert sought revenge by setting fire to one of his tormentor's houses, a fire which in the end burned six wood frame houses in the village. Community justice still exerted itself in mid-nineteenth century rural Canada West, usually in a more violent and unpredictable manner than official justice, and often with unplanned results.

The Niagara cases all involved the official justice system even if the magistrates seemed determined to try to prevent them from proceeding to trial. On 3 December 1838 the town wardens of Wainfleet filed a statement with the Niagara clerk of the peace that William Cochrane of Wainfleet Township was 'a man of unsound mind and a Dangerous Character to go at Large.' He had repeatedly abused his wife Elizabeth, who had been forced to seek refuge among her neighbours. Elizabeth filed her own deposition before the local magistrate on 29 March 1839, reporting an assault which had taken place the previous December. Her husband had struck her three times, thrown her on the floor, choked her, and she feared he would have killed her had not their son intervened. Elizabeth Cochrane felt she could not return home without being in great danger of further injury or death. She added that she was not filing the complaint against her husband 'out of any hatred, malice or ill-will ... but purely for the preservation of her person and children from further danger.'[22]

Elizabeth filed her deposition after the magistrate had issued a warrant to commit her husband to jail for refusing to find sureties and keep the peace towards his wife. Faced with the judicial warrant and his wife's deposition, William, a farmer, changed his mind and signed a recognizance for £20 to keep the peace towards Elizabeth. This spared him from jail and also kept him out of court, since the magistrates apparently had no desire to prosecute him for domestic assault. Elizabeth had been married to William for thirteen years. Presumably she had endured other violent episodes without seeking the protection of the town wardens or going to the magistrate. The wardens, without any other legal weapons of their own, tried to suggest that William Cochrane's conduct implied insanity and that on those grounds he deserved to be incarcerated. That tactic did not succeed.

Although peace bonds are not mentioned in the studies by Backhouse, Errington, and McKenna, they appear to have been the standard method used by Niagara magistrates to shackle abusive husbands. Peace bonds may also have been used more than we realize in other parts of Upper and Lower Canada. Susan Lewthwaite, for instance, mentions them in her article on 'Violence, Law and Community in Rural Upper Canada.' The use of the recognizance, or peace bond, in her words, 'demonstrated that there was no overt desire to punish the transgressor, but nevertheless conveyed the message that his behaviour would no longer be tolerated.'[23] In his study of the work of the justices of the peace in the district of Montreal from 1764 to 1830 Don Fyson uncovered three hundred complaints of wife beating, almost all of which were resolved with the husband being bound over to keep the peace. Here, too, the cases were hidden from public view and rarely reached the level of a court trial.[24] Annalee Golz has confirmed that even in more modern times the criminal courts 'were less inclined to punish violent husbands than to endeavour to mediate marital relations ...'[25]

In April 1828 Mary McMahon, who was illiterate, found someone to help her write a petition to the magistrates claiming that since her husband, John, had been released from jail he had used violent and threatening language against her, maltreated her, torn her hair, and even threatened to kill her.[26] John McMahon had been confined since 1 March, pending trial for an assault. For reasons which are not clear from the records, he was not tried at the April quarter sessions but kept in jail until July and then released. His wife's petition may have influenced the magistrates to hold McMahon in jail for another three months without trial.

Jailing men for wife-beating appears to have been the exception rather than the rule in Upper Canada. While John Weaver's examination of Hamilton jail records turned up one James Hall, 'a nasty drunkard and wife beater who occasionally turned to theft, [and who] compiled a local record from 1837 to 1849 that ranks him as one of the more vicious characters encountered by authorities,'[27] it is not clear whether Hall was jailed for wife-beating or for his other crimes. By the end of the century, in cities like Hamilton, which had Police Magistrates Courts, wife-beating cases were either resolved through mediation or, in serious instances, punished by incarceration and whipping.[28] In the earlier period in Niagara incarceration was occasionally resorted to, but no physical punishment was added.

In December 1830 Jane Baker, a Queenston housewife, appeared before Alexander Hamilton, the local magistrate, and related her harrowing circumstances in a deposition:

> on Saturday evening last past, she was sitting at home in her house in Queenston aforesaid when her husband, Daniel Baker, came in and asked her for something to eat ... she told him to look on the table ... he ordered her out of the chair, brought out the table and began to eat ... he shortly after rose up and struck her on the head – she then told him that if he struck her again he must abide by the consequence – in reply he swore that if that was the case she should have more of it, and then proceeded to beat and kick her more violently ... he then threw a tin basin at her, which she picked up, and then made a pass at her with a knife which she parried with the basin and the knife glancing struck the child sitting on her knee – on the head ... she made her escape with the child to a neighbouring house where she has been confined to her bed under the doctor's care.[29]

She told the magistrate she feared for her life and asked, in legal terms, for 'surety of the peace.' The fact that Jane went to the magistrate for 'surety of the peace' suggests that either she, or her neighbours, were familiar with peace bonds. Her doctor may also have played a key part in alerting the local magistrate. The tale itself is an all too familiar one. Jane, who had no resources of her own, had to rely on her neighbours to post security on her behalf. The magistrate compelled her husband to post a peace bond of £50 sterling and to appear at the next quarter sessions in January. By January a temporary calm apparently reigned in the Baker household, because no indictment was preferred. The magistrates were content to bind Daniel to keep the peace for a year.

The calm was short-lived. Jane filed a second deposition on 21 March 1831, recounting another terrifying incident. On the previous Saturday night, 19 March, while they were in bed, her husband had 'jammed her with his knees in bed – Struck her with his fist on her Shoulder, took hold of her and jammed her a Second time against the Wall, kicked the chair from under her, Stuck a knife into the wall close to her face as if he intended to strike her with it ...' She then fled the house to seek refuge with her father. Daniel denied the assault and accused his wife of assaulting him. He explained the incident by saying that Jane 'left the house in a passion without a cause.'[30] The documents make no mention of alcohol, but because the incident occurred on a Saturday night it was likely a factor. This time the magistrates indicted Daniel for assault and he was tried at the March quarter sessions. The all-male jury found Jane's testimony more credible than her husband's and Daniel was convicted. He was sentenced to one month in jail and he was to remain in custody until he could produce security to post a peace bond for a year.

Daniel Baker was not the only husband tried at the March quarter sessions for domestic assault. Sylvester Glynn, a Grantham labourer, faced the same charge after beating his wife and threatening her life. Elizabeth Glynn did not prosecute her husband and may not even have given evidence at his trial. The charge was brought by the local magistrate, James Black, and corroborated by testimony from Nathaniel Blackmer, a cooper, and Peter Darby, a carpenter. Black had acted 'as much for our Lord the King as himself.' In his role as keeper of the king's peace, he had summoned the local constable and together they had tried to arrest Glynn. It was no easy task. After the initial assault, Glynn 'did furthermore with an Axe in one hand and a Knife in the other threaten to murder his said Wife – and also the said James Black and John Smith, Constable, in their attempt to prevent his further injuring his said wife and in their attempt to take him into custody.'[31] Glynn, like Baker, was found guilty and he received the same sentence, a month in jail and security for a year's peace bond.

In this second case Elizabeth Glynn appears only as the silent victim. We do not hear her voice at all in the court documents and are left wondering whether any charge would have been brought against Sylvester Glynn if the magistrate had not been determined to act upon the evidence brought before him.

Violent husbands and fathers could be jailed without trial on a warrant for committal issued by the local magistrate or sheriff. A case found among the papers of one of the sheriffs of the Niagara district, Alexander Hamilton, suggests how the law could respond. On 23 June 1832, Jacob Misner the younger succeeded in having his father committed to jail for violent and threatening behaviour to other members of his family.[32] It is not difficult to read between the lines here and find wife abuse. When Jacob Sr's behaviour became intolerable, his son took matters into his own hands and went to the sheriff for assistance. It is highly probable that Hamilton knew the family and was familiar with the father's behaviour. He procured a warrant to commit the senior Misner to jail. Although the case never came to trial, the family was given a short respite. The Niagara jail records indicate that a Jacob Misner spent nearly a month in jail, from 23 June to 16 July 1832 that summer.[33]

Informal processes of the law could be and occasionally were used to deal with extreme cases of domestic abuse. Much more common, however, was the case of Margaret Anderson. Anderson filed a deposition before James Black on 12 January 1831 that she had been violently assaulted by her husband. Black issued a warrant for William Anderson's arrest, but at this point the story ceases: Anderson was not arrested and no trial took place.[34] Elizabeth Lampman found herself in a similar position. She went to her local magistrate on 4 March 1832 and deposed that her husband had 'frequently threaten'd to put an end to her life and on the last day of February past, he said if any one got a Stick of Wood for her, except her Father's people, he would put an end to them and to her – and further that She is dayly [in] fear of her life.' The magistrate sent the deposition to the clerk of the peace in Niagara, along with recognizances for the appearance of the parties at the next quarter sessions court. Again no trial ensued.[35]

Sarah Taylor, the wife of Robert Taylor, a Niagara innkeeper, appears briefly in the Niagara court records in 1832. Apparently another victim of abuse by her husband and at least one other male, Sarah was determined to fight back. She was put in the Niagara jail on 7 July

1832, charged with threatening to burn down her husband's house and taking his life. Although the documents do not specify this, Robert was probably responsible for his wife's arrest. A week later the magistrate, Dr Muirhead, cancelled the charge and released Sarah from jail after she found bail and posted a bond for good behaviour for six months. At the beginning of June 1832 Moses Goodfellow, a Niagara farmer, had been charged with assaulting her, but this case did not proceed to trial at the quarter sessions when the grand jury found no bill.[36] Again, we are left with a number of questions. Was this a domestic dispute which the court felt should be settled between the parties? Were there other complications because of the tavern and the likely influence of alcohol? Whatever the real reasons for Sarah Taylor being forced to spend a hot July week in the Niagara jail, she does not reappear in the Niagara court records.

A case in 1833 reveals two in-laws using the law as a weapon in a bitter domestic quarrel. Ann Smart of Stamford, wife of Robert, brought a charge of assault and battery against her son-in-law, William Rees, in March 1833, alleging that William had arrived at her house drunk and threatened to kill anyone 'who should prevent him from dragging his wife from the House where she had been confined for four months.' Ann tried to stop him and in protecting her daughter she was assaulted. But just before the trial was to take place, the Stamford magistrate, R.H. Dee, wrote to Charles Richardson, the clerk of the peace for the Niagara district, saying that Robert Smart and his son-in-law had 'come to an amicable adjustment of their quarrel.' William's wife left her parents and returned to her husband, and the indictment against him was dropped.[37] The cause of the quarrel and the role played by the women in resolving it are not revealed. The court documents mention only the men in the resolution, a marked illustration in itself of the subordinate status of women in nineteenth-century Niagara marriages. What is clear is that the threat of an imminent court appearance hastened a solution to a lengthy and acrimonious domestic dispute. Again, alcohol appears as a significant element in the story.

More tragic is the unknown fate of Mary Doyle, a housewife from Grantham (St Catharines). On 28 November 1834 several witnesses testified that they saw Mary's husband, John, about nine o'clock in the morning, beating her with a club that had nails in it. The men who witnessed this act of savagery followed the Doyles into their house to rescue Mary, who was by then bleeding profusely from her head. Doyle was heard to swear 'he would be the death of the woman.'[38] A constable was summoned and John Doyle was charged with assault and battery on the evidence of the male witnesses. By the time of his trial, however, he had disappeared, probably having forced his wife to accompany him. Mary remains another silent victim. We never hear from her directly; our knowledge of her circumstances derives solely from the testimony of the men who witnessed the attack.

Even more shocking is Ellen Fitzgerald's brutal treatment at the hands of her husband, and the blunt rejection of assistance when she finally turned to the lieutenant governor for help in May 1835. Ellen's husband John had been arrested several years earlier for a murder he had allegedly committed in Ireland in the early 1820s. While waiting for the Colonial Office to return him to Ireland to face trial, John Fitzgerald had been imprisoned first in Niagara and then in Toronto. Then, for some reason not clear from the records, he had been permitted to return to his home in Niagara. Whether the brutality he exhibited towards his wife was related to his imprisonment or the continuation of a long-established pattern is unknown, but his treatment of her reveals a degraded brute. Ellen described what he did to her in her petition to the governor: 'he beat, kicked and took one of my hands and held it in the fire, until it was severely burnt; choked and undertook to cut my throat, with a Razor he took out of his hat which he would have effected, had he not taken compassion on the Prayers of a little son of mine.'[39]

Ellen understandably feared for her life and tried without success to convince one of the Niagara magistrates to bind her husband over to keep the peace. Attached to her petition was an affidavit from the district high constable detailing the cold and unfeeling reaction of local magistrates who were either 'very busy' and 'could not attend' to her urgent plea or who 'refused to interfere in the business.' Ellen's petition begged the governor 'to direct' or 'command' the uncooperative Niagara magistrates to restrain her husband. The petition has the supporting signatures of two Niagara physicians, who confirmed that they had visited Ellen and found that 'she had been most unmercifully beaten and otherwise ill treated (by as she says her Husband.)' Ten other local residents had signed the petition, at least six of whom were women. Female signatures on a petition to the governor were unusual in themselves. Keith Johnson has found only two examples of women petitioning the lieutenant governor for protection from abusive or improvident husbands between 1815 and 1840. As he says, 'most women submitted petitions only when they had no alternative, not because they were weak, helpless, or incompetent, but because to act otherwise would have been, in the social circumstances of the day, disturbingly unconventional.'[40]

Sir John Colborne's terse instructions to his secretary convey no sympathy whatever for the plight of Ellen Fitzgerald. Hers was just another of the hundreds of petitions that regularly crossed his desk. He dealt with it quickly, as he did other petitions on legal issues: 'Acquaint the petitioner that she should apply to a magistrate.' The secretary referred her petition to the Niagara magistrates themselves on 3 June 1835 'for any observations they may be pleased to make.'[41] Their reply has not survived. Even in this case, which cried out for executive intervention, the lieutenant governor was unwilling to override the actions of the local magistrates.

Peace bonds remained the only legal option available to battered wives in the Niagara district long after the union of the Canadas in 1841. Under English law, magistrates had ample powers to impose peace bonds on wife-beaters, and they did so in other jurisdictions. When magistrates were given the power to deal with minor cases summarily in 1834, fewer depositions appear in the quarter sessions records. Magistrates who wished to could now issue peace bonds on their own. For example, Jacob Keefer, the Thorold magistrate, issued a peace bond to George Turney on 1 May 1841 binding him to keep the peace for a year with his wife.[42] Because this was not a conviction, it was not published with the annual schedule of summary convictions in the district and thus received no publicity in the district newspapers. Both Mary Jane and George Turney avoided the embarrassment of a trial in which their marital problems would be made public, and Mary Jane received whatever protection came with the peace bond and her husband's forced appearance before the local magistrate.

George Turney's peace bond cost him only £20, but in 1842 William McKenzie of Stamford was forced to pay £50 for a peace bond towards his wife, Mary Ann. Magistrate John Mewburn of Stamford also imposed an unusual term: McKenzie was bound either for life or until the death of Queen Victoria.[43] Magistrates had considerable leeway in establishing the amount and term of the peace bonds they imposed and could, like Mewburn, exercise considerable ingenuity. In 1836 Mewburn had convicted James Mullingham for abusing and threatening his wife, Phoebe, in particular for 'turning her out of doors.'[44] In this instance Mewburn did not impose any fine, but

Mullingham had to pay the court costs. What stands out again is the discretion magistrates exercised in these cases of domestic assault.

The magistrates' powers to deal with so-called minor cases under summary jurisdiction resulted in at least two other convictions for assault against husbands for abusing their wives. Nathaniel Cooper of Thorold was convicted by Jacob Keefer for assault and battery on his wife, Elizabeth, in July 1835. Cooper had thrust her into the family fireplace, used abusive and threatening language and hit her with a broomstick. The magistrate fined him £2 10s. and costs.[45] A Clifton labourer, Robert Wood, was convicted in March 1835 by his local magistrate, Ogden Creighton, for assaulting his wife, Sarah. He had seized her 'by the hair of her head without provocation and did drag her thereby and also inflict upon her several severe blows with his fist, and did also kick her with his foot and otherwise maltreat and abuse her.' Wood also received a fine of the same amount and was ordered to pay costs.[46] These convictions were published as part of the schedule of summary convictions which appeared after every court of quarter session, but there was no indication in this schedule that the assault had been a spousal one.

In 1845 Stamford constable John Bunting arrested his neighbours, George Kitson, an innkeeper, and Kitson's wife, Lucinda, on a charge of causing an affray. Kitson had been abusing his wife, and when Lucinda cried out 'murder' it woke Bunting up. He went over to his neighbours and found Kitson threatening Lucinda with a knife. The testimony of another witness, George Baker, adds further detail:

On Monday evening, 8 September, as Mrs. Kitson was going to the front door, Mr. Kitson gave her a shove. Mrs. Kitson asked what he had done that for and said she would make him suffer for that in the morning and went up stairs to bed. Mr. Kitson went up stairs and told her to come down. He would not allow her to sleep up there. She came down and said she would have a smoke before she went to bed. Mr. Kitson said she should not. Mrs. Kitson was standing by the table with a knife and a plug of Tobaco in her hand. Mr. Kitson gave her a push towards the bedroom door. She then took a chair and threw it at him and picked up a piece of Lath and struck him. Mr. Kitson then picked up a stick of stovewood and attempted to strike her but did not do it. He then caught hold of her and threw her down on the floor and Mrs. Kitson cried out, 'murder' ... Afterward Mrs. Kitson was standing with a small case knife in her hand and Mr. Kitson said if she took a knife he would take a knife too. Got the large carver knife and was standing by her with the knife drawn when the Constable came in.[47]

Both George and Lucinda were bound over to keep the peace on a recognizance of £20. Their trial was scheduled for the November quarter sessions, but the Kitsons were discharged and the case did not go to trial. Bunting, the Stamford constable, may well only have brought the charge because the Kitsons' conduct interfered with his sleep. The magistrates clearly regarded the affair as a private marital dispute that should be resolved out of court.

One female plaintiff sought the assistance of a lawyer. In 1836 Mary Manly swore a complaint drawn up by counsel against her husband, Walter, to whom she had been married for twenty years. She claimed that there had been a long pattern of 'cruel, barbarous and inhuman' conduct towards her, which on 10 February had culminated in a life-threatening episode. Walter 'in a violent passion tore her clothes and threatened to kill her and threw her down out of the door of the House in which they live and then dragged her by the hair of the head into the House.'[48] Mary was afraid she would be murdered if she returned to her home, and wanted her husband to post a peace bond. Her deposition contained the standard but important statement that she was not complaining about her husband's treatment 'out of any hatred, malice or ill will ... but purely for the preservation of her life and person from further danger.' The insertion of this phrase at the advice of the lawyer suggests that a deposition that implied hatred or malice on the part of the wife would receive little sympathy from the magistrates. The records are silent on the results of Mary's action. The case never went to trial, presumably because a peace bond was posted.

What conclusions can we draw from these cases? The first and most obvious is that there was far more family violence, especially spousal abuse, in the Niagara district than can be detected from contemporary newspapers or records of trials at the quarter sessions and assizes. None of these cases received any newspaper publicity and only two came to trial. The low number of formal prosecutions itself calls for explanation. Constance Backhouse correctly reminds us that 'nineteenth century law provided an almost perfect example of a formally patriarchal institution ... women were barred from all direct control over the legal system – as voters, legislators, coroners, magistrates, judges and jurors.'[49] Decisions on the prosecution of cases of spousal abuse rested with the all-male magistracy which clearly preferred to deal with this social problem informally, if at all. Ann Alexandra McEwen discovered that only two cases of assault were tried at the assize level in Niagara prior to 1838. Of the 372 assault cases tried at the quarter sessions level in the period 1828–46, only two involved spousal abuse;[50] of the more than 500 cases tried at the assize level up to 1850, none was for wife-beating. In Niagara, prosecution for spousal abuse occurred only when all other options had been exhausted and often, we suspect, not even then. The incidence of trials for spousal abuse cases thus does not provide an accurate reflection of the incidence of abuse.

In her Montreal study Kathyrn Harvey identifies at least 45 out of 349 cases reported by the *Montreal Star* as dropped 'because the victim failed to substantiate the charge.'[51] Many women simply could not afford to have their husbands put in prison. As Harvey says, 'They were forced to weigh the loss of his contribution to the family economy against their own physical well being.'[52] The family economy model in which the man earned the wages and the woman remained at home severely restricted the wife's options when it came to protecting herself against physical violence from her spouse. The same limitations likely applied in the pre-industrial world of the Niagara district, making women reluctant to bring charges in the first place and even less willing to proceed with a prosecution.

In Niagara, the legal system only deigned to notice spousal abuse when the victim enlisted male support outside the family or when the abuse became intolerable to neighbours or the local magistrate. Women who lived outside the district capital of Niagara were even less likely to contemplate charging their husbands with assault, given the costs of travel. Few women were prepared to risk visiting a magistrate to seek a peace bond and it was a rare wife, indeed, who was prepared to formally charge her husband with assault. Even Ellen Fitzgerald's petition to the governor was likely initiated by one of her physicians, since Ellen herself was illiterate, very ill, and in a state of shock. The colonial criminal justice system as it operated in the Niagara district offered minimal assistance to victims of spousal abuse, so little in fact that the victims have become almost invisible to posterity.

AFRICAN CANADIAN VICTIMS

A significant number of African Canadians were caught up in the tentacles of the Niagara district courts, a disproportionate number in relation to population figures. As in mid-nineteenth century Halifax, African Canadians were over-represented in court statistics.[53] Most of the African Canadian members of the Niagara community were recent refugees from the United States and slavery. The legal freedom they found in this northern sanctuary did not free them from the rigours of the British colonial justice system, or from racial persecution.[54] Jason Silverman has written that the American fugitive slave arriving in Upper Canada 'often found a segregated society, along with antagonism and resentment ... Many Canadians deeply shared the prejudices and racial practices of their American neighbours; an attitude which ultimately manifested itself in anti-black newspaper attacks, discriminatory legislation, and an educational system reminiscent of the antebellum American North and the later Jim Crow South.'[55] These refugees were promised equality under British law, but even the legal records perpetuated the discrimination they suffered.

Every time an African Canadian appeared before the Niagara courts as offender, prosecutor, or witness, or was entered on the jail list, the magistrate, clerk of the peace, or jailer would make a note of his or her race. Indeed, in Niagara being an African Canadian was apparently sufficient to disqualify an individual from jury duty. A Thomas Hart was listed as one of the petit jurors for the July quarter sessions in 1828. The clerk wrote 'Blackman' beside his name and Hart was not chosen to serve on the jury.[56] Among the odours of the district jail one was not mentioned in public: the odour of discrimination. A quarter sessions grand jury presentment in April 1828 recommended that '*white people*' be confined separately from 'people of colour in different apartments.'[57] This did not happen, but the grand jury undoubtedly reflected feelings of the prisoners themselves, feelings they did not hesitate to endorse.

African Canadians did seek justice for themselves in the courts. Sometimes they succeeded in obtaining guilty verdicts, but their success could be illusory. Often the penalties handed down were nominal. Reuben Jackson, described as a Niagara labourer, brought a prosecution for assault against William Moffatt, a Niagara innkeeper, at the April quarter sessions in 1828. Moffatt was found guilty, but he was fined a token one shilling and court costs.[58] John Isaiah, an African Canadian labourer in Niagara, was more fortunate in a prosecution at the October sessions in 1830. He had been assaulted by William Turman, another labourer, who had beaten him 'with a club on the head, knocked him down and afterward jumped on his body with his feet.' Turman was found guilty and fined £3 and court costs.[59] The magistrates generally tended to be less severe in punishing innkeepers than labourers, but in assaults involving two labourers there is no evidence that the punishment meted out to African Canadians differed from that handed out to whites.

Following the 1837 Rebellion the government established a military force on the Niagara Peninsula to maintain order and to protect the frontier from raids or incursions from the United States. When a company of African Canadian soldiers was stationed in Thorold their commander had to turn to the local magistrates for assistance in controlling the conduct of some of the local citizens, as the black troops were apparently the object of open racism. In 1845 William Roberts, the commander, filed a deposition before local magistrate Duncan McFarland complaining of the conduct of George Gordon, a Thorold innkeeper who called the soldiers 'all manner of names and characters.' Roberts told the magistrate he had filed the complaint not 'from malicious motives but to preserve order and decorum and prevent a serious breach of the peace.' The case never went to court, but the innkeeper was required to post a peace bond of £50. In this case, the threat of further legal action may have headed off a worse incident.[60]

Young African Canadian males were prime suspects in theft cases. Once accused, they were immediately arrested and remanded to the Niagara jail until the next quarter sessions. Without resources to bail themselves or guarantors to provide surety, they could languish in jail for lengthy periods. Harkless Livers, described simply as 'a negro boy,' was arrested and committed on 9 March 1830 for petty larceny. He had allegedly stolen an axe worth two shillings, which he claimed he took by mistake. The charge was dropped at the quarter sessions, likely because of the absence of the prosecutor, and Livers was released from jail on 26 March 1830.[61] In a case tried ten years later, thirteen-year-old Reuben Gunn was not as fortunate. Gunn was arrested on 11 February 1840 for stealing a bridle and headstall worth five shillings from John Brown, a Queenston tavern keeper. After spending more than a month in jail waiting for his trial Gunn was tried at the March quarter sessions, found guilty, and sentenced to two further weeks of solitary confinement.[62] Solitary confinement was an unusually severe punishment for an act of petty theft, and was doubtless imposed both to intimidate Gunn and to send a message to potential thieves. Since African Canadian youths were commonly suspected, a racial element in the sentence also seems apparent.

Racial prejudice was confirmed by Mr Justice Sherwood in sentencing Isaac White to one month's imprisonment at hard labour for larceny at the Niagara spring assizes in 1844. The judge told White, an African Canadian, that fugitives from American slavery 'come to this country for protection; they are kindly received and admitted to all the privileges of the white inhabitants ...' If instead of working industriously, 'so many of them continue to perpetrate offences against the laws, it may be found necessary before long to send them back again, instead of offering them asylum.'[63] The implied threat of repatriation may not have been given wide circulation, but the sentiments of one of the colony's leading justices were unmistakeable.

In contrast, two local Niagara magistrates in Dunnville had a complaint brought against them in 1846 for refusing to bind an African Canadian named Barley Wafield to keep the peace after he had allegedly threatened a neighbour, W.H. McEwan. The magistrates had responded that they 'were anxious to discourage rather than promote litigious proceedings among the people from hasty words or occasional quarrels.' Upon investigation they had discovered that McEwan 'was the aggressor by abusing the other man on account of his colour. Wafield has been here for many years and has conducted himself well – we were satisfied [he] would harm no one if let alone.'[64] In this case the magistrates acted to prevent a racist act from escalating into a larger dispute or possible assault.

African Canadians constituted no more than 2 per cent of the population of the Niagara district, but they exceeded that percentage as victims of murder. Ann Alexandra McEwen reconstructed ten murder cases and found that in two of them the victims were African Canadians. In one, an African Canadian was murdered during a charivari in St Catharines in 1841. The charivari was aimed at another African Canadian man who had married a white woman, but William Brown found himself in the middle of the mob, who pursued him and killed him during a fight. One participant at the trial, in which the accused was found not guilty, confessed that the mob had 'run down a D-n nigger, but he was not the right one.'[65] The testimony reinforces the powerful racist feelings that lurked just beneath the surface among some of the population in the district.

The difficulties experienced by African Canadian members of the Niagara community in finding justice for themselves even from the lower court of quarter sessions are illustrated in three cases described below, each in its own way highly unusual. John Strong brought a charge of assault against a white female resident of Niagara during the October quarter sessions in 1829. As noted earlier, men rarely prosecuted women for assault. Strong had been passing Mary Fountain's house, knocking on her picket fence with his walking stick, when Mary emerged with an axe. She struck him and cut him under the right eye. Strong claimed he had not even spoken to her prior to the attack. The jury found Mary Fountain not guilty.[66]

Elizabeth Thompson, a married African Canadian housekeeper living in Bertie township, backed by both her husband and her white employer, charged a neighbouring white carpenter, Adam Snyder, with assault and intent to rape at the October quarter sessions in 1830. The complaint she swore was an eloquent testimonial to her own vulnerability, and that of many other females, in what could be a lonely and terrifying frontier society. Thompson had been left alone in charge of the house on 20 July 1830, and she discovered Adam Snyder 'skulking about the barn.' She returned to the house; Snyder followed and forced his way in. He 'took hold' of her, 'wishing if possible to take improper liberties with her as a married woman which he knew.' She resisted and succeeded in eluding his grasp. At that point, Snyder 'pulled down the flap of his pantaloons and shewed her his private parts ... and laughed at her, she feeling at the same time determined to resent the insult.' Thompson wanted him arrested and tried, out of fear of what he might do in the future. Whether she would have brought the complaint without the support of her husband and her employer will never be known, but her statement was not sufficient for the grand jury. They sided with the white male accused, returning a finding of no bill, and Adam Snyder escaped even a trial.[67]

At the March quarter sessions in 1840 two St Catharines innkeepers and a butcher faced a charge of riot and assault following an affray the previous October. Between 2 and 3 a.m. on 16 October they had allegedly visited the house of Alfred Talbot, an African Canadian labourer, on the pretext that they wanted him to play the fiddle for them. Badly frightened by the antics of the interlopers, who were probably drunk, Talbot tried to escape, but they caught him, severely beat him, and in the process broke his arm. One of the St Catharines magistrates wrote to the clerk of the peace just prior to the court date requesting that the case be held over until the next assizes. He confirmed 'that a violent assault was made in the night time upon the man by breaking into his house and leaving him nearly lifeless, but by whom I know not.'[68] Talbot lacked his most material witness for the trial, which went ahead anyway in March. The three accused were all acquitted.

Some individuals in the Niagara district did go out of their way to dispel rumours about the criminality of the African Canadian population. Following an article in the *Niagara Chronicle* in 1844, planting suspicion on local African Canadians for a robbery which had taken place in a Niagara store on 23 September, the store owner, Henry Charles, wrote a letter to the editor saying that 'as an act of common justice to the coloured population of our town, I wish to inform the public that I have not the least reason to suspect any of that class of the community of having been in any way concerned in the robbery of my store.'[69]

Henry Charles's letter testifies to a fairer attitude towards the African Canadian inhabitants of the Niagara district. In the cases of John Strong, Elizabeth Thompson, and Alfred Talbot, however, African Canadians who applied to the law to right an apparent wrong failed to win justice. How many others were deterred from even trying because of the expense and trouble involved in prosecution, or a conviction of the futility of any attempt? While African Canadians could and did obtain justice in some instances, in Niagara they were more likely to be victims of crimes, or to be prosecuted and convicted, than they were to find legal redress for wrongs done to them. The cases discussed in this chapter graphically illustrate that the criminal law in the Niagara district, as in the rest of Upper Canada, was applied unevenly. Women and African Canadians faced far more difficulties in attempting to secure justice for themselves in colonial Niagara. The constitutional guarantee of equality for all under British law proved to be badly flawed in practice.

9

Criminal Boundaries

Magistrates and sheriffs in the Niagara district often viewed the United States as a source of criminality of all kinds. Prostitutes were suspected of regularly coming over the border from Buffalo; horse thieves were thought to cross the frontier and then flee back again riding their stolen animals; coiners and forgers might attempt to free their fellow gang members from the Niagara jail. In the aftermath of the War of 1812, and again following the Mackenzie Rebellion, the British government and its colonial officials reinforced garrisons along the frontier to ward off further violence. Both military officers and civilian magistrates in the Niagara district in these periods blamed Americans for terrorist or criminal acts. When one of the locks of the Welland Canal was blown up in September 1841 by two kegs of gunpowder a British military officer wrote, 'it is generally thought the villains were from Buffalo.'[1]

Recent historiography on early Canadian – United States relations suggests that we should re-examine traditional interpretations of the impact of the United States and Americans on the historical evolution of Upper Canada.[2] If David Moorman is correct in arguing that within Upper Canadian historiography 'a consistent theme has been the rejection of American ways,' new interpretations are challenging that view.[3] A doctoral thesis on the Niagara region written in the United

States argues that 'the Niagara border runs more naturally north and south than east and west.'[4] Many nineteenth-century criminals would have agreed. Examining how the border was utilized, especially by those caught up in the nets of justice, offers a unique perspective upon both the criminal justice system of the period and the larger themes of early Canada-U.S. relations.

BORDERLANDS

There has always been a constant interaction between the systems of justice found on either side of the border. Throughout its history the border has been used by Americans and Canadians alike to circumvent 'inconvenient' laws or societal norms.'[5] Robert Lecker, introducing a book of historical essays on Canadian-American borderland regions, points out that 'the border is important, mainly because it creates a region of interaction, but also, to a lesser extent, because it is the element of division.'[6] The Upper Canadian-American border during the colonial period illustrates just how the interaction and division constantly played off against each other. In his path-breaking study of the criminal justice system in Hamilton John Weaver not only finds elements of the British legacy, he also discovers American influences along with what he terms 'indigenous tinkering.' As he says, various influences give the institutions of law and order in Ontario communities 'a complicated and hybrid quality.' He emphasizes that 'in its criminal justice activities, as in so much else, Hamilton was a North American city.'[7] What was true of Hamilton was true of the province as a whole. The criminal boundaries of Upper Canada, even in its colonial days, reflect a North American reality in which both criminals and officials used the border for their own ends. The political frontier was not always a barrier to criminals or fugitives and it could provide benefits to officials charged with upholding the law.

The perception of the boundary between Canada and the United States has changed dramatically over time. Travel across the border has become commonplace, creating an easy and automatic sense of familiarity with the other. By the 1930s an estimated 30 million border crossings occurred annually. Today when we cross the border to the United States at Niagara Falls or Fort Erie, or when we enter Canada from the United States, our awareness of passing from one country to another derives primarily from a change in symbols like flags, or from our experience with the officious bureaucracy of customs and immigration found on both sides of the border. As early as the turn of the twentieth century Adam Shortt taught his Queen's students that the boundary line between Canada and the United States was imaginary. One of those students, after going on to Chicago for further study, wrote to him to acknowledge the truth of Shortt's observations. Swanson added, 'really the people of Ontario and New York State have far more in common than the people of Ontario and Quebec,' a comment that resonates with much more impact in the aftermath of the 1995 Quebec referendum and the North American Free Trade Agreement than it did at the beginning of the twentieth century.[8]

If the boundary line was believed by some to be imaginary at the beginning of the twentieth century, can we trace this perception back any further? One of the earliest American historians of immigration to North America, Marcus L. Hansen, shrewdly observed that 'immigrants viewed the continent as a whole.' Hansen went on, 'it was not the United States and Canada. It was all of America to them.' Another historian of Canada, J.B. Brebner, carried the idea further still. Immigrants were 'capable of allegiance to one country one day and to another the next.'[9] The title of their book on immigration, *The Mingling of the Canadian and American Peoples*, signals their continentalist approach.[10] Early historians of Canadian-American relations, many of them authors of the books in the Carnegie Series, thought in terms of a North American nationality or, in Carl Berger's words, 'a common North American individualism.'[11]

Reginald Stuart's far-reaching analysis of U.S. expansionism from the American Revolution to the Treaty of Washington (1871) posits a succession of geographically distinct borderlands gradually evolving across the continent. By the mid-nineteenth century, the most important, from an economic point of view, were to be found in the centre of the continent, especially what he terms the Great Lakes Commercial Borderlands.[12] Many things besides trade joined the people of these borderlands. Their ties grew progressively closer in mid-century as Britain and the United States abandoned the hostility of the War of 1812 for new accommodative measures, from the Webster-Ashburton Treaty of 1842 to the Reciprocity Treaty of 1854. The true borderlanders, according to Stuart, were those 'who saw no real distinction between provincials and Americans.'[13]

However much the notion of a common North American individualism lying just beneath the surface on both sides of the border may seem to be a seductive interpretive framework for early nineteenth century Canadian-American relations, it should not be given a completely free rein. True borderlanders existed, but even by the 1840s they were far from a majority. Cross-border contacts became both broader and deeper, but the border itself never disappeared. In Upper Canada British law, British institutions, and British concepts of justice had sunk deep roots, giving the border both a political and a cultural configuration.

Philip Buckner argues that in this period people on both sides of the political border 'knew on which side they belonged and, equally importantly,` who belonged on the other side.'[14] Like dangerous chemicals, the border regions could prove to be highly unstable, as in 1837–8, bringing Britain and the United States much closer to possible conflict than either desired. The border remained part of the ever-present political, social, and economic reality of Upper Canada, especially in a district like Niagara.

We may be much less conscious today of fundamental differences between the two separate countries than our predecessors were in the early nineteenth century. During the period when Upper Canada was a separate colony, 1791–1840, an era marked by war and rebellion, visitors and inhabitants alike commented knowingly on the contrasts between British North America and the United States.[15] Especially for British travellers arriving in Upper Canada from the United States, the border could induce strange transformations and cause outpourings of patriotic hyperbole. Captain Basil Hall, an intrepid British globetrotter and writer, described what it felt like to cross from New York to Niagara in 1827, after only six weeks in the United States: 'The air we breathed seemed different, the sky, the land, the whole scenery, appeared to be altered; and I must say, that of all the changes I have ever made in a life of ceaseless locomotion, I have seldom been conscious of any transition from one country to another more striking than this.'[16]

Not all British travellers to Upper Canada found the Britishness of the colony upheld as strongly as they would have wished. Patrick Shirreff, an East Lothian farmer who visited Niagara in 1833, could not hide his disappointment with Upper Canada. He remarked condescendingly that 'the manners and customs of the people were essentially Yankee, with less intelligence, civility and sobriety.'[17] Yet there was still a sense of vivid differences between the British colonies and the United States, differences originating in Upper Canada with a Loyalist culture reinforced by the experience and memories first of the

American Revolution and then of the War of 1812. Underlying the perceived cultural difference, of course, was a conviction of the unquestioned superiority of the monarchy and British institutions found north of the border, matched on the southern side by an equally aggressive pride in Republican ideals and institutions, as well as a widespread belief that the Canadas would someday become part of the United States. Even the failure of the 1837 Rebellions did not squelch this conviction.

When we strip away the layers of British-American hostility and Upper Canadian Loyalism we find a reaffirmation of the idea of a common North American nationality or individualism, a ready willingness on the part of many individuals to move when their interests or circumstances dictated, regardless of whether moving involved switching national allegiances. This does not diminish the importance of the border, but it raises the question of how deep-rooted contemporary allegiances were. Re-examining the early frontier relations between Upper Canada and the United States from the perspective of the people themselves may lead us to view this period in larger, more continental terms rather than through the more partisan British imperial lens.

The border between the United States and Upper Canada in the early nineteenth century was much more than a boundary line between Republic and Empire. The frontier areas on both sides witnessed not only the increased traffic brought by growing trade, population movements, and the tourist magnet of Niagara Falls, but also clashes between rival states and armed incursions during two periods of war and heightened tension, 1812–14 and 1837–8. What then was the interaction between justice and the frontier?

Apart from periods of war and armed rebellion, when restrictions on the usual access to the border were expected, if not always totally accepted, it was assumed that movement across the border was open to anyone. Individuals freely crossed the boundary line, including immigrants, although legal commerce was tied up in the tariffs of the old colonial system until the middle of the century. When anything occurred to interrupt this free passage, reaction was quick and forceful. The outbreak of cholera in the summer of 1832 prompted emergency measures on both sides of the border in an attempt to prevent the rapid spreading of the disease. The Board of Health at Youngstown imposed a fifteen-day quarantine on any vessels arriving from Canada, which drew an immediate yelp of outrage from the captain of the aptly-named steamboat, *Canada*. After his passengers were forbidden to land on the American side two days in a row, Captain Richardson wrote to the lieutenant governor, requesting his intercession with the Americans. Trumpeting self-righteous indignation, Richardson described the American action as a 'public calamity.' He could hardly believe that the Americans could display 'such selfishness, such pusillanimousness of soul, such shrinking from the calamities of human nature, such extreme uncharitableness towards fellow human beings ... in these times of distress.'[18] Richardson was not content merely to write blistering protests about American actions, as the Upper Canadian officials in Niagara discovered to their chagrin. When they imposed regulations for the same purpose, ordering vessels to stop fifty yards from the town wharf so that a health officer could visit them, Richardson ignored the order and landed his vessel, thereby undermining the credibility of the Niagara Board of Health, as its secretary was quick to complain to the lieutenant governor.[19] The governor in turn informed the Niagara officials that they had the legal authority to prevent anyone landing in violation of the regulations and left it to them to enforce the regulation against the obstreperous Captain Richardson. Fortunately for all concerned, the cholera outbreak itself rapidly dissipated, permitting a return to normal commercial travel across the border. This incident reveals how quick individuals were to challenge restrictions to border crossings that appear quite normal to us, and how difficult it was for government officials to enforce even minimal interference with usual movements across the border. Richardson's complaint may have arisen solely from the frustration of an entrepreneur thwarted by the actions of the authorities. Whether or not he had wider public support his protests gained him instant notoriety if little satisfaction.

It was not merely fugitives and criminals who showed great ingenuity in navigating around the difficulties posed by the state frontier. Joseph Adams was a veteran British sailor who had served in the Royal Navy during the War of American Independence. He then left the navy and settled in the United States. In 1827, being, as he put it, 'Old and Infirm,' Adams crossed over from New York State to Kingston and applied for a pension from the naval commandant there. To prove his questionable loyalty to Britain, he attached a supporting statement signed by sixteen of his neighbours from Kingsburg, New York, written seven years earlier. They swore that during the War of 1812 Adams had been 'quite obnoxious to the People here,' and had been 'repeatedly refused the Priviledge of Voting at our Elections for Officers of our Government.'[20] Whether this unusual proof of loyalty was sufficient to obtain a pension is unknown, but it illustrates the lengths the residents of Kingsburg were prepared to go to rid themselves of an unwanted neighbour. For them, as for others, the other side of the frontier was viewed as a convenient receptacle for outcast members of society.

Just as there was a growing traffic in legitimate commerce and population flows, so there was also a complicated pattern of illegal movements across the border. Criminals escaping justice or jail regularly fled from one jurisdiction to the other; soldiers deserted or tried to desert by fleeing across the border; African slaves crossed into Upper Canada seeking freedom; and goods were smuggled across the border then as they are now. The illegal movements tended to concentrate in three regions where there was a close proximity between communities on each side of the border: Kingston, the Niagara region, and the area of Amherstberg and Sandwich opposite Detroit.

Illegal border crossings gave rise to acts of private or community justice as well as the constant efforts of authorities to maintain official justice. Community and official justice did not always coincide in Upper Canada. Even official justice was by no means homogeneous. Differences commonly arose between military and civilian interpretations of justice and between the views of top government officials such as the lieutenant governor or the attorney general and the local magistrates. A brief survey of the issues of extradition, banishment, desertion, and smuggling will serve to illustrate the complexity of relationships between the political border and the illegal movements of people and goods across it.

EXTRADITION

At the local level, magistrates on the Upper Canadian side of the border had by the 1830s developed a close and effective working relationship with their counterparts on the American side. When John Fitzgerald, the Irishman suspected of committing a murder in Waterford, Ireland, in the early 1820s, was discovered to be working as a tavern keeper in Niagara in 1832, he quickly slipped across to the United States to escape arrest. In this case the Niagara magistrates were able to issue a warrant and persuade the American officials to arrest Fitzgerald within a day. He was returned across the frontier to the Niagara jail and ultimately sent home to Ireland to face trial.[21] Without the Americans' prompt action the Canadian authorities would have lost Fitzgerald.

Charles Eliot, an Upper Canadian magistrate at Sandwich opposite Detroit, wanted to act in the same cooperative manner in November 1832, when he received a request from the Michigan authorities to return two men, James Walker and William Bird, suspects in a series of thefts on the Detroit shore. Eliot obligingly had the men arrested and jailed prior to being turned over to the Americans. But when he asked the government officials at York to issue the necessary instructions, a wall of legal roadblocks suddenly appeared. Eliot was understandably anxious to facilitate cross-border cooperation in the return of suspected criminals. He pressed his case forcefully with Sir John Colborne, the lieutenant governor. 'In justice to the Americans I must declare that they have ever evinced extreme eagerness to protect us from the mischief attending the escape of such hardened monsters: they have most readily arrested and resigned, at our request, both murderers and thieves. How merited then, would be the reproach upon us, were we in no one instance to alternate with them?'[22] Colborne promptly turned the matter over to his attorney general, Henry Boulton, who issued an opinion stating that without solid evidence to implicate the accused men in a crime he could not support the local magistrate.[23]

To resolve the impasse the government arranged for an unusual legal hearing, in which the attorney general acted as private counsel for the prisoners and the solicitor general acted for the Crown, before one of the province's King's Bench judges, James Macaulay.[24] The government's objective was to obtain a definitive judicial ruling on the province's legal obligation to return fugitives to the United States. Justice Macaulay's lengthy judgment reviewed all the available legal precedents, including American ones. Macaulay found nothing in the warrant of committal of the suspects to verify that they were, indeed, American citizens. He concluded in the absence of such evidence that they were British subjects, entitled to the full protection of British law, and specifically to the rights granted by the Habeas Corpus Act. Macaulay ordered the release from jail of the two suspects under Habeas Corpus, which prevented their being sent to a foreign country for trial, in spite of the general impression of their likely guilt in the cross-border thefts. Walker and Bird were both identified in the court documents as African Canadian. Other than this identification there is no indication that race played any part in the outcome of this case.

The government must have been disappointed in its hope of securing judicial clarification, as Macaulay wrote that every U.S. request to transfer a fugitive 'must be decided on its own peculiar features & merits.' Cases of murder might be dealt with more expeditiously, but Macaulay stressed that the Upper Canadian courts must carefully scrutinize 'in each instance the nature of the offence – the degree of proof – the political character of the fugitive – the promptness of the pursuit & application' before a fugitive could be transferred to the United States.[25] Macaulay also concluded that there was no existing law or treaty governing the transfer of fugitives between territories of the United States and Upper Canada. Jay's Treaty (1794) had originally provided that anyone charged with murder or forgery could be turned over to the other country, but Article 27 containing this clause had expired in 1803 and had never been renewed.[26] The superior legal officials and judges at York, by now all Upper Canadians, were determined to apply British law in each case, even if this meant disrupting the harmonious local networks of cross-border judicial cooperation. Solicitor General Hagerman summed up the law for the lieutenant governor, following Mr Justice Macaulay's ruling. 'The power to surrender fugitives from a foreign country – *such fugitives being subjects of that Country – is Discretionary with the Government*, but that discretion was never exercised in sending away subjects of His Majesty or residents within his dominions ...'[27]

Charles Eliot, the Sandwich magistrate who had originally raised the question with the government, was dumbfounded by the outcome. When he heard about it in January 1833, Eliot was in the midst of another complicated case involving forgers operating on both sides of the border. He pleaded for guidance on what he should do in future and wrote, plaintively, 'what shall I say on this liberation to His Excellency, Governor Porter [of Michigan] after his prompt & effectual exertions to serve us? And how can we now apply to him for Crofts, alias Crawford, who has passed so many forged bills on our side & to so many of our poorer Inhabitants, & against whom I have conclusive testimony?'[28] Eliot's credibility was badly damaged as the story of the release quickly spread on both sides of the border, and he found himself vilified by at least one of his fellow magistrates for arresting suspects at the instigation of the Americans. Eliot's latest dilemma, how to prosecute the suspected forger, Crofts, was made worse by the fact that an American grand jury had not been able to indict Crofts because of a lack of evidence. As Eliot informed the lieutenant governor,

Crofts 'has been astute enough never to pass a forged Bill on his own side of the river.'[29]

This time, however, the attorney general was firmly on the side of the magistrate. The evidence was 'so strong and flagrant' that Eliot was ordered to apply immediately to have Crofts transferred to Upper Canada for trial. Should the Michigan laws require a formal request from the lieutenant governor, Attorney General Boulton recommended that this request be complied with. Where forgers were concerned, 'it is evidently the Interest of both Countries to put down this Nefarious System of fraud which is practised with too much Success by gangs of Villains infecting both sides of the Water.'[30] But Eliot had not waited for instructions from the Upper Canadian capital. He had visited the governor of Michigan to lay before him all the evidence he had gathered, and Governor Porter ordered Crofts to be imprisoned until a formal application for transfer arrived from the Upper Canadian government.

Eliot, who strongly believed in reciprocity of treatment across the border, was immensely relieved to hear of a new Upper Canadian law outlining the conditions for the return of fugitives to the United States. This statute would help to reassure the American authorities that the return of criminals would be reciprocated. Eliot asked for extra copies of the law to give to the American authorities, 'whose ever prompt compliance with our wishes indubitably merits our warmest thanks.'[31] The Fugitive Offenders Act, which came into force early in February 1833, gave the government all the legal powers required to return those 'charged with Murder, Forgery, Larceny or other crime' to the United States upon application through the proper authorities.[32] This Act governed all extradition proceedings between Upper Canada and the United States until it was superseded by the Webster-Ashburton Treaty of 1842.

The attorney general had adopted a much more cautious stance a few months earlier, when he received a request from Niagara to apply to the New York authorities for the return of the crew of the steamship, *Niagara*, as escaped felons. Not satisfied with the information he had been given, Boulton ordered a thorough investigation by Niagara magistrate Alexander Hamilton. This investigation revealed that a labour dispute over wages had led the crew to seize the vessel and sail her to the American side. There they succeeded in obtaining a large amount of the unpaid wages. Boulton agreed that in law the crew had acted 'most improperly,' but he found no grounds for a formal application to the New York governor for their return as fugitive felons who had committed an act of piracy.[33]

BANISHMENT

Upper Canadian government officials did not view the frontier solely as a source of problems. They were quick to use the proximity of the border when it suited their purposes, and undesirables were banished to the United States. The modification of British criminal law by the Upper Canadian Legislature in 1800 to incorporate banishment as a criminal punishment was a conscious recognition of the ease and economy of transferring Upper Canada's criminals south of the border. It was also, as the law itself stated, an acknowledgment that transportation overseas in official Upper Canadian eyes was either 'inapplicable' or could not be implemented without 'great and manifest inconvenience.'[34] John Weaver, in his study of the criminal justice system in Hamilton, argues that banishment 'was never a satisfactory form of punishment,' and Peter Oliver, in his landmark history of prisons and punishment in nineteenth-century Ontario, concludes that banishment as a punishment was 'severely flawed.'[35]

From the perspective of the criminals affected, banishment, an Upper Canadian variant on transportation, was a far less severe punishment and highly preferable to an alternative like execution. Not until 1842 was banishment formally replaced by imprisonment in Canadian law. In practice, however, the opening of the Kingston Penitentiary in 1835 meant that many criminals who might earlier have been banished were sent to Kingston instead. The following year the British government opened Van Diemen's land to North American colonies, and a number of Upper Canadian criminals were transported there, including many convicted for their part in the 1837–8 Rebellions.

The outbreak of cholera in 1832 gave a new twist to the Upper Canadian government's use of banishment. Many prisoners confined in local jails and fearing for their safety, petitioned the lieutenant governor for pardon. He referred these petitions to Chief Justice Robinson for his advice, and Robinson recommended banishment for the prisoners convicted of the more serious crimes. In one instance the local sheriff protested against any pardon for the convicted rapist John Standish, but Robinson's view prevailed on the grounds that banishment for life would dispose of Standish more effectively than 'protracting his imprisonment.'[36] Sheriff Jarvis eventually recommended a two-day pardon to enable Standish to reach Queenston or Niagara, which the lieutenant governor was pleased to endorse. The banishment would serve both to reduce the possibility of cholera spreading through the gaols and rid the colony of another felon.[37] The magistrate who had committed him reported to the lieutenant governor that Standish's threats to wreak revenge on his prosecutor and all the others involved in bringing him to justice had occasioned 'a good deal of excitement and apprehension' in Brantford, where the offence had been committed, as rumours of his possible banishment circulated long before the decision was made.[38]

The royal pardon on condition of banishment had really become a vehicle for dumping Upper Canada's unwanted prisoners on her neighbour's frontier, in the full expectation that they would find a new home somewhere in the United States. Banishment could be controversial in Upper Canada, as the Standish affair had proved. A grand jury in the Gore District protested to the lieutenant governor that the practice had 'a most baneful effect ... upon the moral Condition of the people of this District' because several of those banished had returned. They were seen by their neighbours as having escaped the punishment of the law. The grand jury argued that this would 'have the effect of encouraging the vicious and unprincipled to go on in Crime with a hope of impunity.'[39]

Banishment as a substitute for pardon was not uncommon even before the appearance of cholera. Francis Morgan, a prisoner in the Bathurst jail in 1832, had escaped death through the governor's prerogative and after more than a year of prison wrote to the lieutenant governor again, petitioning for a pardon on the grounds that he was 'so worn out and emaciated, from the want of fresh air, that he is a perfect Shadow and rack'd in his bones with the most acute pains.'[40] Instead of receiving a pardon, Morgan was banished from the province with an escort to the border. The proximity of the frontier allowed the government to reduce the expenditure of imprisoning serious felons in local jails by banishing convicts from Upper Canada in response to pardon petitions. The likely destination of banished criminals was not always made explicit in these proceedings, but there could be little doubt it was the United States. The criminals themselves could either make a new start somewhere in the United States or try to return, after a suitable period, to Upper Canada, risking recapture and a worse fate.

On rare occasions, the usually cumbersome judicial process was capable of producing surprises. One occurred in what first seemed an ordinary appeal from a prisoner seeking the lieutenant governor's clemency. Samson Catlett had been sentenced to a prison term in September 1829, for shooting a cow. He was still serving his sentence in the district jail at Sandwich at the beginning of 1831. Someone prepared a petition for him and the jailer attested that Catlett's mark was, in fact, his signature and agreement to the contents. The petition described him as 'a half Indian' and asked for clemency. Sir John Colborne annotated the margin, 'Banished from the Province & liberated.' This was a revealing conjunction, because for prisoners like Catlett liberation often equalled banishment. Shortly after Catlett was freed Colborne received another petition in connection with his case, this time from sixty-two inhabitants of Amherstberg, where Catlett had been living. This petition asked the lieutenant governor to revoke the banishment. It now turned out that Catlett was a freed slave and these Upper Canadians plainly told their governor that 'he cannot pass into the American States but with the certainty of being immediately subjected again to Slavery.'[41] Colborne acceded to this unusual but eloquent plea of the local community and granted Samson Catlett a full pardon.

Catlett was lucky in that Upper Canada's chief justice, John Beverley Robinson, to whom his original petition had been referred, took an unusually long time to reply to the lieutenant governor. Robinson was not inclined to recommend a pardon, and his reasons illuminate what may have been widely held views among the Upper Canadian elite. 'If the man has left the Province, I think I would leave him where he is – they have too many such people about Amherstberg already. He was detected in killing a cow on the common with the intent of stealing the carcass – a very common offence among the blacks and one which it is very necessary to put a stop to.'[42] Robinson also had analysed the signatures on the petition. He found that scarcely any of the local magistrates had signed, an inauspicious omen for the petitioner, although 'some very good names' from the community might warrant government action. By the time Robinson's opinion was received, however, the pardon had already been granted and it thus had no influence on the outcome of Catlett's case. It nonetheless sheds considerable light on the way in which the Upper Canadian government made pardon decisions.

We rarely hear what the criminals themselves felt about being forced to move from one state to another. In one case in which an Upper Canadian sought refuge in the United States to avoid imprisonment on a murder charge, we do have a letter from the fugitive justifying his action. John Ward had escaped to Michigan early in 1830 and wrote a letter home. Although intended for his family, this letter ended up in the hands of government officials. His explanation has a certain logic, viewed from his desperate position: 'i think it is better for me to keep my liberty untill i Can have my trial. It will make it no better if i Should ly in prison untill then.'[43] For Ward, as for the other criminals or criminal suspects who fled across the border seeking sanctuary, the boundary was a minor obstacle, easily overcome. In another instance, the prospect of banishment was more attractive than a continued stay in the prison at Kingston. Abraham Welden had been confined for seventeen months. He petitioned the lieutenant governor to release him, saying 'I am Contented to leave this province if you were to Send me.'[44] Colborne released and banished him, ridding the district jail of a long-time and expensive prisoner.

It was not only male prisoners who made use of the United States as a sanctuary. Margaret Murtaugh had been convicted of selling liquor illegally in Kingston and fined. She could not pay the fine, and rather than go to jail she fled to the United States, even though her husband was seriously ill. After her husband died, Murtaugh petitioned the lieutenant governor for a pardon so she could return to Kingston. Sir John Colborne sought the advice of the local magistrates. They could not recommend a pardon, given 'the contempt for the law' Margaret had displayed,'[45] and Colborne accordingly rejected her plea, leaving her with a choice of finding money to pay the fine or remaining in the United States.

Some convicts openly used the United States as a temporary refuge. David Underhill was convicted in the Gore district in 1829 of assault and battery and sentenced to three months' imprisonment and a fine. On the way from court to the jail he escaped and fled to the United States, where he remained nearly a year. Then he quietly returned to his family, apparently hoping to escape notice. This ploy was unsuccessful. Underhill was recaptured and taken to prison. He was then able to use compassionate circumstances, a likely terminal illness, poverty, and a pregnant wife, to appeal successfully for clemency.[46]

Perhaps no case displayed Colborne's callous attitude to banishing criminals to the United States as the belated attempt to capture a man named Sirus Bartgeri, wanted for the rape and murder of Margaret Bunchwith in the summer of 1831. After the suspect had evaded a constable who had tried to capture him, Sheriff Jarvis of the York district asked the lieutenant governor to post a reward. Jarvis was convinced that Bartgeri had fled to the United States, 'and the probability is that a reward may bring him from the U. States.' The reply to Jarvis, relayed through the governor's secretary, was a blunt and final rejection of the idea, 'as it is probable he will quit the Province, to which it is not desirable he should return.'[47] Instead of putting all the resources of the state to work to capture the chief suspect in a crime of appalling brutality, the governor was content to let the apparent murderer cross the border unpursued and remain in the United States. It did not matter what happened to Bartgeri as long as he did not return to Upper Canada.

Whether banishment was an effective punishment is a difficult question to answer, since the Upper Canadian authorities neither analysed its use, nor kept statistics of the number banished and those who returned. The absence of American complaints suggest the numbers were small enough to escape official notice. An indication that banishment was held in contempt by some Upper Canadian politicians is found in the report of the Select Committee of the Legislature in 1831 recommending the construction of the Kingston Penitentiary. Hugh Thompson, the author and MPP from Kingston, and a strong advocate of the penitentiary, wrote, 'Banishing the province is so nonsensical that nothing need be said on the subject; it is no punishment to a rogue to order him to live on the right bank of the Niagara river instead of the left and it is cruelly unjust to our neighbours to send among them thieves, robbers and burglars, to exercise their iniquitous callings in a country, where, not being known, they cannot be guarded against.'[48] At least some prisoners viewed banishment as a genuine punishment. George Martin received a very severe sentence of five years' banishment for a small theft, but remained in the Niagara jail because he did not leave the country as ordered. Martin later petitioned the court to be freed, using the time he had served and patriotism as his rationale. He 'could not persuade himself to leave a country an alegiance [sic] to which he has held ever since he knew what alegiance [sic] was.'[49]

Chief Justice Robinson remained a proponent of banishment until feasible alternatives emerged in the middle of the 1830s, principally the new Kingston Penitentiary. And his colleague, Justice James Macaulay, found himself without any other option after three felons he sentenced at the Niagara assizes to respective terms of five years in the Kingston Penitentiary were returned in the spring of 1835 because the penitentiary was not yet ready to receive them. He changed the punishment for each convict to fourteen years' banishment.[50] Two of these returned within two years and had to be recaptured, an indication of one of the major weaknesses of banishment. Nevertheless, until the opening of the penitentiary, Robinson and his judicial colleagues continued to support banishment. It offered a cheap, ad hoc alternative for government officials anxious to avoid either long and costly imprisonments in overcrowded local jails or a rash of public hangings which might attract unwanted political attention to the colony's largely inherited system of criminal laws. Banishment thus served as a ready safety valve for the Upper Canadian colonial government from 1800 to the mid-1830s, however flawed or unsatisfactory this punishment may seem in retrospect.

DESERTERS

The American border was a powerful magnet for deserters from the British army, which was stationed at posts along the frontier from Kingston to Detroit. One of the earliest European travellers to visit Upper Canada, the Duc de la Rochefoucauld Liancourt, a French nobleman in exile from revolutionary France, understood why British soldiers would want to desert. 'The ennui naturally arising from the dull and secluded manner of living in garrisons, where they find neither work nor amusement, and the slight attention shewn them by most of the colonels, darken still more, in their view, the dismal picture of their situation. They emigrate accordingly into the United States, where they are sure to find a settlement, which, if they choose to work, cannot fail to make them rich and independent.'[51] He also reported that the British officers had private bounty arrangements with neighbouring Indian tribes for returning deserters.[52]

Capturing deserters could involve unofficial military expeditions across the border. In 1809, Americans engaged in at least two serious military incursions to recapture deserters who had slipped over the frontier to Upper Canada. A small American raiding party crossed the border near Ogdensburg at the end of January and succeeded in seizing three deserters. This provoked a passionate, albeit anonymous, complaint to the lieutenant governor, Francis Gore, calling on magistrates to be 'active and firm and Staunch to our Glorious Constitution and prevent any of its Laws to be perverted and trod upon.'[53] In other words, the maintenance of the British constitution required that formal justice through the magistrates and courts replace informal and vigilante justice. Another challenge to the constitution occurred a few months later, when an American deserter, Isaac Underhill, was killed at the beginning of May in Elizabethtown (Brockville) while trying to escape from a detachment of the 6th regiment of United States infantry who were trying to take him back to the United States.[54] These thinly disguised military raids ceased after the War of 1812, except in the period following the Mackenzie Rebellion, although desertions continued to provoke acts of informal and arbitrary community justice on both sides of the border.

The number of British deserters rose rapidly after the War of 1812 had concluded. Immediately following the end of the war complaints about British army deserters being seduced by the Americans mounted. One British sergeant, marching from Kingston to Montreal, 'deserted accompanied by no less than 50 soldiers, horses being stationed on the American side of the River St. Lawrence to favour their escape.'[55] Richard Preston, in his study of Kingston before the War of 1812, discovered that 'a successful breakaway by one deserter always proved infectious and would be followed by others.'[56] British officers professed to be mystified by the continuous desertions. One wrote in Kingston in 1801, 'I have done every thing in my power to find out the cause of this Spirit of Desertion without Effect.'[57] Some deserters were promptly recruited into the U.S. army, although the Americans insisted that they officially discouraged the practice. John Richardson, writing in the 1840s about his years in the Canadas, claimed that 5,000 British soldiers had deserted for the United States in the years between 1815 and 1838. The main centres of this unofficial emigration movement were Niagara, Kingston, and Amherstberg. Richardson, the author of one of Canada's earliest novels, Wacousta, had his own unlikely explanation for the rash of British desertions: he blamed the institution of libraries in several British posts. Libraries 'tend to give to the soldier especially an unduly exalted opinion of himself and to induce a contempt for the position he occupies.'[58] Ironically, the libraries had been instituted to try to prevent the desertions by providing the soldiers with an alternative to unrelieved boredom.

Peter Burroughs has written the most thorough account of British desertion in nineteenth-century British North America. He tabulated figures for the Canadas of 6,000 desertions between 1815 and 1840, an average annual desertion rate of over 5 per cent of the army establishment.[59] The highest annual desertion rates occurred in the mid-1830s. Desertions occurred for many different reasons but, as Burroughs stresses, some soldiers had enlisted deliberately to have their fares paid to North America with a clear intention of staying there by deserting to the United States. British officers especially blamed the Irish. Lieutenant Governor Arthur wrote to the British government in 1838, 'They all have relations or friends settled in the States, and what will bind an Irish Soldier if he has the opportunity of seeing his *cousin*.'[60] The real causes were more mundane and easily understood. British soldiers were no less attracted than civilians to the United States, 'where wages were known to be higher than those prevailing in Canada or in Britain itself and where good land was readily available to purchasers of limited means.'[61] For these deserters, crossing the frontier opened the gate to a new life free from the confines of the military. The movement of soldiers was not entirely one way, nor were the military authorities on either side of the border content to let it continue unchallenged, even if most of their efforts to stop it were unsuccessful. Magistrate Alexander Hamilton reported the capture of two deserters to their commanding officer at Fort George in 1832 and added that the ferrymen on the Niagara river would capture deserters in return for a reward of £5.[62] A British missionary witnessed an incident at Youngstown, New York, in 1832 in which an Irish deserter from the American army at Fort Niagara attempted to reach the British side of the river. Some Upper Canadians saw him and rushed into the water to rescue the Irishman from his American pursuers. The Canadians yelled at the 'Yankees that unless they instantly desisted and retired within their own jurisdiction they should be thrown into the water.'[63] The rescue was successful.

Ann Alexandra McEwen found that in the Niagara district the authorities prosecuted the crime of enticing soldiers to desert with much greater vigour in the years immediately following the Rebellion, 'when the stability of Upper Canada seemed at greatest risk.'[64] All but one of the cases tried at the assizes for enticing to desert occurred in the three-year period 1838–41, and every person who stood trial was convicted on at least one count. Like the colony's judges, the governors of Upper Canada during this period, nearly all of them military officers, regarded the crime of enticing to desert as a most serious one and dealt harshly with anyone convicted of it. Albert Spear was twenty years old when he was convicted of trying to help a soldier to desert to the United States at Amherstberg. Pleading for a pardon after spending fourteen months in the district jail, Spear claimed he had been intoxicated when the offence occurred. The lieutenant governor referred the petition to Judge L.P. Sherwood, who had presided at the trial. Sherwood replied with an argument he must have known would appeal to Colborne who, in his capacity as governor, also commanded the British forces in the colony. 'When it is considered that the facility of passing the frontier of the province from Amherstberg into the United States is a great inducement to desertion, and that the hope of assistance creates confidence in those inclined to desert, the public good seems to require examples to be made of such persons ...'[65] Colborne agreed and rejected the petition.

SMUGGLING

Smuggling was rampant across the border between the United States and Britain's Canadian colonies. The major reason was British insistence on maintaining the mercantilistic system of customs duties in the colonies until Britain finally shifted to free trade in 1846 and then signed the Reciprocity Treaty with the United States in 1854. The Duc de la Rochefoucauld Liancourt observed the impact in the 1790s. 'The high duty laid by England upon all the commodities exported from her islands proves a powerful encouragement to a contraband trade with the United States, where, in many articles, the difference of price amounts to two-thirds.'[66] Key foodstuffs like tea could not be imported directly from the United States without duties because of the monopoly retained by the East India Company. The incentive to smuggle was irresistible. William Lyon Mackenzie wrote of personally witnessing a tea smuggling operation from Youngstown, New York, to Fort George right under the noses of British soldiers who made no effort whatever to intervene. He concluded that smuggling tea and other American goods across the border, especially at Niagara, 'must have been nearly universal.'[67]

American treasury officials, perhaps even more than the British, tried their utmost to put a stop to smuggling across the border, but officials on both sides could intercept only a trickle of the huge stream of smuggled goods regularly crossing the line. One American official described the contraband trade across the Niagara frontier in 1808: 'Smuggling is carried on from Lewiston to Canada to a considerable extent, and disgusting and humiliating as the practice is to every feeling that is American, it is almost as publicly transacted as any common avocation.'[68] Cross-border trade, both legal and illegal, steadily increased in the first half of the nineteenth century. The locals, especially those living next to the frontier, refused to equate smuggling with crime. It was just another and very lucrative form of the expanding commercial opportunities presented by the border.[69]

Smugglers did not always escape the clutches of the magistrates and customs officers. A bizarre episode along the Niagara frontier illustrates the hazards of a smuggling mission gone awry. On 5 December 1825, at about ten o' clock at night, Robert Grant, the collector of customs in Queenston, heard that three wagons had just passed through the village. Suspecting smugglers, he took a constable with him and immediately set off in pursuit. They caught up with the suspects at a barn near St Catharines around midnight. Grant seized the wagons and discovered that they contained metal stoves and boxes of window glass, all manufactured in the United States. While there must have been a ready market for American stoves and window glass in Upper Canada, these are not the first objects to come to mind when we think of cross-border contraband in this period. We can, however, infer the value of these items from the subsequent actions of the smugglers. They would not give up their booty without a fight, and attacked the collector of customs and his constable with stones, poles, and rails. The constable claimed that 'he rather got the better' of one of his assailants, but when another tried 'to deprive him of his eyes' he gave in. The smugglers escaped temporarily with all their goods, except for a stove which fell out of the back of one of the wagons as they fled.

Robert Grant petitioned the quarter sessions court at Niagara early in January 1826 for a full criminal prosecution in this case, which the court endorsed. The case was tried at the fall assizes in Niagara. The chief culprit, William Terrybery, a forty-two-year-old St Catharines innkeeper who was apparently well known to the local authorities, was convicted on the charge of rescuing smuggled property and sentenced to three months' imprisonment and a $25 fine. Terrybery was one of the very few of what must have been a steady stream of smugglers along the Niagara frontier in this period to be caught, successfully prosecuted, and imprisoned. Had he not resisted arrest in such a violent manner, he would likely have escaped with only the confiscation of his smuggled goods. Those convicted of enticing soldiers to desert regularly appear on the jail returns of border districts like Niagara, especially in the latter 1830s, but Terryberry stands out in being convicted and jailed for smuggling.[70]

Two of the crimes discussed in this chapter, desertion and smuggling, fall into the category of social crime, defined by the British legal historian J.A. Sharpe as 'a conscious, almost a political, challenge to the prevailing social and political order and its values.'[71] Acts defined as criminal by the authorities were seen as either legal or justifiable by the individuals or groups carrying them out. This was certainly true where smugglers or deserters were concerned, but there are some significant differences between the social crimes of colonial British North America and those described in the rich literature on eighteenth-century England.[72] Community support often sided with the smuggler and the deserter rather than the customs officer or the soldiers charged with enforcing these unpopular laws, but desertion and smuggling across the national border were probably less class-based activities than, say, poaching in England. Neither crime, moreover, led to political violence in British North America as did some early-nineteenth-century social crimes in England.

Criminals, smugglers, deserters, and other nineteenth-century outcasts moved regularly across the Upper Canadian-United States border, only to disappear as quickly as water through sand. In their own unique way they were continentalists, operating with a North American individuality, not confined and certainly not shackled by political boundaries. Even Upper Canadian government officials, whose task was to enforce the laws and regulations that made the boundary a very real political frontier, discovered the utility of permeability when it came to banishing prisoners. For these officials the border both offered a convenient and cheap solution to the vexing dilemmas of overcrowded local jails and proved the source of nagging and insoluble problems like smuggling or desertion. Criminals and officials alike quickly learned how to manipulate the political frontier for their own purposes.

10

Hands Across the Border

Four years after the abolition of slavery within the British Empire in 1833, the government of Upper Canada authorized the return of Solomon Moseby, a fugitive slave, to Kentucky. Moseby had stolen his master's horse and ridden to Buffalo, where he had then crossed the frontier into Upper Canada and, as he believed, to freedom. Alexander McLeod, the deputy sheriff of the Niagara district, took Moseby into custody and confined him in the Niagara jail, waiting for orders to deliver Moseby into the hands of his former American master, who had journeyed to Upper Canada to reclaim him. But the local population of African Canadians were not going to let a brother who had successfully made the journey to freedom on British soil be returned by British authorities to slavery. Led by their preacher, Herbert Holmes, a group of determined men and women mounted a vigil at the jail for some three weeks in late August and September 1837 to prevent the authorities from sneaking Moseby across the border. When McLeod finally received the orders to extradite Moseby, he surrounded himself with special armed constables and soldiers from the British detachment at Fort George. With this armed escort, he then tried to deliver Moseby to the Americans. What happened next constitutes the first race riot in Upper Canada.

The African Canadians gathered outside the Niagara jail succeeded in aiding Moseby to escape custody; he then eluded the Upper Canadian authorities and eventually reached Britain. But the cost for the liberators was high. Herbert Holmes and another of Moseby's rescuers were shot dead, and several others were wounded in the mêlée. Upper Canada's reputation as a safe haven for escaping American slaves was placed in serious question, as was the reputation of British justice.

The Moseby episode has been examined from the perspective of the fugitive slave laws and diplomatic relations between Britain and the United States.[1] But there are a number of layers to the Moseby affair, and previous historical accounts have not done justice to the organizational capability of the African Canadian community. Within this community, the role of African Canadian women first in deciding to resist the colonial authorities and defend their hard-won freedom and then in leading this resistance deserves closer attention. Anna Jameson's contemporary account and the first historical reconstruction by Janet Carnochan on the sixtieth anniversary of the Moseby rescue in 1897, provide important clues to a very different version of this story.[2]

The population of Niagara, like other parts of Upper Canada, included African Canadians even before the colony was officially created in 1791. According to one estimate 300 African Canadians lived in the region in 1791, many of whom were still legally slaves who had come as forced migrants with their Loyalist masters.[3] Others were legally free or indentured servants. Because of its border location, Niagara had also been the site of a number of attempts to return or to sell slaves. In one of the most notorious instances Chloe Cooley had been sold to a new American owner in March 1793 after being forcibly transported across the Niagara river by her owner, William Vrooman, of Queenston. This episode played a key part in convincing Lieutenant Governor Simcoe, himself an abolitionist, to pressure the Upper Canadian Legislature into passing an act in 1793 to prevent any further slave importations into Upper Canada, and to set in motion a timetable leading to the abolition of slavery within the province long before Britain took any action on this issue.[4] In the War of 1812 some of the African Canadians in the Niagara area joined a Coloured Corps which fought at Queenston Heights and Stoney Creek, helping to defend their adopted land against the invading Americans.[5]

Niagara's proximity to the United States and the financial potential of the sale of Africans into slavery meant that kidnappings of free or freed African Canadians were an ever-present threat. William Lyon Mackenzie relates a tragic tale of the kidnapping of a former African American slave from Queenston in the early 1830s, condemning the people who stood by and did nothing: 'To the everlasting disgrace of the inhabitants of Queenston, they stood by, many of them, and allowed the poor African lass to be placed by main force on board the ferry-boat which was to carry her back into slavery of a far worse nature than she had formerly experienced.'[6] Kidnappings of ex-slaves in the Niagara region were not uncommon. What was new in Moseby's case was the role played by the colonial authorities.

Before turning to the events surrounding the attempt to hand Moseby over to his American captors, it is necessary to examine the government of Upper Canada's decision to extradite him. Upper Canada had been receiving an increasing number of slave refugees from the United States, an estimated 12,000 by the time slavery was abolished in the British Empire in 1833. The Thornton Blackburn case of 1833, involving another escaped slave from Kentucky, established a precedent for refusing American requests to return slaves who had found freedom in Upper Canada. Escaping from slavery in the United States could not in itself constitute a crime in Upper Canada, where slavery did not exist, as the attorney general of Upper Canada had advised.[7] African Americans who had found refuge in Canada still felt insecure. Slave catchers had been active north of the border as well as in the United States and legislation passed in Upper Canada in 1833, the Fugitive Offenders Act, now provided for the extradition of criminals from foreign countries. Would this Act be used to justify returning slaves to their former owners in the United States?

Solomon Moseby's former owner, David Castleman, from Fayette County, Kentucky, arrived in Niagara late in August 1837, accompanied by three men, including Daniel Kelley of New York. Castleman had taken care to bring with him a formal request from the governor of Kentucky for the return of men who had allegedly committed crimes in Kentucky, along with a grand jury indictment and other documents from the Kentucky courts. James Boulton, a lawyer in Niagara, assisted Castleman and his companions in presenting their case both to the Upper Canadian courts and to the government.[8] Boulton was employed by the deputy sheriff to handle all the legal business of the sheriff's office.[9] From their arrival in Upper Canada, the local authorities offered the Kentucky men any help they needed, including the services of the sheriff's lawyer, suggesting a strong bias towards slave owners rather than fugitive slaves. Boulton wrote a letter of introduction for Daniel Kelley to the lieutenant governor's secretary, obviously to expedite their claim. It seems clear from the extant evidence that

Castleman was looking not only for Solomon Moseby but also for Jesse Happy, another fugitive slave from Kentucky. On 7 September Castleman was in Hamilton swearing a complaint against Happy for horse stealing, implying that his trip to Upper Canada had been carefully planned as a slave-catching venture.[10] As one of the slaveholding states bordering the northern free states, Kentucky was anxious to put a stop to runaway slaves escaping to Canada.[11]

Once the documents had been laid before the magistrates and the two fugitive slaves had been arrested and lodged in the Niagara and Hamilton jails, the Upper Canadian government was approached to issue the orders for their respective extraditions. The cases arrived in Toronto separately. The government chose to treat them individually instead of examining them together. Moseby's case arrived first, on 5 September, and was turned over to the attorney general, C.A. Hagerman, for his opinion. Hagerman, who was preoccupied with the vexed question of the Clergy Reserves, replied the next day with a very brief opinion. He believed there was 'sufficient proof' of Moseby's guilt as a horse thief, and under the Fugitive Offenders Act he advised the lieutenant governor to deliver Moseby to the American authorities, enclosing a warrant for his signature. The Executive Council concurred with Hagerman's view and also recommended Moseby's extradition. Neither Hagerman nor the Executive Council paid any attention to the letter Moseby's lawyer had submitted on his behalf or the petitions that had been sent in to support him.

The fact that Moseby had a lawyer is in itself remarkable and testifies to the influence and financial support of Niagara's African Canadian community. Given the role played by Herbert Holmes, the pastor and leader of the African Canadian resistance, in the Moseby case, it is highly likely that Holmes was the person who organized the legal defence and hired Moseby's lawyer, Alexander Stewart. Moseby's lawyer wrote to the lieutenant governor with his own interpretation of what had happened. He found it incredible that four men could have travelled 1,500 miles from Kentucky to Upper Canada at an expense of some $400 merely to bring to justice a slave charged with stealing a horse worth $150. This, said Stewart, was 'a pretext too preposterous to merit refutation.' His explanation was that U.S. slaveholders had become 'seriously alarmed' about the flow of fugitive slaves to the Canadas and saw the Fugitive Offenders Act as a tool they could use, in Stewart's words, to gratify 'their cupidity.' Stewart hoped the lieutenant governor, Sir Francis Bond Head, would see through their machinations and use the discretion granted to him in the statute to free Moseby. After pointing out that Moseby had a reputation in Upper Canada for 'sobriety, honesty and industry,' he appealed to Bond Head's British patriotism. Stewart could not believe that the Fugitive Offenders Act would be used to support slavery, 'which is our proudest boast that England was the first among the nations of the earth to abolish.'[12]

The petition sent to the lieutenant governor by African Canadians from Niagara reaffirmed the arguments of Moseby's lawyer. They were convinced that the charge of horse theft was a 'fraudulent artifice.' As soon as his former owners succeeded in returning him to the United States they would drop the horse stealing indictment in order to return Moseby immediately to slavery. To corroborate their belief, they told Bond Head they had offered Moseby's former owner, David Castleman, $1,000 in the presence of Moseby's lawyer to cover the expenses of the Kentuckians and the lost horse. Castleman had refused the offer. Herbert Holmes was one of the seventeen signatories of this petition, implying that he had a role in offering the money to free Moseby. The petition from the white inhabitants of Niagara contained 117 signatures, including those of many of the magistrates and prominent members of the community. They argued that Moseby could not be guilty, either morally or legally, of the charge against him, because, as a slave, he had not been a free agent. Since he now resided in Upper Canada, Moseby was a free man according to the British constitution. If the lieutenant governor returned him to Kentucky, he would lose that freedom and his case would set a precedent 'whereby no runaway slave will either now or henceforth be safe in a British colony.'

The white inhabitants of Niagara wanted to defend the principle of the British constitution according to which all British colonies provided sanctuary for refugee slaves, and in order to do this, they asked the lieutenant governor to refer the issue to the British government for a legal ruling.[13] Bond Head did refer the larger issue of returning fugitive slaves to the British government, but he replied to the petitions that 'this land of liberty cannot be made an Asylum for the guilty of any colour.' He was convinced that Moseby was guilty of horse theft and, for this reason, resolved to return him to the American authorities.[14] Two years later, after resigning as lieutenant governor, Bond Head published a collection of his despatches. He included without comment the one he had written on fugitive slaves, referring to it in the table of contents as 'Curious Questions respecting Fugitive Slaves.'[15] In 1839, the problems of fugitive slaves paled beside the Rebellions in Upper and Lower Canada in the minds of the British government and their colonial administrators. For Bond Head, the issue had become a mere colonial curiosity.

The government's stand on Moseby's case was clear. Moseby was a criminal even if his crime had been committed in the context of escaping from slavery, and under the 1833 statute he had to be extradited to the United States. Bond Head's despatch to London on the issue of extraditing slaves referred only to the case of Jesse Happy, but among the arguments he summarized opposing his action was the one raised by the white inhabitants of Niagara. Under slave law, slaves were not recognized as men and '... actually existed as brute beasts in moral darkness, until on reaching British soil they suddenly heard for the first time in their lives the sacred words, "Let there be light, and there was light." From that moment it is argued they were created *men*, and if this be true, it is said they cannot be held responsible for conduct prior to their existence.' In this moral debate over who was 'the blackest criminal,' 'the dealer in human flesh versus the stealer of horse-flesh,' Bond Head, while appearing to sympathize with the fugitive slaves, actually placed himself on the side of the slave owners by supporting the extradition of criminals, whether slave or free.

The government of Upper Canada's decision to authorize the extradition of Solomon Moseby, whom it regarded as a criminal, had been very clear, but two days later it received a similar application on behalf of David Castleman requesting the extradition of Jesse Happy, again for horse stealing. Both the attorney general and the Executive Council examined the request for Happy's extradition much more carefully. While still endorsing the request, because of the allegations of horse theft, they expressed reservations, claiming that there were significant differences in the two cases. The most important concerned when the alleged offence had been committed. In Solomon Moseby's case, the offence had apparently occurred only a few months earlier; in Jesse Happy's case the crime had allegedly been committed four years previously and the grand jury indictment was dated June 1835, more than two years prior to the application for extradition. Hagerman also thought he should draw attention in Happy's case to the fact that Happy risked a double punishment as a fugitive slave, the punishment imposed for the offence itself and the possibility of being returned to slavery. He had not made this point in his legal opinion on

Solomon Moseby. The Executive Council elaborated on the same points in its recommendation to the lieutenant governor before suggesting that a referral to Britain would be advisable.[16] Bond Head decided not to order Jesse Happy's extradition until he had received advice from London on the overall policy of slave extradition, and Happy thus remained in jail. Before the British government replied, however, the Executive Council of Upper Canada reconsidered the Happy case and recommended his release. The evidence submitted was insufficient to determine his guilt. Jesse Happy was ordered to be released from the Hamilton jail on 14 November 1837.

In his original despatch to the British government the lieutenant governor had included a legal opinion from the chief justice of the province, John Beverley Robinson. Bond Head's request for a separate legal opinion indicated how seriously he and his government took the larger question of policy on slave extradition and the applicability of the Fugitive Offenders Act in cases of fugitive slaves. Robinson was not at all impressed with the humanitarian arguments advanced by the African Canadian community and their supporters. He was willing to admit that slavery 'politically considered is a great evil' and 'morally wrong,' but he could not countenance admitting slaves into Upper Canada who had murdered their masters, burned their masters' houses, or stolen their masters' goods. Robinson believed in reciprocity with the United States when it came to extradition. If Upper Canada held itself out 'as a place of refuge for atrocious criminals from other Countries,' it could 'expect consequences fatal to its own security and independence.' Robinson was opposed both legally and morally to such a position, and his strongly argued opinion left no doubt whatever of his stand on slave extradition.[17]

What actually happened at the Niagara jail on the day Solomon Moseby was to be handed over to the American authorities? Contemporary newspaper accounts, legal records, Anna Jameson's account, and the first historical chronicle of the affair permit a reconstruction of what occurred while raising some important questions.[18] Chronologically, the first report of what took place is found in the *Niagara Reporter* of 14 September 1837. Written two days after the event by an eyewitness the report opens by questioning the lieutenant governor's decision to turn Moseby over to the American authorities 'without ever giving the unfortunate slave the chance of showing the motives of the miscreants who were pursuing him, and in open defiance of the emphatic language of British laws and British justice: "Slavery cannot exist on British ground."' The reporter thus places the moral issue of returning a slave to slavery, in open contravention of the British abolition of this evil, in the forefront of his story. He then goes on to detail Deputy Sheriff McLeod's attempts to carry out the orders he was given. 'The Deputy Sheriff saw how thoroughly every man of true British feeling, whose blood was warmed with the sacred flame of Liberty, condemned in unqualified terms the conduct of His Excellency. This expression of public feeling shown in language not to be misunderstood, that a rescue would be attempted, and for his protection, called upon the constables to assist him in this, we must say, dirty business.' Local feeling clearly ran high and in opposition to the government's action. The reporter described the scene in front of the jail,

> where [a] more motley assemblage was never to be seen in our recollection; about a hundred coloured people and forty or fifty of them females drawn up in battle array at the Gaol gates ready to seize the man as soon as out of the gate. But to our impressible astonishment, up marched a non-commissioned officer of the Royal Artillery and three of his men with their arms and armaments, ordered by our magistrates to assist the Sheriff ... Gracious heavens, we exclaimed, are we in a British colony? What, four forlorn soldiers brought to maintain the supremacy of the laws? Where, Mr. Sheriff, is your posse? ... A community always on the alert to maintain the Majesty of the laws, stood aloof. Not one person of any claim to respectability would step forward to assist the officer and those constables *whose duty compelled them to be on the spot*, [who] were armed with rusty muskets without flint. The Sheriff in an attempt to seize one of the coloured men, being resisted, ordered the soldiers to charge. The men advanced and to our surprise entered into the thick of a justly infuriated mob. But had not that mob been actuated by more human motives than some other heartless miscreants on the ground, the lives of the soldiers might have been destroyed in a moment. They forbore with Christian fortitude, exclaiming, 'don't hurt the poor soldiers.' Now we would merely ask for information what would have been the feelings of those magistrates had those soldiers fired into the collection of men, women and children, how could they answer for the blood that would have resulted in such an event? We envy not their reflections.

At this stage, a reprieve occurred when a letter arrived from Toronto indicating that the Executive Council was reconsidering Solomon Moseby's extradition at the request of the lieutenant governor. The crowd dispersed 'after giving three cheers – and we are now fully convinced that no power can take a human being from Canada, no matter what his colour, for here, Thanks be to God, man is practically "Free and Equal."' The reporter, along with the crowd which had shown such restraint in the face of military provocation, must have been quickly disillusioned, for the rhetoric about British freedom proved hollow. The Executive Council and the lieutenant governor held to their previous decision and ordered the deputy sheriff to deliver Moseby to the Americans. This led to a repetition of the scene already described, but with a very different outcome. In the reporter's words, 'As soon as the prisoner was outside the gate he disengaged himself from his irons and jumped from the Waggon and escaped. The Deputy Sheriff ordered his assistants to fire when two coloured men were shot dead and two wounded.'

What this reporter does not say is that the Riot Act had been read before the soldiers opened fire. The deputy sheriff had not only ordered the soldiers to fire on the crowd, he had also ordered the arrests of anyone who could be rounded up. Those arrested were initially charged with riot, a serious felony. McLeod's clerk gave a deposition about one of the men charged, William McIntyre, an African Canadian. Henry Long, the clerk, reiterated that McIntrye, 'did with many other colloured people to the number of eighty or ninety, assemble near the Court House with the avowed intention of obstructing the Deputy Sherriff in delivering up Solomon Moseby to the authorities of Kentucky.'[19] McIntyre's own deposition hints at a more sinister interpretation. 'On that day I did not hear the Riot Act read and I was standing quietly when McLeod struck me with [a] dirk. Then I went away to Hammitt's Tavern and got my cheek dressed and came to Town and did not return to the gaol afterwards untill the next day.'[20] McIntyre spent ten days in jail before receiving bail. The sheriff reported later that six African Canadians and four white men had been arrested and indicted for felony in connection with the Moseby escape. Only one of the African Canadians, described by the sheriff as 'by no means the most dangerous,' was found guilty of any offence. McIntyre and four others were tried and acquitted after the jury had deliberated all night. When the deputy sheriff tried to swear in extra constables to assist him, he met with outright resistance. One man said he would 'see McLeod d----d first,' while another said he would prefer to assist the African Canadians. The judge who later listened to the witnesses wrote, 'it is more like a Rout than a Riot...'[21]

After the acquittal of all but one of the African Canadians, a jury acquitted all the whites who had been charged. The jury, composed solely of white people from Niagara, exhibited far more independence in its decisions to acquit all but one of those arrested than the ruling elite anticipated. The circumstances of Moseby's escape and the public reaction to it, including the jury decisions, suggest that historians may need to re-examine the history of black-white relations in this period of Canadian history.

Sheriff Hamilton later tried to explain these surprising events to the lieutenant governor's secretary. All he could say was that sympathy for Moseby and hatred of slavery 'pervaded not only the Blacks, but the greatest proportion of the Whites in the vicinity, even to the Juries themselves, rendering verdicts of acquittal in the face of the strongest evidence ever offered in a Court of Justice ...'[22] The local white community had its own sense of what constituted justice and jurors were prepared to defy the governing elite of the province. This defiance reflected the broad support the African Canadians had generated for their position.

The magistrates also ordered a coroner's inquest to probe into what had led to the deaths and injuries. McLeod, far from an impartial witness, poured scorn on the testimony of the African Canadians: 'such a mass of contradictory evidence I have never heard of – no two have told their tale the same way; that is of the Negro party.'[23] Certainly the jurors had great difficulty reaching a verdict, which required seventeen hours of deliberation. They concluded that the death of pastor Herbert Holmes had been justifiable homicide but could not determine on the basis of the evidence presented whether Jacob Green's death had been justifiable or not.[24]

The *Christian Guardian*, published in Toronto, offered a different interpretation of events: 'The Deputy Sheriff, enraged at the obstruction which he met with, on attempting to pursue the prisoner, ordered the military to fire upon the crowd, which they did, killing two and wounding several others.' The *Guardian* went on to deliver its own verdict on McLeod's actions: '... the Deputy Sheriff in ordering the military to fire upon an unarmed assemblage of persons who offered no violence to him or his assistants, and that, too, as we are credibly informed, several minutes *after* the escape of the prisoner, exceeded his authority, and is exceedingly culpable, if not guilty of the capital offence charged by the Inquest.'[25] One of the local doctors, testifying for the defence in the later trials for riot, stated that the deputy sheriff had acted 'with impropriety that day.'[26] Here was a basic issue of justice the inquest had not really answered. Had the deputy sheriff acted in an arbitrary and indefensible manner, or had he been justified in ordering military force to quell the crowd? If he had acted arbitrarily, had he ordered the military to fire minutes after the escape took place to cover up the fact that it had occurred and to protect his own position?

The *St. Catharines Journal* took issue with the *Guardian*, accusing it of warping the facts and attacking 'the very foundation of social order' by disguising its views 'under the sacred garb of Christianity.' The *Journal* accused the black population of 'mobocracy.' The African Canadians had violated the laws and ordinances 'of the country which affords an asylum for the oppressed of their race who flee from slavery to this land of refuge, where all those who demean themselves in a quiet, upright and orderly manner, are treated with the utmost kindness and respect.' By 'resisting officers of the law in the performance of their duty' this mob had committed a crime for which the *Journal* had no doubt that they deserved the severest punishment.[27] In these two papers we find radically opposed accounts of what happened outside the jail, as well as very different interpretations of the leading actors, the deputy sheriff and Niagara's African Canadian population. The *St. Catharines Journal* speaks for the conservative elite both in its attack on the more radical *Guardian* and in its opposition to mob action against the forces of law and order.

Anna Jameson, in *Winter Studies and Summer Rambles*, describes the conduct of the African Canadians of Niagara, 'animated and even directed by the females,' as 'really admirable for its good sense, forbearance and resolution.' Unarmed, they were determined to confront the British authorities in defence of their peoples' freedom. The British officials opened fire and caused deaths and casualties, in the name of law and order, but their real purpose was to return an escaped slave to his American captors. Jameson wrote, 'it was the conduct of the women which, on this occasion, excited the strongest surprise and interest. By all those passionate and persuasive arguments that a woman knows so well how to use, whatever be her colour, country or class, they had prevailed upon their husbands, brothers and lovers to use no arms, to do no illegal violence, but to lose their lives rather than see their comrade taken by force across the lines. One woman had seized the sheriff, and held him pinioned in her arms; another, on one of the artillery-men presenting his piece, and swearing that he would shoot her if she did not get out of his way, gave him only one glance of unutterable contempt, and with one hand knocking up his piece, and collaring him with the other, held him in such a manner as to prevent misfiring.'[28] Jameson was so intrigued by the conduct of the African Canadian women that she went out to interview one of their leaders, a twenty-five-year-old escaped slave from Virginia known as Sarah or Sally Carter. Carter did not try to hide her anger at what the British had done. 'I thought we were safe *here* – I thought nothing could touch us *here*, on your British ground, but it seems I was mistaken, and if so, I won't stay here – I won't – I won't. I'll go and find some country where they can't reach us! I'll go to the end of the world, I will.'[29]

Sally Carter's faith in British justice and her belief that the sanctuary offered to refugees from American slavery in British territory was absolute had both been shattered. A sense of deep betrayal echoes through her words as recorded by Anna Jameson. The female leadership of the African Canadians during this crisis that had so impressed Jameson was not even discussed in their conversation. Jameson, a member of the British gentry and the estranged wife of a leading official of the Upper Canadian government, contented herself with reporting Sally Carter's words and did not pursue further the implications of such unique female leadership. Jameson may have had her own reasons for not wishing to appear too radical.

Another nineteenth-century account, by long-time Niagara resident and author William Kirby, has Mrs Carter addressing the crowd in front of the jail day after day. She was a natural leader, 'whose fiery speeches roused the multitude to frenzy. The women were particularly excited. They stood in solid phalanx before the gaol gates singing negro hymns, praying and encouraging the men never to allow the fugitive to be delivered up to his masters.' On the day of Moseby's escape Kirby claims Carter 'stood on a wagon, calling on the people in the wildest strain of impassioned oratory to rescue the captive, and never to give him up while they had life.' While Sally Carter roused the crowd with her oratory, another woman, 'a powerful black woman seized the deputy sheriff, Alex. McLeod, round the waist and held him fast so he could not get away.'[30] African Canadian women played a key part in preventing the authorities from returning Moseby to his former owner. They may also have prevented the number of casualties from escalating. As one of the local magistrates testified at the ensuing trial, 'the women made the most noise.'[31]

What is apparent from both Jameson's account and Kirby's later retelling is the pervasive feeling of resistance against a manifest injustice, a feeling shared by many in the Niagara district, both black and white. The two racial communities seemed united in their sense that a violation of a sacred principle of British justice had taken place, although they expressed their feelings in quite different ways. Any whites who sympathized with the Kentucky slave owner or with slavery more generally were careful to keep quiet. Early in her account Jameson articulated this fundamental principle of British justice, even if the tale she recounted displayed its hollowness: 'Here, as in all British dominions, God be praised! The slave is slave no more, but free and protected in his freedom.'[32] Jameson confirmed the widespread support for granting runaway slaves the full protection of British law and abhorrence at the thought of a refugee from slavery being returned to his master. The white population of both Niagara and St Catharines, where the majority of the African Canadian population of the district lived, resorted to the traditional and common method of protest to the government, petitions to the governor signed by leading inhabitants, including the mayor of Niagara and some of the magistrates. One of the petitions focused on the probable fate of Moseby if he was returned to his master, who had been heard to say that he wanted to make an example of Moseby to deter other Kentucky slaves from trying to escape. Theirs was a humanitarian plea to save Moseby from 'a torturing death ... under the lash or at the stake.'

Janet Carnochan's later chronicle (1897) of the events of September 1837, based on interviews with some of the people who had been alive at the time, adds some important details about the reaction of the local white community. She wrote that 'the majority of the whites were opposed to the surrender, but did not want to interfere.' She also discovered that Moseby had friends among the jail guards, which may have aided his eventual escape, and that two magistrates from St Catharines organized another petition to the governor which had no more success than the one from Niagara. The white captain of the local ferry that ran between Niagara and Lewiston had been approached by the deputy sheriff to take Moseby across in his boat. Captain Richardson replied that 'no vessel commanded by him would be used to convey a man back to slavery.' Carnochan also found out that members of the local white community in Niagara had given practical aid to blacks trying to block Moseby's extradition. The Niagara whites were willing to supply the black protesters with food and shelter, even if they were not prepared to join in their vigil in front of the jail.[33] They would not go as far as engaging in open resistance against constituted British authority, but many believed a grave injustice was being committed and were willing to express their opposition through petitions and private acts of assistance.

Carnochan's most important contribution, however, is to shed light on the extensive organization and determined struggle of Niagara's African Canadian community as they did everything in their power to resist the return of a fellow fugitive slave. She is able to relate the oral history still extant in the city. The commitment of the African Canadians to rescue Moseby, 'to live with him or die with him,' was vividly remembered by a few survivors sixty years later, in much the same way as war memories live on. As Carnochan states, the African Canadians had 'a well organized plan,' probably orchestrated by Herbert Holmes. All members of the community were summoned 'to come to the rescue at once, and nobly they responded.' African Canadians were willing to sacrifice what little they had to assist in rescuing Moseby from jail. Carnochan also emphasizes the difficulties and dangers involved in the journeys to summon help. These summons went out 'by boys and girls ... often in the night, over nearly impassable roads' to all the little communities making up the Niagara district.

The recruiting was very successful, as some hundreds of the African Canadian community made their way to Niagara and assembled in front of the jail. At the later trial, the deputy sheriff testified that the crowd numbered between three and four hundred. There were so many that temporary huts were erected for what Carnochan calls a 'blockading army.' The siege lasted 'for three weary weeks,' with many false alarms. The plan extended to how this little army of besiegers planned to thwart the escape. In Carnochan's words, 'a wooden bridge crossed some low ground near the jail and the idea of the blacks was to use no violence, but the women were instructed to stand on the bridge forming a solid mass so that there would be some time taken up in dispersing them, which would cause a diversion and give time and opportunity for the prisoner to escape in the confusion. The women sang hymns.'[34] When the actual attempt to extradite Moseby occurred and violence did break out, African Canadians did not hesitate to defend themselves. Rails removed from local fences 'were stuck in the waggon wheels,' giving Moseby his opportunity to escape, and 'a stone in a stocking formed a formidable weapon for the women.' Some of them, 'worked up to a high pitch of fury, did "grievous bodily harm" to some of the officials who never liked to have this episode referred to afterwards.' Carnochan wrote in praise of those African Canadians living in Niagara who had exhibited 'moral heroism' and 'struck a blow for freedom.'

How did African Canadians living in other parts of Upper Canada react to these events? As Allen Stouffer has pointed out, an Upper Canadian Anti-Slavery Society had been formed in Toronto in January 1837. In retrospect, the two slave cases of Solomon Moseby and Jesse Happy seem ideal for a public campaign, had the Anti-Slavery Society been trying to make its mark. The lack of such a campaign owed to what Stouffer terms the 'faltering leadership' of the society and later to the climate of general repression which ensued following the outbreak of the Mackenzie Rebellion.[35] The willingness of the Upper Canadian government to return fugitive slaves to the United States added greatly to the insecurity of African Canadians in Upper Canada. As Stouffer describes they appointed a physician, Thomas Rolph, to lobby on their behalf in London, trying to secure the right of any fugitive slave charged with a crime to be tried by an Upper Canadian jury rather than extradited. The memorial Rolph presented on behalf of the African Canadians of Upper Canada to Lord Durham reflected their view that the sacrifice of two of their brothers to free Solomon Moseby would not be in vain if the end result was to establish the legal principle of the Canadas as a sanctuary for fugitive slaves from the United States. This campaign did not succeed, although, after a long and frustrating exercise of lobbying, Rolph was able to persuade the British government to remove horse-theft and robbery from the list of extraditable crimes eventually incorporated into the Webster-Ashburton Treaty of 1842.[36]

What happened to Solomon Moseby and Alexander McLeod, and how do their respective fates fit into an interpretation of what occurred in Niagara in 1837? Moseby eluded his pursuers and escaped the country with a reward of £100 sterling on his head. He apparently made his way to Britain and eventually returned to Niagara. Janet Carnochan found that he was no longer welcome among the African Canadians there, perhaps because of the loss of Holmes in the attempt to rescue him. Another account, however, has Moseby living quietly for the rest of his life in St Catharines and Niagara.[37]

Alexander McLeod's subsequent activities are better known, as they relate to the Mackenzie Rebellion which occurred a couple of months later. McLeod had been a 'schoolmaster serjeant' with the 12th Royal

Lancers for some sixteen years and had taught in a school in Edinburgh before migrating to the Canadas. He then spent two years as a store-keeper in Toronto. When he applied to become Niagara's deputy sheriff he came with good references and apparently was just the sort of person the sheriff, Alexander Hamilton, was looking for.[38] Hamilton, as we have seen, lived in Queenston and did not want to move to Niagara. McLeod became his deputy in 1834. With an active deputy sheriff anxious to make his reputation, Hamilton could avoid difficult things like the Moseby case. As discussed in chapter 2, McLeod later claimed that he had been the 'Sheriff de facto.' [39]

One of the unusual aspects of the Moseby affair is that we hear so little from or of the actual sheriff of the Niagara district. Alexander Hamilton did write to the lieutenant governor's secretary just after the events at the Niagara jail, warning the governor not to take any notice of exaggerated reports of the circumstances of the death of a black prisoner. The governor would receive 'a circumstantial account' of what had happened as soon as the coroner's inquest had been completed.[40] Living in Queenston, Hamilton was apparently unaware that the prisoner had escaped and that the deaths were those of two men trying to assist his escape. In any case, his chief concern was to protect his own reputation.

It took nearly three months for Hamilton's report on the events to arrive in Toronto, and by then the government was preoccupied with the storm clouds of a political rebellion in Lower Canada that would shortly spread to Upper Canada. Hamilton argued that the disastrous outcome could have been much worse. He could have called in the militia but chose not to because he was afraid that the jail would have been broken into and all the dangerous criminals let loose, 'many of them of desperate character.' He also repeated to the lieutenant governor what was common knowledge in Niagara, that a lot more blood might have been shed 'from the settled determination of the Blacks to stake their lives on the issue' if the authorities had succeeded in returning Moseby.

Hamilton stressed the bloodshed he claimed to have prevented rather than attempting to explain how the actions of his deputy and the others had contributed to the bloodshed that occurred. He defended McLeod and his officers, 'who acted with perfect firmness and propriety and the utmost forbearance that the case would possibly admit.'[41] Hamilton's delay in sending the report and the report itself reflect his continuing efforts to protect his reputation rather than providing the circumstantial report he had promised. In the end, Hamilton did not investigate any aspect of the affair on his own, preferring instead to rely on the combined evidence of McLeod's account and newspaper testimony of the coroner's inquest.

Long after the events had taken place McLeod wrote a brief memoir, the only extant account of his perspective, of what happened at Niagara in September 1837. To understand the significance of this memoir, McLeod's subsequent and even more controversial role in the *Caroline* affair must be mentioned. McLeod was in Toronto when the Mackenzie Rebellion broke out later in 1837, and he helped to disperse Mackenzie's forces at Montgomery's Tavern with what one historian has branded 'a reckless charge ahead of the main forces into the rebel ranks.'[42] After Mackenzie escaped to New York, McLeod apparently combined military spying for Britain with his duties as deputy sheriff, and on one of his trips to New York he learned that a U.S. steamboat, the *Caroline*, would be used to supply Mackenzie and his men on Navy Island in the Niagara river. On the basis of this information a raid was launched against the *Caroline*.[43] The vessel was destroyed and one of the boat's crewmen, Amos Durfee, was killed. In 1840, when McLeod was no longer a deputy sheriff, he was arrested in Lewiston and charged with Durfee's murder. At the trial held in Utica, New York, in 1841, however, the prosecution could not bring any credible evidence to prove that McLeod had even been part of the *Caroline* expedition.

McLeod's arrest and trial brought Britain and the United States close to hostilities. Albert Corey has termed the McLeod case 'the most troublesome issue' to arise between Britain and the United States during the whole Rebellion era, from 1837 to 1842.[44] In the result an American jury took only twenty-eight minutes to acquit McLeod, clearing the air between the two countries. McLeod's biographer states that following the acquittal McLeod, 'returned to the relative obscurity from which he had so bizarrely emerged.'[45] He spent many years pursuing compensation first from the Canadian government and then from the British government, eventually receiving a pension of £200 in 1855 to compensate him for the suffering he claimed to have endured. He was appointed a justice of the peace in 1866, several years before his death, finally achieving the public status he had always sought.

What was not mentioned at the time, nor in most accounts since, is that Amos Durfee, the dead crewman of the *Caroline*, was an African American. Whether or not McLeod had anything to do with Durfee's death, the fact that he was charged and tried for the murder of an African American in the United States was surely an historical irony which could not have escaped him, given both the role he had played in trying to return a fugitive slave to slave owners and the excessive patriotism he manifested during the Mackenzie Rebellion. A large part of McLeod's later life was spent presenting himself as a victim, someone who had suffered imprisonment and financial hardship for services on behalf of the British Empire. His memoir has to be read in this light, as a document written to make others aware of what he had endured and why he deserved recompense.[46] His quest for justice included petitions to the Legislature in 1845 and a trip to Britain in 1853 to plead his case in person before any British officials and politicians who would listen to him.[47]

What is most remarkable in McLeod's sparse account is what he omits: 'I was ordered by the Government to surrender a horse thief to the authorities of the United States, I was attacked on the road by 200 men and the prisoner rescued. My party consisted of myself, three constables and four privates of the Royal Artillery. We killed two of the assailants and wounded twelve. These affairs and others of a similar nature were highly approved of by the Provincial Government but they procured me a host of enemies on both frontiers. I became marked for future vengence ... [sic].'[48] McLeod was correct in saying that the government approved his conduct and supported his actions, although government support was not as wholehearted as he believed: Bond Head's successor as lieutenant governor of Upper Canada, Sir George Arthur, described McLeod privately as 'altogether a scheming kind of gentleman.'[49] Arthur was quite cynical about McLeod's motives prior to his arrest in the United States, believing that McLeod was not above creating what the lieutenant governor called 'a little excitement' in order to 'raise for himself not only a great deal of sympathy, but a little money.'

In his account of the events of September 1837 McLeod leaves out entirely Moseby's name, his identity as an escaped slave, and the composition of the crowd, especially the large number of women in it. He also omits the indignity he had experienced of being held captive by one of the female protesters. McLeod, acutely sensitive to any real or imagined injustices he had suffered himself, was highly selective in recounting instances in which others might have suffered injustice at his hands. McLeod's memoir casts the events in which he had been involved as a classic law and order tale, with the sheriff as the law and

Moseby as a horse thief. All the other details could be and were forgotten. McLeod painted himself as a wronged martyr to the British imperial cause, certainly not as a man who might have to contend with his own conscience over his actions in Niagara in September 1837.

The most obvious conclusion to draw from this sad and little-known episode of Canadian history is that the African Canadians living in the Niagara region had been victims of British injustice. Two had died and others had been wounded in a successful attempt to prevent a fugitive slave being returned to his former owner. The loss of Herbert 'Hubbard' Holmes was a bitter blow to the fledgling refugee community of African Canadians living near Niagara. It deprived them of their teacher, pastor, and leader, a man who had distinguished himself in the service of his people. Moseby was the chief beneficiary of the action. He escaped from custody, and even if he did later return to the Niagara district, as two of the narratives relate, he was never arrested again as a fugitive slave or on the original charge of horse stealing.

William Kirby, after recounting the tale of Solomon Moseby, told his readers that 'this was the last attempt ever made by a Governor of Canada to surrender a fugitive slave on any pretence.' He was not correct in this conclusion: in 1841 Nelson Hackett was extradited to Arkansas for nearly identical reasons.[50] Kirby also believed that 'the sympathy of the whole Province was on the side of the slave, and the people were glad to hear of his rescue.'[51] Nothing more is heard of David Castleman, who, we surmise, returned to Kentucky having been unsuccessful in both of his attempts to recapture fugitive slaves. His extradition requests had not only failed, they led in the end to a reconsideration of British policy which actually made it more difficult for American slaveholders to recapture slaves who fled to Canada.[52] Moseby was not of course the only fugitive slave whose fate was tangled up in the laws of the United States and the British colonies. Shadrach Minkins, the first runaway slave to be arrested in New England under the 1850 Fugitive Slave Law, was rescued in Boston in 1851 and then escaped to Montreal, where he found refuge.[53] An even more spectacular case occurred during the United States Civil War when a Canadian court ruled that a fugitive slave, John Anderson, should be returned to the United States for killing a friend of his during a fight when Anderson escaped. The ensuing public outcry forced a reconsideration and Anderson was permitted to remain in Canada.[54]

The Moseby affair succeeded in raising awareness of the plight of fugitive slaves in Upper Canada, and African Canadians set about persuading the British government to give them greater security. On both sides of the Atlantic, abolitionists now urged more protection for fugitive slaves arriving in the Canadas. Thomas Rolph, the lobbyist whom the African refugees enlisted to carry their message to Britain, not only used the case in his efforts with the British government, he also took the details of Solomon Moseby's plight to the world anti-slavery convention held in London in 1840 as a powerful and vivid example of the lengths to which American slaveholders would go to recapture their escaped slaves in British colonies. At the annual meeting of the British and Foreign Anti-Slavery Society in May 1841 a petition was sent to Lord Palmerston, the British foreign secretary, demanding that measures be taken to prevent any recurrence of what had happened to Solomon Moseby.[55] As mentioned above, the Webster-Ashburton Treaty of 1842, setting out the conditions of extradition, did not include horse theft in part because of Rolph's lobbying and Palmerston's memory of the Moseby case.

Alexander McLeod is now largely remembered in connection with his murder trial in the United States, not in connection with the deaths he was responsible for in Niagara. And because the Mackenzie Rebellion followed so soon after the Moseby episode, details of the latter event either have been conflated with the Rebellion or faded from view in the history of Upper Canada. A recent Web site incorporates the Solomon Moseby case into a larger multicultural interpretation of the Mackenzie Rebellion.[56] This conflation originated in McLeod's account of the events of September 1837. But since the whole Moseby episode occurred prior to the outbreak of the Rebellion, we must separate it from the later events, not fuse the two together. Both McLeod's memoir and the web site distort historical reality.

The many versions of the Solomon Moseby story, and the way in which they have come into being, offer a telling commentary on Canadian historiography. The African Canadians of Niagara had demonstrated to the whole colony their determination to protect the freedom promised to them by British law. In spite of the abortive Moseby extradition and their bitterness at being betrayed by British authorities, a number of African Canadians were still prepared to serve in the militia during the Mackenzie Rebellion to help to protect Upper Canada from a possible invasion by the United States. Such an invasion would have been an even greater threat to their security. Those who had been jailed during the Moseby riot and Jesse Happy, who had been incarcerated in Hamilton, were released to join a newly created coloured corps which saw service on the Niagara frontier and was later used to police the Welland Canal.[57] African Canadian loyalty to Britain was in the end much stronger than the support British officials had offered them in the face of attempts by American slave owners to recapture their fugitive slaves. African Canadians were prepared to forgive British injustice in order to preserve their freedom from slavery, even though they had been made aware of the need to be constantly on guard to protect their newly won liberty.

Conclusion

When Anna Jameson first visited Niagara in the winter of 1837, she wrote poetically about the snow-covered land. She was struck by 'the deep, monotonous tranquillity which prevailed on every side,' and how the country appeared 'so exquisitely pure and vestal-like.' This made the tales she had heard even more unlikely. She could hardly 'believe that this whole frontier district is not only remarkable for the prevalence of vice, but of dark and desperate crime.'[1] Jameson's romanticism may have heightened the contrast, but she does emphasize that in colonial Niagara both vice and crime were to be found in abundance. Since the goals of the British system of justice instituted in the colony from its beginning were to encourage Christian morality and to suppress crime, Jameson's findings could suggest that the system had failed. The truth is more complex and it takes us to the roots of what British justice in Upper Canada meant and how it worked.

First, it is important once and for all to dismiss a myth invented by some of the Loyalist historians writing early in the twentieth century. Colonel George Denison expressed this myth most forcefully in his presidential address to the Royal Society of Canada in 1904. Eulogizing the early Loyalists he stated that the Loyalist spirit 'is shown in the remarkable freedom from crime of this country in its early years. The pious, God-fearing men who had made such sacrifices for their principles, were a community almost free from crime.'[2] Denison, who had been a police magistrate in Toronto, conjured up an imaginary golden age in which the country was nearly free from crime, doubtless to contrast with the late-nineteenth-century crime-ridden society he was all too familiar with in Toronto and to promote the Imperial Federation Movement. No such golden age existed, however, and proves Anna Jameson a more trustworthy witness than the later police magistrate. Loyalist Niagara, in common with the rest of Upper Canada, had high levels of certain crimes, most notably personal assaults. Some of them, often where alcohol was involved, revealed savage levels of brutality.

If the golden age theory has to be dismissed, we must equally dismiss some of the corrective historiography. It has been argued that law and order was maintained solely because of 'the zeal and commitment of the authorities who controlled the government apparatus.'[3] But maintaining law and order in the Niagara district was in truth a cooperative venture, requiring the support of the population as well as the active commitment of the magistrates, the sheriff, and the constables recruited in each local community. Some recent historiography has focused on high-profile political trials for perjury and sedition, including the Gourlay trial in 1819 and the Randal trial for perjury in 1825. These cases have been cited as illustrations of 'the repressive uses of criminal law as well as the possibilities and limits of counter-hegemonic struggles in the criminal courts.'[4] But both cases were exceptional. The vast majority of the criminal cases heard in the Niagara courts did not have their obvious political implications, and it is to these cases that we must turn in order to discover the more usual patterns of British justice in the colony.

Although the system of justice introduced into Upper Canada in 1792 was to be completely British, with the modifications made over the subsequent fifty years it began to assume more hybrid features. As we have seen, the first lieutenant governor, John Graves Simcoe, had great ambitions for the new colony. Over time, his lofty ambitions were toned down as colonial realities set in, although the implicit belief in the superiority and uniqueness of the British legal implantation never vanished. Simcoe did not succeed in proving to the Americans that they had been wrong in choosing to separate from Britain, but British institutions guided by British principles did take root in Upper Canada, including Niagara. While Simcoe's attempt to create a colony modelled on British lines did not work out precisely as he had planned, the colony remained loyal to Britain, resisting American invasion during the War of 1812 and rejecting the lure of Rebellion in 1837. The officials charged with maintaining law and order always understood that what they were maintaining was British law and order.

The legal system was also supposed to embody British social gradations, especially the distinctions which land and wealth had given the privileged classes in England. In Upper Canada, these distinctions were artificially created in the early years of the colony through large land grants to a favoured few, but over time they became less noticeable. In Britain these distinctions had placed a notable stamp on the justice system, but in Upper Canada, if Niagara is an accurate guide, the possession of land and wealth did not affect the administration of justice in a similar way. North American geography, the presence of the democratic United States across the Niagara river, and the nature of the pioneering settlements which made up the district all worked to level the social distinctions taken for granted in Britain. There was greater agreement on the primary purpose of the criminal justice system: 'to maintain order and to protect property.'[5] The social distinctions created by the possession of property may not have been as substantial in Upper Canada as in the mother country, but it was never doubted that the duty of the criminal justice process was to protect property.

The selection of the Crown's agents, the men who implemented the system of justice, ensured that those with substantial property interests, would preside over the district courts. The legal and political community rooted in the districts of Upper Canada gave a particular shape to the system of criminal administration and local government. Most of the men who enforced justice in the districts in the earliest days of the colony had no legal training. While professionalization of the system would later became the norm, justice was self-taught for most magistrates into the third decade of the nineteenth century. The criminal justice system was part of a local government, which as we have seen was also placed in the hands of the magistrates, and fiscal constraints affected the administration of justice. In Niagara, as in the remainder of Upper Canada, the deliberate integration of justice with local government went unchallenged until the reform opposition of the 1820s and 1830s. As the issues faced by the local magistrates became more complex, however, and as a steady stream of immigrants arrived in the colony, the strains in the system became increasingly evident, even to those in charge. A growing confusion of roles and responsibilities was not cleared up until local government was placed in the hands of elected officials. In Niagara, this did not occur until after the union of the Canadas in 1841.

By the middle of the nineteenth century, the various elements of the eighteenth-century system of English justice and local government instituted in the Canadas had changed or begun to change as they had in Britain. The districts were abolished in 1849, local government was transferred over time to elected town and township officials, and from 1841 the authority of magistrates on the court of quarter sessions was subordinated to an appointed district judge who had to be a professionally trained lawyer. The grand jury tradition of the quarter sessions courts gradually faded away, and the local constables were slowly replaced by municipal and township police forces. A tradition of local administration of criminal justice was replaced by a more professional system administered by the province.

Even during the colonial period, criminal justice was not applied uniformly across the colony, as local studies such as this reveal. There was a strong local context to the way the law was implemented. Community feeling often expressed itself powerfully through petitions or presentments of quarter sessions grand juries and certainly influenced the way in which the justice system functioned. The active involvement of juries, especially grand juries, in a wide variety of criminal justice and social welfare matters, testifies to the close connection of the local community and its system of justice. Operation of the system was also dependent on a small number of local men who served as constables for limited periods. Even by the 1840s the people of the Niagara district were far more intimately involved with the courts, as jurors, witnesses, plaintiffs, or accused, than their descendants. Legal processes infused elements of local government right down to social welfare.

Knowledge of legal processes was much more widespread in the colonial period than it has subsequently become. Increasing professionalism has removed the pervasive participation in the legal system which characterized the colonial period. While that close connection helped to cement a feeling of ownership it also gave rise to contested views about how the system should operate. The community was anything but passive or even united in its viewpoint. The criminal justice system functioned in a public arena in which issues were vigorously debated and agreement was often difficult to find. Nevertheless, the principles, practices, and culture of British law and British justice were firmly implanted in Upper Canada during the early colonial period. The Niagara district provides solid evidence of the extent and depth of this legal implantation.

Early Upper Canadian legal historians have debated at length the extent of corruption and partiality in the colonial justice system. There was certainly much to complain about in the administration of justice in the colony and Upper Canadians were at times vociferous critics of the legal system. The Niagara district has assumed a particular importance in this debate because some of the more obvious 'outrages' occurred in a small number of court cases tried there. The debate has focused especially on cases at the assize level, but Robert Fraser concludes as well that 'the actions of magistrates either singly, or in concert within quarter sessions were a perennial, deep seated, province-wide grievance.'[6]

The reformers' complaints about the justice system in Upper Canada echoed those of the British reformers prior to the 1832 Reform Bill. Political agitation in Britain, including 'an apparently universal outcry' against the justices of the peace, brought no immediate change in the judicial system. Sydney and Beatrice Webb concluded that magistrates in Britain were left after 1832, 'unchanged in their unrepresentative character, unchecked in their irresponsibility, unfettered in their powers of expenditure and unreformed either in the method of their appointment or in the secrecy of their procedure.'[7] In Upper Canada the complaints of William Lyon Mackenzie and his fellow reformers likewise had no immediate effect, although they may have hastened changes in both local government and the operation of the criminal justice system made after the union. Local government was reformed in Britain in 1835, removing it from the justices of the peace, and this example would be followed in the Canadas.

In Upper Canada prior to the Mackenzie Rebellion, because the magistrates were leading property holders and often men with close connections to the government officials, a few court cases assumed the character of political and partisan struggles. This was certainly the case in the sedition trial of Robert Gourlay in 1819, but political overtones are also evident in a few civil trials. In 1827, for instance, William Forsyth attempted to sue for damages over an episode arising from his fencing in land overlooking Niagara Falls to ensure that tourists wanting to view the Falls would have to enter his property and, presumably, visit the inn he owned. The lieutenant governor, Sir Peregrine Maitland, ordered the military to tear down the fence. Forsyth rebuilt it and military forces tore it down a second time. Forsyth failed to win any damages from government officials, including the district sheriff, for their actions.[8] Paul Romney, who has provided the fullest account of this particular legal saga, concludes, 'Justice was probably more unequal in the Niagara District than elsewhere.'[9] This conclusion is open to question. There were certainly blatant inequalities in the administration of justice at all levels in Niagara, as this book illustrates, but arguably they were rooted more often in the status or race of individuals who appeared before the courts than in the political partiality of magistrates or judges. The notoriety of certain cases gives the Niagara district a particular prominence, but in the vast majority of cases the justice dispensed in Niagara probably differed little from that meted out in the rest of the colony.

If we are to move beyond the paradigms inherited from the political struggles of the colonial period and the subsequent historiography, we must rely on more focused local studies of the operation of the justice system. Susan Lewthwaite's examination of the magistrates of the Newcastle district contends 'that there is nothing glaringly *wrong* with most of what went on at the local level of criminal justice administration.'[10] Donald Fyson concludes from his examination of the justices of the peace in the Montreal district that the criminal justice system there, even though 'riddled with barriers and biases,' was one 'which many people still turned to and came in contact with.' Its 'whole essence was fluidity and ambiguity,' making it impossible to characterize with rigid models.[11]

Similar conclusions might be drawn about the operation of the justice system in Niagara. On the basis of her study of the assize court, Ann Alexandra McEwen concluded that in Niagara, 'people of all callings participated in the workings of the judicial system: justice was being done and being seen to be done.' Peter Oliver has stated that his own analysis supports these findings. McEwen also determined that the law in Niagara 'functioned in such a manner as to reinforce the values of a generally conservative society while at the same time upholding popular ideas of justice, equitability and fairness.'[12] Frances Ann Thompson discovered that in Niagara 'local elites ruled autonomously of York control,' and she went to some length to stress that her conclusions depart 'from structural or ideological arguments which emphasize York-centred control of the province through constitutional structure, ideology or patronage.'[13] These studies of the criminal justice system in the Niagara and Newcastle districts of Upper Canada, and the Montreal district in Lower Canada, like my own, reach different conclusions about the nature and operation of the system than those found in earlier studies that concentrated on a few notorious cases at the assize levels or on trials for sedition, treason, and libel. If corruption and partiality were endemic in the colonial justice system, this should be evident at the lowest level, where the largest number of people came into contact with the law. Appointments of magistrates and sheriffs were certainly partisan, and magistrates obviously pursued their own particular interests. Widespread corruption, however, is a different matter entirely.

Justice could certainly be applied unequally in the Niagara district, as many inhabitants discovered to their cost, but similar inequalities existed elsewhere in the colony and indeed throughout British North America in the same period. Equality before the law was trumpeted as a basic principle of the British law, but the real barriers to equal treatment remained unaltered throughout the colonial era. Serious obstacles existed for minorities, women, and those too poor to employ lawyers to assist them. In these cases, full justice gave way to gelded justice.

Nevertheless, in the vast majority of the cases heard before the courts in the Niagara district, both at the level of the quarter sessions and the assizes, the outcome was based on a determination of the law as understood by magistrates and juries. Gender and racial discrimination often denied justice to women and African Canadians. But there is little evidence of widespread corruption and partiality in the justice system. It may thus be necessary to reconsider long-dominant hypotheses about the nature of Upper Canadian colonial justice.

Notes

INTRODUCTION

1 *Dictionary of Canadian Biography*, 5:755.
2 Simcoe to Dundas, 12 Aug. 1791, *The Correspondence of Lieut. Governor John Graves Simcoe* ... ed. E.A. Cruikshank (Toronto: Ontario Historical Society, 1923), 1:43–51.
3 William Blackstone, *Commentaries on the Laws of England* (Oxford: Clarendon Press, 1773), 4:59.
4 Archives of Ontario (AO), 6th Report of the Bureau of Archives of Ontario (Toronto, 1909), 18, speech by Simcoe, 15 Oct. 1792.
5 Simcoe to Dundas, no. 11, 6 Nov. 1792, *Correspondence*, 1:251–2.
6 AO, 4th Report of the Bureau of Archives of Ontario (Toronto, 1907), 181, Proclamation, 11 Apr. 1793.
7 AO, 6th Report of the Bureau of Archives of Ontario (Toronto, 1909), 22, speech by Simcoe, 31 May 1793.
8 Norma Landau, *The Justices of the Peace, 1679–1760* (Berkeley and Los Angeles: University of California Press, 1984), 45.
9 J.M. Beattie, *Crime and the Courts in England, 1660–1800* (Princeton: Princeton University Press, 1986), 5.
10 Clifford Geertz, *Local Knowledge: Further Essays in Interpretive Anthropology* (New York: Basic Books, 1983), 167.
11 Jim Phillips, 'Recent Publications in Canadian Legal History,' *Canadian Historical Review*, 78 (2) (June, 1997), 236–57 at 253. Philip Girard rein-

forces this theme in his article, 'Themes and Variations in Early Canadian Legal Culture: Beamish Murdoch and his *Epitome of the Laws of Nova Scotia*,' *Law and History Review*, 11 (1) (Spring, 1993), 101–44.

12 Clive Emsley, *Crime and Society in England, 1750–1900*, 2nd ed. (London and New York: Longman, 1996), 13.

13 Edward L. Ayers, *Vengeance and Justice: Crime and Punishment in the 19th-Century American South* (New York and Oxford: Oxford University Press, 1984), 9–33.

14 Susan Lewthwaite, 'Pre-Trial Examination in Upper Canada,' in Greg T. Smith, Allyson N. May, and Simon Devereaux, eds., *Criminal Justice in the Old World and the New: Essays in Honour of J.M. Beattie* (Toronto: Centre of Criminology, University of Toronto, 1998), 85–103; 'Violence, Law and Community in Rural Upper Canada,' in Jim Phillips, Tina Loo, and Susan Lewthwaite, eds., *Essays in the History of Canadian Law*, vol. 5, *Crime and Criminal Justice* (Toronto: Osgoode Society, 1994), 353–86; 'Law and Authority in Upper Canada: The Justices of the Peace in the Newcastle District, 1803–1840' (PhD thesis, University of Toronto, 2000); Peter Oliver, *'Terror to Evil-Doers': Prisons and Punishments in Nineteenth-Century Ontario* (Toronto: Osgoode Society, 1998); John C. Weaver, *Crimes, Constables and Courts: Order and Transgression in a Canadian City, 1816–1970* (Montreal and Kingston: McGill-Queen's University Press, 1995); Ann Alexandra McEwen, 'Crime in the Niagara District, 1827–1850' (MA thesis, University of Guelph, 1991); Frances Ann Thompson, 'Local Authority and District Autonomy: The Niagara Magistracy and Constabulary' (PhD thesis, University of Ottawa, 1996); Donald Fyson, 'Criminal Justice, Civil Society, and the Local State: The Justices of the Peace in the District of Montreal, 1764–1830' (PhD thesis, Université de Montréal, 1995); James K. Wilson, 'The Court of General Quarter Sessions of the Peace: Local Administration in Pre-Municipal Upper Canada' (MA thesis, McMaster University, 1991).

15 Robert L. Fraser, ed., *Provincial Justice: Upper Canadian Legal Portraits from the Dictionary of Canadian Biography* (Toronto: Osgoode Society, 1992), lxvii.

16 Ibid, xvi.

17 Peter Oliver, 'The Place of the Judiciary in the Historiography of Upper Canada,' in G. Blaine Baker and Jim Phillips, eds., *Essays in the History of Canadian Law in Honour of R.C.B. Risk* (Toronto: Osgoode Society, 1999), 449.

18 F. Murray Greenwood and Barry Wright, *Canadian State Trials: Law, Politics, and Security Measures 1608–1837* (Toronto: Osgoode Society, 1996), 38.

19 These issues have been explored most fully by Paul Romney in a number of writings, most notably, *Mr Attorney: The Attorney General for Ontario in Court, Cabinet, and Legislature, 1791–1899* (Toronto: Osgoode Society, 1986); 'From Constitutionalism to Legalism: Trial by Jury, Responsible Government, and the Rule of Law in the Canadian Political Culture,' *Law and History Review* 7 (1989), 121–74; 'From the Types Riot to the Rebellion: Elite Ideology, Anti-legal Sentiment, Political Violence, and the Rule of Law in Upper Canada,' *Ontario History* 79 (1987), 113–44; and 'Very Late Loyalist Fantasies: Nostalgic Tory "History" and the Rule of Law in Upper Canada,' in W.W. Pue and Barry Wright, eds., *Canadian Perspectives on Law and Society* (Ottawa: Carleton University Press, 1988), 119–47.

20 Landau, *The Justices of the Peace*, 2.

21 The court records are described in C.J. Shephard, 'Court Records as Archival Records,' *Archivaria* 18 (Summer, 1984), 124–8. They can found in the Ontario Archives (AO) R.G. 22, Series 372.

1 The Paradise of Upper Canada

1 John N. Jackson, *Names Across Niagara* (St Catharines, Ont.: Vanwell Publishing, 1989), 30–1.

2 Figure 1 is taken from R. Louis Gentilcore's 'The Niagara District of Robert Gourlay,' *Ontario History* 54 (4) (1962), 228. Gentilcore adapted it from Gourlay's own book, *Statistical Account of Upper Canada*, 2 vols. (London, 1822).

3 J. Wreford Watson, 'The Influence of the Frontier on Niagara Settlements,' *Geographical Review* 38 (1) (1948), 113–19.

4 For a series of essays on life in the capital during these years, see Richard Merritt, Nancy Butler, and Michael Power, eds., *The Capital Years: Niagara-on-the-Lake, 1792–1796* (Toronto: Dundurn Press, 1991).

5 W.G. Dean, ed., *Economic Atlas of Ontario* (Toronto: University of Toronto Press, 1969), Plate 99.

6 Isaac Weld, *Travels Through the States of North America and the Province of Upper and Lower Canada, 1795, 1796, 1797* (London, 1800), 2:83.

7 Bruce G. Wilson, *The Enterprises of Robert Hamilton* (Ottawa: Carleton University Press, 1983), 6; Douglas McCalla, *Planting the Province: The Economic History of Upper Canada, 1784–1870* (Toronto: University of Toronto Press, 1993), 250, table 2.1.

8 McCalla, *Planting the Province*, table 2.1.

9 Gourlay, *Statistical Account of Upper Canada*, 106.

10 M.M. Quaife, ed., 'The Chronicles of Thomas Verchères de Boucherville,'

in *War on the Detroit* (Chicago: Lakeside, 1940), 168–9, cited in George Sheppard, *Plunder, Profit, and Paroles: A Social History of the War of 1812 in Upper Canada* (Montreal and Kingston: McGill-Queen's University Press, 1994), 172.

11 Wilson, *The Enterprises of Robert Hamilton*, 164–5.

12 Sheppard, *Plunder, Profit, and Paroles*, 125.

13 Robert Gourlay, *Statistical Account of Upper Canada*, reprint ed. (New York: Johnson Reprint Corporation, 1966), 1:237.

14 AO, R.G. 22, Series 372, 2–3, 'Return of the Population of the District of Niagara, 31 May 1828.'

15 McCalla, *Planting the Province*, 253, table 3.1.

16 AO, Ms. 180, Aggregate Census Returns, Upper Canada, 1824–1850.

17 J. Wreford Watson, 'Urban Developments in the Niagara Peninsula,' *Canadian Journal of Economics and Political Science* 9 (4) (1943), 463–86 at 464.

18 Gourlay, *Statistical Account of Upper Canada*, 1:135; Gentilcore, 'The Niagara District of Robert Gourlay,' 228–36.

19 AO, Ms. 180, Niagara District Census.

20 William Lyon Mackenzie, *Sketches of Canada and the United States* (London: E. Wilson, 1833), 89.

21 E. Morris Sider, 'The Early Years of the Tunkers in Upper Canada,' *Ontario History* 51 (2) (1959), 121–9.

22 Arthur Garatt Dorland, *A History of the Society of Friends (Quakers) in Canada* (Toronto: MacMillan, 1927), 63–76.

23 J.S. Moir, 'Early Methodism in the Niagara Peninsula,' *Ontario History* 43 (2) (1951), 51–8.

24 Peter A. Russell, *Attitudes to Social Structure and Mobility in Upper Canada, 1815–1840* (Lewiston: Edwin Mellen Press, 1990), 201–2.

25 Robert Fraser, 'Like Eden in Her Summer Dress: Gentry, Economy and Society: Upper Canada, 1812–1840' (PhD thesis, University of Toronto, 1979), 218.

26 Figure 2 is taken from Gentilcore, 'The Niagara District of Robert Gourlay,' 230.

27 For the roads of early Niagara, see Andrew Burghardt, 'The Origin and Development of the Road Network of the Niagara Peninsula, Ontario, 1770–1851,' *Annals of the Association of American Geographers* 59 (3) (Sept. 1969), 417–40.

28 Cecil J. Houston and William J. Smyth, *Irish Emigration and Canadian Settlement: Patterns, Links and Letters* (Toronto: University of Toronto Press,

1990), 57; J. Lawrence Runnalls, *The Irish on the Welland Canal* (St Catharines: St Catharines Public Library, 1973), 18–32.

29 John N. Jackson, *The Welland Canals and Their Communities: Engineering, Industrial and Urban Transformation* (Toronto: University of Toronto Press, 1997), 65–9.

30 H.V. Nelles, 'Loyalism and Local Power, the District of Niagara, 1792–1837,' *Ontario History* 58 (1966), 112.

31 Donald Creighton, *The Commercial Empire of the St. Lawrence, 1760–1850* (Toronto: Ryerson Press, 1937), 251.

32 Louis L. Babcock, *The War of 1812 on the Niagara Frontier* (Buffalo: Buffalo Historical Society, 1927).

33 David A. Gerber, *The Making of an American Pluralism, Buffalo, New York, 1825–1860* (Chicago: University of Illinois Press, 1989), 5.

34 Ibid., 16.

35 *Farmer's Journal and Welland Canal Intelligencer*, 5 July 1826.

36 McCalla, *Planting the Province*, 138, map. 7.1.

37 Gourlay, *Statistical Account of Upper Canada*, reprint ed., vi.

38 Francis Hall, *Travels in Canada and the United States in 1816–1817* (London: Longman, 1818), 205.

39 John Howison, *Sketches of Upper Canada* ... (Edinburgh, 1821), 66. See also 220, where he describes the Niagara district as 'the richest part of the province.'

40 Anna Brownell Jameson, *Winter Studies and Summer Rambles in Canada* (Ottawa: New Canadian Library 1990), 56.

41 Mackenzie, *Sketches of Canada and the United States*, 295.

42 Marjorie Freeman Campbell, *Niagara, Hinge of the Golden Arc* (Toronto: Ryerson Press, 1958), 3.

43 *Farmer's Journal and Welland Canal Intelligencer*, 13 Dec. 1826.

44 Patrick Shirreff, *A Tour through North America; together with a comprehensive view of Canada and the United States*, reprint ed. (New York: Benjamin Blom Inc., 1971), 95.

45 Jameson, *Winter Studies and Summer Rambles*, 40.

46 Ibid., 220.

47 *Lord Durham's Report on the Affairs of British North America*, ed. with an introduction by Sir C.P. Lucas, 3 vols. (New York: Augustus Kelly, reprint ed. 1970), 2:212.

48 Ibid., 3:357.

49 Sir Francis Bond Head, *A Narrative* (London: J. Murray, 1839), 467–9.

50 AO, R.G. 22, Series 372, 35–28, James Cummings to Charles Richardson, 12 Aug. 1839.

51 NA, M.G. 24 E1, Merritt Papers, vol. 14, Jacob Keefer to W.H. Merritt, 28 Feb. 1839.
52 Pierre Berton states that even by 1845 Niagara Falls was attracting close to 50,000 visitors annually. Pierre Berton, *Niagara: A History of the Falls* (Toronto: McClelland & Stewart, 1992), 80.
53 Patricia Jasen, 'Romanticism, Modernity, and the Evolution of Tourism on the Niagara Frontier, 1790–1850,' *Canadian Historical Review* 72 (3) (September, 1991), 283–318 at 306.
54 Watson, 'The Influence of the Frontier on Niagara Settlements,' 118.
55 Janet Carnochan, *History of Niagara (In Part)* (Toronto: W. Briggs, 1914), 1.
56 William Kirby, *Annals of Niagara*, 2nd ed. (Toronto: MacMillan & Co., 1927), 324.

PART ONE

1 John C. Weaver, *Crimes, Constables and Courts: Order and Transgression in a Canadian City, 1816–1970* (Montreal and Kingston: McGill-Queen's University Press, 1995), 269.

2 Courts, District Rulers, and Crown Servants

1 34 Geo. III (1794), c. 2.
2 41 Geo. III (1801), c. 6.
3 Margaret Banks, 'Evolution of the Ontario Courts, 1788–1981,' in David Flaherty, ed., *Essays in the History of Canadian Law*, vol. 2 (Toronto: Osgoode Society, 1983), 500–3.
4 J.H. Aitchison, 'The Courts of Requests in Upper Canada,' in J.K. Johnson, ed., *Historical Essays on Upper Canada* (Toronto: McClelland and Stewart, 1975), 86–95.
5 Sydney and Beatrice Webb, *English Local Government*, vol. 1, *The Parish and the County* (Hamden, Conn.: Archon Books, 1963), 295–6.
6 59 Geo. III (1819), c. 5.
7 James K. Wilson, 'The Court of General Quarter Sessions of the Peace: Local Administration in Pre-Municipal Upper Canada' (MA thesis, McMaster University, 1991), 32–5.
8 AO, R.G. 22, Series 372, 32–19, draft minutes of court of quarter sessions 2 July 1838 and 6 Aug. 1838.
9 Ibid. 49–26, court order, July 1843.
10 AO, R.G. 8, Box 11, Charles Richardson to the Hon. D. Daly, 1 Dec. 1845.
11 Sydney and Beatrice Webb, *The Parish and the County*, 422.

12 J.K. Johnson, *Becoming Prominent: Regional Leadership in Upper Canada, 1791–1841* (Montreal and Kingston: McGill-Queen's University Press, 1989), 64. See also J.H. Aitchison, 'The Development of Local Government in Upper Canada, 1783–1850' (PhD thesis, University of Toronto, 1953), 28–32.

13 Wilson, 'The Court of General Quarter Sessions of the Peace,' 56–7.

14 AO, R.G. 22, Series 372, 31–10, Draft minutes of court of quarter sessions, 13–16 March 1838.

15 Sydney and Beatrice Webb, *The Parish and the County*, 281.

16 Aitchison, 'The Development of Local Government in Upper Canada,' 28; Sydney and Beatrice Webb, *The Parish and the County*, 319–86.

17 6 Vict. (1842), c. 3, 'An Act for the Qualifications of Justices of the Peace.'

18 H.V. Nelles, 'Loyalism and Local Power, the District of Niagara, 1792–1837,' *Ontario History* 58 (2) (1966), 99–114 at 100.

19 Frances Ann Thompson, 'Local Authority and District Autonomy: The Niagara Magistracy and Constabulary' (PhD thesis, University of Ottawa, 1996), 75.

20 Bruce G. Wilson, *The Enterprises of Robert Hamilton* (Ottawa: Carleton University Press, 1983), 48.

21 Johnson, *Becoming Prominent*, 75.

22 Thompson, 'Local Authority and District Autonomy,' 91.

23 NA, R.G. 5, B7, vol. 5, Application of Bartholomew Tench, 2 May 1843. Magistrates were pluralists in other districts besides Niagara. See Wilson, 'The Court of General Quarter Sessions of the Peace,' 37.

24 Aitchison, 'The Development of Local Government in Upper Canada,' 33.

25 AO, Ms. 75, Russell Papers, Hamilton to Russell, 8 Aug. 1799, cited in Ann Alexandra McEwen, 'The Nelles Family of Grimsby: A Study in Local Loyalism' (undergraduate thesis, University of Guelph, Nov. 1987), 22.

26 AO, R.G. 8, Box 11, David Thompson to the Hon. D. Daly, 17 Nov. 1845.

27 AO, Ms. 74, R8, Merritt Papers, pkg. 59, #40, List of Niagara magistrates, 1833.

28 NA, R.G. 5, B 28, vol. 3, C.A. Hagerman to provincial secretary, 4 June 1838.

29 AO, Ms. 74, R8, Merritt Papers, pkg. 60, #81, List of surviving justices of the peace compiled by Charles Richardson, Clerk of the Peace, 9 Nov. 1842.

30 Ibid. pkg. 59 & 60, J.W. Macaulay to Merritt, 4 July 1838; Andrew Thompson to Merritt, 4 Aug. 1838; William Ball to Merritt, Oct. 1842; R. Kilborne to Merritt, Oct. 1842; John Patterson to Merritt, 4 Oct. 1842; John Ball to Merritt, 6 Oct. 1842; T. Hixson to Merritt, 10 Oct. 1842. For Merritt's biography see *Dictionary of Canadian Biography*, 9: 544–8.

31 NA, R.G. 5 A1, Upper Canada Sundries, vol. 165, pp. 90262–65, Merritt to John Joseph, 22 Apr. 1836; Thompson, 'Local Authority and District Autonomy,' 66–7.

32 AO, R.G. 8, Box 11, William Hamilton Merritt to the Hon. D. Daly, 22 Dec. 1845.

33 Banks, 'Evolution of the Ontario Courts,' 510.

34 AO, R.G. 22, Series 372, 53–29, Judge E.C. Campbell to Charles Richardson, 29 Feb. 1844.

35 NA, R.G. 5, A1, Upper Canada Sundries, vol. 90, pp. 50160–1, Alex. McDonnell to Col. Hillier, 14 Oct. 1828; vol. 92, pp. 51119–22, L. Mitchell to Sir John Colborne, 11 Feb. 1829; vol. 92, pp. 51096–9, Richard Phillips Hotham to Z. Mudge, Feb. 1829.

36 Ibid. vol. 126, p. 69515, John Clark to Lt. Col. Rowan, 4 Feb. 1833.

37 Cited in 'Introduction,' Robert L. Fraser, ed. *Provincial Justice: Upper Canadian Legal Portraits from the Dictionary of Canadian Biography* (Toronto: Osgoode Society, 1992), xxxviii.

38 AO, Ms. 74, R8, Merritt Papers, pkg. 60, #79, John Ball to Merritt, 6 Oct. 1842.

39 NA, R.G. 8, Box 12, Charles Richardson to Daly, 5 Feb. 1846.

40 AO, Ms. 74, R8, Merritt Papers, pkg. 60, #80, Thos. Hixson to Merritt, 10 Oct. 1842.

41 Thompson, 'Local Authority and District Autonomy,' 66.

42 NA, R.G. 5, A1, Upper Canada Sundries, vol. 104, pp. 58881–2, Thos. Merritt, Geo. Adams and [?] Butler to John Beverley Robinson, 22 Nov. 1830.

43 Ibid., vol. 104, pp. 58880, J.B. Robinson to Z. Mudge, 14 Dec. 1830.

44 Norma Landau, *The Justices of the Peace, 1679–1760* (Berkeley and Los Angeles: University of California Press, 1984), 69.

45 Ibid., vol. 126, pp. 69511–13, Memorial of inhabitants of Grantham to Sir John Colborne, 15 Feb. 1831.

46 Wilson, *The Enterprises of Robert Hamilton*, 88–100, 191–2; *Dictionary of Canadian Biography*, 6: 3–6.

47 Sydney and Beatrice Webb, *The Parish and The County*, 384, note 2.

48 NA, R.G. 5, A1, Upper Canada Sundries, vol. 106, pp. 60004–6, Abraham Nelles to Chief Justice Robinson, 8 March 1831; vol. 90, p. 49885, Warner Nelles to Major Leonard, 23 Aug. 1828; vol. 96, p. 53713, Warner Nelles to Sir John Colborne, 3 Oct. 1829.

49 Thompson, 'Local Authority and District Autonomy,' 80.

50 E.A. Cruikshank, 'The Government of Upper Canada and Robert Gourlay,' *Ontario History*, 23 (1926), 65–179, Address of Magistrates, 28 Jan. 1819, 167–8; Address of Grand Jury, 28 Jan. 1819, 166–7.

51 NA, R.G. 5, A1, Upper Canada Sundries, vol. 95, p. 53208, William Mackenzie to Sir John Colborne, 11 Aug. 1829.
52 Ibid., vol. 106, pp. 60311–21, petition of Hugh Freel, James MacFarland, John Cox, and other freeholders of Niagara to Sir John Colborne, Jan. 1831.
53 *Spirit of the Times*, 26 June 1830, cited in Fraser, ed., *Provincial Justice: Upper Canadian Legal Portraits*, lxii–lxiii.
54 NA, R.G. 5, A1, Upper Canada Sundries, vol. 107, pp. 60850–1, petition of inhabitants of Haldimand County, 5 May 1831.
55 Ibid., vol. 107, pp. 61106–8, petition of Edward Evans, J.P. 9 June 1831.
56 Bruce Wilson, 'Privilege and Place: the Distribution of Office in the Niagara Peninsula during the Loyalist Period,' *Immigration and Settlement in the Niagara Peninsula*, ed. John Burtniak and Patricia G. Dirks (St Catharines: Brock University, 1981), 27–38; Wilson, *The Enterprises of Robert Hamilton*, 48–57.
57 Wilson, *The Enterprises of Robert Hamilton*, 51.
58 Ibid., 101.
59 E.A. Cruikshank, ed., *Records of Niagara, A Collection of Contemporary Letters and Documents, 1812* (Niagara: Niagara Historical Society #43, 1934), 18 and 56.
60 AO, Ms. 503, Robert Nelles Papers, Commission to Abraham Nelles and William Crooks, 1817.
61 NA, M.G. 24 E1, Merritt Papers, vol. 14, D. McDougal to W.H. Merritt, 1 March 1838.
62 NA, M.G. 24 I 26, Hamilton Papers, vol. 47, Charles Richardson to Niagara magistrates, 20 June 1832; Richardson to Hamilton, 20 June 1832.
63 NA, R.G. 5, A1, Upper Canada Sundries, vol. 118, p. 66125, minutes of the Special Session of the Niagara Court of Quarter Sessions, 25 June 1832.
64 Ibid., vol. 118, James Clarke to Lt. Col. Rowan, 24 July 1832.
65 Ibid., vol. 120, pp. 66750–4, James Clarke to Lt. Col. Rowan, 17 Aug. 1832, encl. D. Thompson to James Clarke, 9 Aug. 1832.
66 Ibid., vol. 121, pp. 67224–7, presentment of Niagara grand jury, 14 Sept. 1832.
67 W.C. Keele, *The Provincial Justice or Magistrate's Manual* ... (Toronto, 1835), 262.
68 AO, R.G. 22, Series, 372, 41–3, account of James Cummings, J.P., 11 July 1840.
69 Thompson, 'Local Authority and District Autonomy,' 72; R.G. 22, Series 372, 10–1, autopsy on Isaac Ducket, July 1831.
70 Jameson, *Winter Studies and Summer Rambles*, 58.

71 NA, M.G. 24 I 26, Hamilton Papers, vol. 44, King vs. Edward Walker, 26 Oct. 1829.

72 Ibid., Dwight Coft vs. Luther Dunn, 21 Nov. 1829.

73 AO, R.G. 22, Series 372, 10–27 & 10–42, David Thompson to Charles Richardson, 12 July 1831; King versus Thomas Foster, July 1831.

74 NA, R.G. 5, A1, Upper Canada Sundries, vol. 101, pp. 57282–4, J. Muirhead to Z. Mudge, 24 July 1830.

75 AO, R.G. 22, Series 372, 7–2, Boulton to Charles Richardson, 14 July 1830.

76 NA, R.G. 8, Box 6, Dr. John Mewburn to B. Higginson, 4 Oct. 1843.

77 J.A. Sharpe, *Crime in Early Modern England, 1550–1750* (London: Longman, 1984), 30–1.

78 NA, Pamphlet #1534, 'Proceedings of the Legislative Council of Upper Canada on the Bill sent up from the House of Assembly, entitled an Act to amend the Jury Laws of this Province' (Toronto, 1836), 26.

79 Lawrence M. Friedman, *Crime and Punishment in American History* (New York: Basic Books, 1993), 28.

80 *The Colonial Advocate*, 1 July 1824, cited in Barry Wright, 'Sedition in Upper Canada: Contested Legality,' *Labour/Le Travail* 29 (1992), 7–57 at 53, note 155.

81 Johnson, *Becoming Prominent*, 18–19.

82 Ibid., 81.

83 Thompson, 'Local Authority and District Autonomy,' 89.

84 Thomas Merritt's biography can be found in the *Dictionary of Canadian Biography*, 7:602–3. Surprisingly, the entry does not mention his dismissal as sheriff or the likely reasons for it.

85 NA, R.G. 5 A1, Upper Canada Sundries, vol. 96, pp. 54033–5, Thomas Otway Page to Major Hillier, 1 June 1820.

86 E.A. Cruikshank, 'The Government of Upper Canada and Robert Gourlay,' *Ontario History* 23 (1926), 65–179 at 175, Maitland to Bathurst, 19 Aug. 1818. For a biography of Maitland see D.B. Read, *The Lieutenant Governors of Upper Canada and Ontario, 1792–1899* (Toronto: William Briggs, 1900), 116–29.

87 Cruikshank, 'The Government of Upper Canada and Robert Gourlay,' 174–5, Maitland to Bathurst, 19 Aug. 1818. See also Wright, 'Sedition in Upper Canada: Contested Legality,' 7–57 and Wright, 'The Gourlay Affair: Seditious Libel and the Sedition Act in Upper Canada, 1818–19,' in F. Murray Greenwood and Barry Wright, *Canadian State Trials: Law, Politics, and Security Measures, 1608–1837* (Toronto: Osgoode Society, 1996), 487–504.

88 I am indebted to the *Dictionary of Canadian Biography* for providing the

information on Richard Leonard from the files of individuals who were
not included in the published volumes.

89 NA, R.G. 5 A1, Upper Canada Sundries, vol. 82, pp. 44810–12, Leonard
to Major Hillier, 28 Feb. 1827. See also vol. 83, pp. 45110–11, Leonard to
Major Hillier, 26 March 1827.

90 Ibid., vol. 83, pp. 45459–61, Leonard to Major Hillier, 26 Apr. 1827.

91 Ibid., vol. 97, p. 54319, Leonard to Chief Justice Robinson, 28 Nov. 1829.

92 Ibid., vol. 83, pp. 45455–8, James Kerby to Major Hillier, 25 Apr. 1827.

93 Ibid., vol. 97, pp. 54314–15, Leonard to Z. Mudge, 28 Nov. 1829.

94 *St. Catharines' Farmers' Journal*, 30 Sept. 1829.

95 NA, R.G. 5 A1, Upper Canada Sundries, vol. 96, pp. 53447–8, petition of
Niagara inhabitants to Lieut–Governor Colborne, 19 Sept. 1829.

96 Ibid., vol. 98, pp. 54960, 55031, 55067, Woodruff to Z. Mudge, with
enclosed petitions, 29 Jan. 1830.

97 *The Niagara Gleaner*, 26 Sept. 1829; Ann Alexandra McEwen, 'Crime in
the Niagara District, 1827–1850,' 82–3.

98 Wilson, *The Enterprises of Robert Hamilton*, 129.

99 *Dictionary of Canadian Biography*, 7:374–6. Biographical details can also be
found in Wilson, *The Enterprises of Robert Hamilton*, and in the Alexander
Hamilton Papers, NA.M.G 24 I 26, vol. 19.

100 NA, M.G . 24 I 26, vol. 46, George Markland to Hamilton, 15 Aug. 1833,
pvt.; Hamilton to Col. Rowan, 16 Aug. 1833.

101 Ibid., Markland to Hamilton, n.d. Aug. 1833.

102 *St. Catharines' Farmers' Journal*, 19 Nov. 1835, cited in Nelles, 'Loyalism
and Local Power, the District of Niagara,' 111.

103 H.C. Boultbee, ' "Willow Bank", the old Hamilton Homestead at
Queenston,' *Welland County Historical Society, Papers and Records*
(Welland, 1938), 5:11–17.

104 AO, R.G. 22, Series 372, 16–35, grand jury presentment, 25 March 1834.

105 NA, Pamphlet # 1982, *Alexander McLeod to the Honorable Sir Allan Napier
McNab, Knight, Speaker of the Legislative Assembly of Canada, 4 Jan. 1845.*

106 NA, M.G. 24 I 26, Hamilton Papers, vol. 46, William Riley to Hamilton,
21 Oct. 1834.

107 Ibid. vol. 67, #70 Hamilton to R.H. Broughton, Committee of Vigilance,
Lewiston, 1 Jan. 1838; #75, Robert Grant to Hamilton, 31 Dec. 1837.

108 Ibid., vol. 67, #219, John Stayner to Hamilton, 25 June 1838.

109 Ibid., vol. 67, # 2 K. Cameron to Hamilton, 18 Dec. 1837; # 4 Macaulay to
Hamilton, confidential, 27 Oct. 1838; # 122, Macaulay to Hamilton,
confidential, 20 June 1838.

110 Ibid., vol. 67, # 1, Macaulay to Hamilton, 1 Aug. 1838.

3 Servants of the Court

1 32 Geo. III (1792), c. 2, 'An Act to Establish Trials by Jury.'
2 34 Geo. III (1794), c. 1, 'An Act for the Regulation of Juries.'
3 NA, Pamphlets #1534, 'Proceedings of the Legislative Council of Upper Canada on the Bill sent up from the House of Assembly, entitled "An Act to Amend the Jury Laws of this Province"' (Toronto, 1836), 5.
4 Ibid., 6.
5 St Catharines Farmer's Journal, 13 Feb. 1828. For a biography of Lefferty, see Dictionary of Canadian Biography 7:496–7. William Lyon Mackenzie certainly did not agree with this method of jury selection. See his criticism in The Colonial Advocate, 1 July 1824, cited in Barry Wright, 'Sedition in Upper Canada: Contested Legality,' Labour/Le Travail 29 (1992), 53, note 155.
6 Ibid., 17–31.
7 NA, R.G. 1, E3, vol. 103, State Papers, Upper Canada, Memorandum on Grand Juries, 10 Oct. 1840.
8 The Niagara Gleaner, 27 Aug. 1825.
9 The phrase, 'Neighbour-Witness,' is used by John Marshall Mitnick in his article, 'From Neighbour-Witness to Judge of Proofs: The Transformation of the English Civil Juror,' American Journal of Legal History 32 (3) (July 1988), 201–35 at 201–2. The term itself derives from Sir John Fortescue's description of the English trial jury in the fifteenth century: 'The witnesses are neighbours, able to live of their own, sound in repute and fair-minded, not brought into court by either party, but chosen by a respectable and impartial officer, and compelled to come before the judge.' J. Fortescue, De Laudibus Legum Anglia, ed. S.B. Chrimes (Cambridge: Cambridge University Press, 1949), 63.
10 Richard D. Younger, The People's Panel: The Grand Jury in the United States, 1634–1941 (Providence: Brown University Press, 1963), 26.
11 Graeme Wynn, 'Ideology, Society and State in the Maritime Colonies,' in Allan Greer and Ian Radforth, eds., Colonial Leviathan: State Formation in Mid-Nineteenth Century Canada (Toronto: University of Toronto Press, 1992), 313; J.R. Pole, 'Reflections on American Law and the American Revolution,' William and Mary Quarterly, 3rd Series, 50 (1) (1993), 123–59 at 133.
12 J.M. Beattie, Crime and the Courts in England, 1660–1800 (Princeton: Princeton University Press, 1986), 320.
13 Norma Landau, The Justices of the Peace, 1679–1760 (Berkeley and Los Angeles: University of California Press, 1984), 50–4.

14 Sydney and Beatrice Webb, *English Local Government*, vol. 1, *The Parish and the County*, 446–56.
15 Alexis de Tocqueville, *Democracy in America* (New York: A. Knopf, 1994), 287.
16 NA, Pamphlets, #1308, 'Report from the Special Committee Appointed to enquire into the manner in which Juries in Criminal Matters have been drawn in Lower Canada, Quebec, 30 March 1830.'
17 AO, R.G. 22, Series 372, 2–37, list of names for grand and petit jurors, general quarter sessions, Niagara, 14 Oct. 1828.
18 AO, R.G. 22, Series 372, 32–4, A. Gordon to Alexander Hamilton, 11 June 1838.
19 NA, M.G. 24 I 26, Hamilton Papers, vol. 48, McLeod to Hamilton, 9 July 1836; Hamilton to McLeod, 24 Aug. 1836.
20 48 Geo. III (1808), c. 13, 'An Act for the better regulation of Special Juries.'
21 NA, M.G. 24 E1, Merritt Papers, vol. 9, Robert Jameson to W. Hamilton Merritt, 29 Aug. 1834.
22 J.C. Dent, *The Story of the Upper Canadian Rebellion* (Toronto: C.B. Robinson, 1885), 1:30–1 and 157n; Paul Romney, *Mr Attorney: The Attorney General for Ontario in Court, Cabinet, and Legislature, 1791–1899* (Toronto: Osgoode Society, 1986), 119–21.
23 AO, R.G. 22, Series 372, 33–14, orders to the sheriff, Dec. 1838.
24 Ibid. 33–15, precept, Dec. 1838.
25 49 Geo. III (1809), c. 6.
26 Ibid., 15–10, William Thorn to Niagara magistrates, 15 Oct. 1833. He was excused from jury service on the grounds of ill health.
27 Ibid., 41–11, filings, March, 1841.
28 Ibid., 45–29, James Cummings to Charles Richardson, 12 Apr. 1842.
29 Frances Ann Thompson, 'Local Authority and District Autonomy: The Niagara Magistracy and Constabulary' (PhD thesis, University of Ottawa, 1996), 42.
30 W.J. Blacklock, 'The Prosecution of Crime in Upper Canada' (MA paper, University of Toronto, 1987), 76.
31 NA, R.G. 5 A1, Upper Canada Sundries, vol. 121, pp. 67224–7, presentment of Niagara grand jury, 14 Sept. 1832.
32 AO, Series 372, 31–9, grand jury presentment, 14 March 1838.
33 For Romney's analysis of this case, see his 'From Constitutionalism to Legalism: Trial by Jury, Responsible Government, and the Rule of Law in the Canadian Political Culture,' *Law and History Review* 7 (1) (Spring 1989), 121–74 at 132–5, and Romney, *Mr Attorney*, 80–2. See also Frances Collins, *A Faithful Report of the Trial and Acquittal of Robert Randall, Esq., a Member of*

the House of Commons House of Assembly in Upper Canada, accused of Perjury, and tried at Niagara, on Wednesday the 7ᵗʰ of September, 1825 (York, 1825).

34 NA, R.G. 5, A1, Upper Canada Sundries, vol. 108, pp. 61059–60, W.H. Merritt to Col. Rowan, 14 Aug. 1833.

35 AO, Ms 74, R8, Merritt Papers, pkg. 59 #43, O.P. Phelps to Merritt, July 1833.

36 AO, R.G. 22, Series 372, 14–45, documents in the case of Thomas Gilleland, William Sanderson, Jacob Hamer et al. for riot and assault, July 1833. The grand jury presentment is found in NA, R.G. 5 A1, Upper Canada Sundries, vol. 131, pp. 72217–22, 13 July 1833. See also *Niagara Gleaner*, 17 July 1833, and the assessment of this case by Thompson in her doctoral thesis, 'Local Authority and District Autonomy,' 105–7. Whether this is simply an instance of the more Tory jurors of Niagara rejecting the complaints of the more pro-American Merritt, as she states, is open to debate.

37 NA, R.G. 5 A1, Upper Canada Sundries, vol. 108, pp. 61452–9, petition of grand and petit jurors, 16 July 1831; petition of William Forsyth Jr 18 July 1831; J. Muirhead to Edward McMahon, 21 July 1831.

38 AO, R.G. 22, Series 372, 10–11 and 10–26, documents in the case of William Forsyth Jr, July 1831.

39 Robert L. Fraser, 'William Forsyth,' *Dictionary of Canadian Biography*, 7:311–15.

40 Patricia Jasen, 'Romanticism, Modernity and the Evolution of Tourism on the Niagara Frontier, 1790–1850,' *Canadian Historical Review* 72 (3) (1991), 283–318 at 300–1; Romney, *Mr Attorney*, 115–21.

41 W.F.A. Boys, *A Practical Treatise on the Office and Duties of Coroners in Ontario*, 2nd ed. (Toronto: Stuart & Rawlinson, 1878), 109–52.

42 AO, R.G. 22, Series 372, 16–43, petition of freeholders of Thorold, Wainfleet, Pelham, and Crowland, 18 March 1834.

43 Ibid., 16–43, court order 26 March 1834.

44 Ibid., 17–6 and 17–8, W.H. Merritt to Charles Richardson, 2 Apr. 1834, court order 15 Apr. 1834.

45 Ibid., 3–7, petition of 24 Pelham residents, 10 Jan. 1829.

46 Ibid., 12–4, Charles Richardson to Edward McMahon, 9 Feb. 1832, enclosing grand jury presentment, Feb. 1832.

47 Ibid., 4–6, grand jury presentment, 18 July 1828.

48 Ibid., 12–7, grand jury presentment, 28 March 1832.

49 Ibid., 34–6, grand jury presentment, 16 March 1839; Oliver, '*Terror to Evil-Doers,*' 63.

50 Ibid., 60–2, Queen vs. Solomon Darney, assault and battery, Nov. 1845.

51 For accounts of the decline of the jury trial in Canada, see Graham Parker, 'Trial by Jury in Canada,' *Journal of Legal History* 8 (1987), 178–89 and Paul Romney, 'From Constitutionalism to Legalism: Trial by Jury, Responsible Government, and the Rule of Law in the Canadian Political Culture,' *Law and History Review* 7 (1989), 120–74.

52 W.C. Keele, *A Brief View of the Township Laws up to the Present Time: with a treatise on the law and office of Constable, the law relative to landlord and tenant, distress for rent, innkeepers, etc.* (Toronto, 1835), 15–22.

53 AO, R.G. 22, Series 372, 42–2, Account of Martin Kearns, Niagara constable, 8 June 1841.

54 Delloyd J. Guth, 'The Traditional Common-Law Constable, 1235–1829: From Bracton to the Fieldings to Canada,' in R.C. Macleod and David Schneiderman, eds., *Police Powers in Canada: The Evolution and Practice of Authority* (Toronto: University of Toronto Press, 1994), 3–23.

55 AO, Pamphlets, 'The Canadian Constables' Assistant: being the substance of a charge to the grand jury of the county of Simcoe, at the April sessions, 1852,' by Judge Gowan, with notes and additions by James Palton, Esq. (Barrie, 1852), 3.

56 Thompson, 'Local Authority and District Autonomy,' 143. Her two chapters on constables in the Niagara district, 135–205, are the most comprehensive examination to be found of this office in early Canadian history.

57 Ibid., 155–70.

58 Ibid., 170.

59 AO, R.G. 22, Series 372, 17–3, appointment of constables, court of quarter sessions, Apr. 1834.

60 Ibid., 12–3, Samuel Birdsall to Charles Richardson, 2 Jan. 1832.

61 Blacklock, 'The Prosecution of Crime in Upper Canada,' 43.

62 AO, R.G. 22, Series 372, 52–9, declaration of Hiram Page, 15 Apr. 1844.

63 Ibid., 49–2, James Perkins to Charles Richardson, 6 May 1843.

64 Thompson, 'Local Authority and District Autonomy,' 190.

65 Ibid., 71–1, account of Andrew Drew, Jan. 1850.

66 Ibid., 51–2, #6, W. Bonnalick to Charles Richardson, 3 May 1844.

67 Ibid., 45–9, account of David Davis, Apr. 1842.

68 Ibid., 36–4, account of Solomon Soper, Dec. 1839.

69 NA, M.G. 24 I 26, vol. 48, Alexander Hamilton papers, McLeod to Hamilton, 14 Sept. 1838.

70 AO, R.G. 22, Series 372, 43–3, James Cummings to D. McDougal, 13 Sept. 1841.

71 Ibid., 26–1, John Page to Niagara magistrates, 10 Oct. 1836.

72 Ibid., 34–6, Major Richard Webb to Charles Richardson, 25 May 1839; James Black to Charles Richardson, 5 June 1839.

73 Ibid., 11–9, petition of thirteen Niagara constables, Oct. 1831.

74 Blacklock, 'The Prosecution of Crime in Upper Canada,' 46.

75 Ernest Green, 'Upper Canada's Black Defenders,' *Ontario History* 27 (1931), 365–91 at 387.

76 *Niagara Chronicle*, 10 Apr. 1844; Ann Alexandra McEwen, 'Crime in the Niagara District, 1827–1850' (MA thesis, University of Guelph, 1991), 55–6 and 111–12.

77 AO, R.G. 22, Series 372, 51–31, grand jury presentment, 4 Jan. 1844.

78 Lieut. Col. Elliott to Assistant Quarter Master General, 13 July 1844, cited in Ernest Green, 'The Fearful Forties in Welland County,' *Welland County Historical Society, Papers and Records* (Welland, 1938), 168–70.

79 Ruth Bleasdale, 'Class Conflict on the Canals of Upper Canada in the 1840s,' *Labour/Le Travailleur* 7 (1981), 9–39 at 39.

80 Blacklock, 'The Prosecution of Crime in Upper Canada,' 49.

81 AO, R.G. 22, Series 372, 16–55, King vs Barney Woolman, March 1834.

82 Ann McEwen, 'Crime in the Niagara District, 1827–1850,' 111.

83 AO, R.G. 22, Series 372, 39–15, Queen vs Samuel Cramer, Sept. 1840.

84 Ibid., 25–7, summary convictions of John Mewburn, Stamford, Oct. 1836.

85 Ibid., 25–1, account of Donald McDonald, 10 Oct. 1836.

86 Thompson, 'Local Authority and District Autonomy,' 192–5.

87 Ibid., 197.

88 AO, R.G. 22, Series 372, 10–15, King vs John Stewart, July 1831; Thompson, 'Local Authority and District Autonomy,' 196–7.

89 AO, R.G. 22, Series 372, 22–1, statement of Jacob Keefer, 6 Jan. 1836.

90 For a comparison with England, see David Philips and Robert D. Storch, *Policing Provincial England, 1829–1856: The Politics of Reform* (London and New York: Leicester University Press, 1999), 11–35.

91 AO, Pamphlets, 'The Canadian Constable's Assistant,' by Judge Gowan (Barrie, 1852), 3.

PART TWO

1 W.C. Keele, *The Provincial Justice or Magistrate's Manual* (Toronto: Upper Canada Gazette Office, 1835), 81–2.

2 David Flaherty, 'Law and the Enforcement of Morals in Early America,' *Perspectives in American History*, V (Cambridge, Mass: Charles Warren Center for Studies in American History, Harvard, 1971), 206.

3 Ibid, 245.
4 Carolyn Strange and Tina Loo, *Making Good: Law and Moral Regulation in Canada, 1867–1939* (Toronto: University of Toronto Press, 1997), 4.
5 J.M. Beattie, *Attitudes Towards Crime and Punishment in Upper Canada, 1830–1850: A Documentary Study* (Toronto: Centre of Criminology, University of Toronto, 1977), 2–3.

4 Enforcing a Christian Moral Order

1 AO, R.G. 22, 16–17, deposition of Bartholomew Tench, 26 Nov. 1833.
2 Ibid. See also Frances Ann Thompson, 'Local Authority and District Autonomy: The Niagara Magistracy and Constabulary' (PhD thesis, University of Ottawa, 1996), 53–4.
3 Susan Lewthwaite, 'Violence, Law and Community in Rural Upper Canada,' in Jim Phillips, Tina Loo, and Susan Lewthwaite, eds., *Crime and Criminal Justice: Essays in the History of Canadian Law*, vol. 5, *Crime and Criminal Justice* (Toronto: Osgoode Society, 1994), 353–86.
4 NA, R.G. 5, B28, Pardon for George Carmichael, 2 July 1839 for shooting to kill at Bartholomew Tench.
5 'A Proclamation for the Encouragement of Piety and Virtue, and for the preventing and punishing of Vice; Profaneness, and Immorality,' *Upper Canada Gazette*, 23 Sept. 1830. I have been unable to find a similar Proclamation issued at the beginning of Victoria's reign but, in any case, the inhabitants of Upper Canada had other things to preoccupy them in late 1837.
6 Ibid.
7 Instructions to Governor Murray, 7 Dec. 1763, *Documents relating to the Constitutional History of Canada, 1759–1791*, selected and edited by Adam Shortt and Arthur G. Doughty, Part 1 (Ottawa: King's Printer, 1918), 192–3. Similar paragraphs can be found in the instructions to subsequent governors general.
8 Leon Radzinowicz, *A History of English Criminal Law and its Administration from 1750*, vol. 3 (London: Stevens & Sons, 1956), 150.
9 Ibid., 170.
10 AO, Robinson Papers, Charge to Grand Jury, Cornwall, 15 Aug. 1831.
11 In the debate over whether to build a penitentiary in Kingston, the most articulate opponent, James Buchanan, the British consul at New York, advocated in 1833 the particular need to strengthen Sunday schools to educate youth 'in a regard for the Lord's Day.' Maintaining the sabbath for Buchanan was a key to preventing crime. For a good discussion of

Buchanan's views, see Russell Smandych, 'Tory Paternalism and the
Politics of Penal Reform in Upper Canada, 1830–34: A "Neo–revisionist"
Account of the Kingston Penitentiary,' *Criminal Justice History* 12 (1991),
57–83 at 74–6.

12 John Strachan, *A Discourse on the Character of King George the Third.
Addressed to the Inhabitants of British North America* (Montreal: Nahum
Mower, 1810), 9.

13 Robert Fraser, *Provincial Justice: Upper Canadian Legal Portraits from the
Dictionary of Canadian Biography* (Toronto: Osgoode Society, 1992), xxxiii.

14 G. Blaine Baker, 'So Elegant a Web: Providential Order and the Rule of
Secular Law in Early Nineteenth Century Upper Canada,' *University of
Toronto Law Journal* 38 (2) (Spring 1988), 184–205 at 188–9. See also David
Howes, 'Property, God and Nature in the Thought of Sir John Beverley
Robinson,' *McGill Law Journal* 30 (3) (1985), 365–413; Patrick Brode, *Sir
John Beverley Robinson: Bone and Sinew of the Compact* (Toronto: Osgoode
Society, 1984); Terry Cook, 'John Beverley Robinson and the Conservative
Blueprint for the Upper Canadian Community,' *Ontario History* 64 (June
1972), 79–94. William Westfall expresses a similar view in his *Two Worlds:
The Protestant Culture of Nineteenth Century Ontario* (Montreal and
Kingston: McGill-Queen's University Press, 1989), 34, when he says that
for Strachan, 'Christianity ... was the cornerstone of social order.' See also
J.M. Beattie's comment in his introduction to *Attitudes Towards Crime and
Punishment in Upper Canada, 1830–1850: A Documentary Study* (Toronto:
Centre of Criminology, 1977), 2; 'Moral order was the indispensable
foundation and guarantor of a stable society ...'

15 John Howison, *Sketches of Upper Canada* ... (Edinburgh, 1821; facsimile ed.,
Toronto: Coles, 1970), 142–3.

16 The Rev. J. Mason to Dr Lee, 5 Feb. 1835, quoted in Peter Russell, 'Church
of Scotland Clergy in Upper Canada: Culture Shock and Conservatism on
the Frontier,' *Ontario History* 73 (2) (June 1981), 88–111 at 99.

17 John Weaver, *Crimes, Constables and Courts: Order and Transgression in a
Canadian City, 1816–1970* (Montreal and Kingston: McGill-Queen's
University Press, 1995), 46–7. For an earlier study focusing on Toronto see
J.R. Burnet, 'The Urban Community and Changing Moral Standards,' in
Michiel Horn and Ronald Sabourin, eds., *Studies in Canadian Social History*
(Toronto: McClelland and Stewart Ltd., 1974), 298–325.

18 Anna Brownell Jameson, *Winter Studies and Summer Rambles in Canada*
(Ottawa: New Canadian Library, 1990), 39–40.

19 AO, R.G. 22, Series 372, 11–44, Rules and Regulations for Inn-Keepers,
5 Jan. 1832.

20 John N. Jackson, *St Catharines, Ontario: Its Early Years* (Belleville, Ont.: Mika Publishing Co., 1976), 210.
21 AO, R.G. 22, Series 372, 15–10, deposition of Lavinia Ferguson, 22 Oct. 1833.
22 *Canada Museum und Allegemeine Zeitung,* 17 Aug. 1837. On Peterson, see also A.E. Bylek, 'Henry William Peterson,' *Waterloo Historical Society* (1931), 250–6.
23 Ann Alexandra McEwen, 'Crime in the Niagara District, 1827–1850' (MA thesis, University of Guelph, 1991), 125.
24 4 Wm. IV c. 4 (1834), An Act to Provide for the Summary Punishment of Petty Trespass and Other Offences.
25 AO, R.G. 22, Series 372, 17–7, Summary Convictions, Thorold, June 1835.
26 Ibid., Series 372, 21–9, Summary Convictions, Thorold, Oct. 1835; 21–12, Summary Convictions, Pelham, Oct. 1835; 21–13, Summary Convictions, Wainfleet, Oct. 1835.
27 Ibid., Series 372, 22–7, Summary convictions, Stamford, Jan. 1836.
28 Ibid., Series 372, 58–16, Summary convictions, Jacob Misener, Wainfleet, July 1845.
29 Ibid., Series 372, 38–9, Summary convictions, Niagara, June 1840.
30 Ibid., Series 372, 18–23, Summary convictions, Stamford, Jan. 1835.
31 Ibid., Series 372, 18–26, Petition to Justices of the Peace in Special Session, 26 Dec. 1834; Edward Kiseley to Charles Richardson, 1 Jan. 1835.
32 Ibid., Series 372, 42–11, Information filed by John Willims before A. Bradshaw and C. Willson, 16 Apr. 1841.
33 Ibid., Series 372, 33–9, Summary convictions, Stamford, Dec. 1838.
34 Ibid., Series 372, 30–13, Summary convictions, Stamford, Nov. 1837.
35 Ibid., Series 372, 26–23, Deposition of Cortland Secord, Thomas Heenan, and Samuel Thorold, 5 Dec. 1836.
36 Ibid., Series 372, 45–12, Conviction of Silas Fowler, Luther Russel, George Enas, and William Stoneman on complaint of Joseph Thompson, St Catharines, 1842.
37 Ibid., Series 372, 59–30, Conviction of Edward Weekly on the prosecution by Edward Taylor, St Catharines, 1845.
38 *Dictionary of Canadian Biography,* 7:497.
39 8 Vict. c. 45 (1845).
40 26 Geo. III (New Brunswick) c. 5 (1786), 'An Act against the Profanation of the Lord's Day commonly called Sunday and for the Suppression of Immorality.'
41 1 Will. IV (New Brunswick) c. 38 (1831).
42 45 Geo. III (Lower Canada) c. 10 (1805); 57 Geo. III, c. 3 (1817); Fyson, 'Criminal Justice, Civil Society, and the Local State,' 444–6.

43 William Westfall, *Two Worlds: The Protestant Culture of Nineteenth Century Ontario*, 6. For an account of the temperance crusades in Canada West see Jan Noel, *Canada Dry: Temperance Crusades before Confederation* (Toronto: University of Toronto Press, 1995), 101–39.

44 Elizabeth Gibbs, ed., *Debates of the Legislative Assembly of United Canada*, vol. IV, Part II, 1844–45, 2025–8.

45 Peter Oliver, 'A Terror to Evil-Doers: The Central Prison and the "Criminal Class" in Late Nineteenth Century Ontario,' in R. Hall et al., eds., *Patterns of the Past: Interpreting Ontario's History* (Toronto: Dundurn Press, 1988), 210.

46 Allan Greer and Ian Radforth, eds., *Colonial Leviathan: State Formation in Mid-Nineteenth Century Canada* (Toronto: University of Toronto Press, 1992).

47 AO, R.G. 22, Series 372, 55–36, Schedule of Convictions, Niagara district, Nov. 1844. John Weaver remarks on the increase of committals for moral offences in the Gore district during the period 1843–51 from 12 per cent of committals prior to 1843 to 35 per cent in the following eight years. See his *Crimes, Constables and Courts*, 46–7. The Niagara district had an increase in convictions but not as dramatic as that found in the neighbouring Gore district. A study of sabbath breaking in Scotland suggests that cases there were in decline by the late eighteenth century. Leah Leneman, '"Prophaning" the Lord's Day: Sabbath Breach in Early Modern Scotland,' *History* 74 (June 1989), 217–31.

48 Ibid., Series 372, Summary convictions, Jacob Misener, Wainfleet, April 1844.

49 Ibid., Series 372, 59–13, Summary convictions, Owen Fares, Humberstone, Nov. 1845.

50 Ibid., Series 372, 58–15, Summary convictions, R.M. Long, Humberstone, July 1845.

51 Ibid., Series 372, 57–29, 58–31, 62–38, Schedules of Summary Convictions, Niagara District, April 1845; July 1845; April 1846.

52 *The Niagara Chronicle*, 30 Nov. 1848, Schedules of Summary Convictions, Niagara District, Nov. 1848.

53 AO, R.G. 22, Series 372, 64–31, Summary convictions, Owen Phelps, St Catharines, Nov. 1846.

54 Ibid., Series 372, 64–21, Summary convictions, Jacob Misener, Wainfleet, Nov. 1846.

55 Ibid., Series 372, 77–5, Summary convictions, Leonard Misener, Wainfleet, Jan. 1850.

56 Ibid., Series 372, 64–16, Summary convictions, Robert Hobson, Thorold, Nov. 1846.
57 Nicholas Rogers, 'Serving Toronto the Good: The Development of the City Police Force 1834–84,' in V.L. Russell, ed., *Forging the Consensus, Historical Essays on Toronto* (Toronto: University of Toronto Press, 1985), 133. See also Weaver, *Crimes, Constables and Courts,* 49–50.
58 AO, R.G. 22, Series 372, 61–33, Petition of Bertie inhabitants, 4 Dec. 1845.

5 Intruders Upon the Precincts of Crime

1 AO, Ms. 44, Robinson Papers, 'Draft of Address by John Beverley Robinson at the Laying of the Foundation Stone of the Asylum for the Insane, Toronto, 22 August 1846.' See also Russell Smandych, 'The Upper Canadian Experience with Pre-Segregative Control' (PhD thesis, University of Toronto, 1989), 266–7.
2 Parts of this chapter and the next have previously appeared in earlier versions under the title, 'The Cold Hand of Charity: The Court of Quarter Sessions and Poor Relief in the Niagara District, 1828–1841,' in W. Wesley Pue and Barry Wright, eds., *Canadian Perspectives on Law & Society: Issues in Legal History* (Ottawa: Carleton Library Series #152, 1988), 179–206.
3 Peter Oliver, *'Terror to Evil-Doers': Prisons and Punishments in Nineteenth-Century Ontario* (Toronto: Osgoode Society, 1998), 46.
4 AO *Supreme Court of Ontario Judges Bench Books, J.B. Robinson, Assizes 1831–34,* R.G. 22, Series 390, September (1832) Box 21, File 3, The King vs Patrick Donnelly. The subsequent references to Robinson's bench book in this case all come from this file.
5 Roger Smith, *Trial by Medicine: Insanity and Responsibility in Victorian Trials* (Edinburgh: Edinburgh University Press, 1981), 20.
6 Joel Eigen, *Witnessing Insanity: Madness and Mad-Doctors in the English Court* (New Haven and London: Yale University Press, 1995), 3.
7 Smith, *Trial by Medicine,* 56–66.
8 Anna Brownell Jameson, *Winter Studies and Summer Rambles in Canada* (Ottawa: New Canadian Library, 1990), 198.
9 NA, R.G. 5, A1, Upper Canada Sundries, vol. 146, 79898, J.B. Robinson, n.d. 1834.
10 Ibid. 79896–7, Niagara grand jury presentment, 27 Oct. 1834; Oliver, *'Terror to Evil-Doers,'* 46.
11 NA, R.G. 5, A1, Upper Canada Sundries, vol. 146, 79898, J.B. Robinson, n.d. 1834.

12 AO, R.G. 22, Series 372, 19–18, court order, 25 March 1835.

13 NA, M.G. 24 I 26, vol 46, Gaol Returns, 1834–38, note by Alexander Hamilton, 27 Nov. 1834.

14 Ibid., note by Alexander McLeod, 1 Jan. 1836.

15 Oliver, 'Terror to Evil-Doers,' 47.

16 Ibid.

17 AO, R.G. 22, Series 372, 30–20, jail orders, 7 Nov. 1837.

18 Ibid. 31–9, Presentment of Niagara grand jury on need for a Provincial Asylum, 14 March 1838.

19 Ibid., 34–6, Niagara grand jury presentment, 16 March 1839.

20 2 Vict. c. 2 (1839).

21 AO, R.G. 22, Series 372, 41–24, jail records, report of Henry Rolls, 23 March 1841.

22 Ibid., 24–12, report of Dr F.W. Porter, 12 July 1836.

23 Ibid., 24–15, grand jury recommendation and magistrates' order, 15 July 1836.

24 Ibid., 23–15, petition of inhabitants of Walpole Township, 9 Apr. 1836; grand jury presentment, 12 Apr. 1836; 23–14, court order, 14 Apr. 1836; 24–1, account of Joseph Evans, 16 May 1836.

25 Edith Firth, The Town of York, 1793–1815 (Toronto: Champlain Society, 1962), note 38, 233–4 and 281–2. See also T.E. Brown, 'Living with God's Afflicted: A History of the Provincial Lunatic Asylum at Toronto' (PhD thesis, Queen's University, 1980), 43–4.

26 NA, R.G. 5 A1, Upper Canada Sundries, vol. 110, 62687–9, Annual report of York Hospital, 28 Nov. 1831.

27 Ibid., vol. 107, 60767–9, memorandum by lieutenant governor Colborne, May 1831.

28 Ibid., vol. 107, 60764–6, Clerk of the Peace, York District, to Z. Mudge, 12 May 1831.

29 Journals of the Legislative Assembly, Upper Canada, 12 Parl., 2nd Session 1836, Appendix 44, 'Petition of Assize Grand Jury for Niagara, 8 Sept. 1835.'

30 C. J. Taylor, 'The Kingston Ontario Penitentiary and Moral Architecture,' Histoire sociale/Social History 12 (24) (Nov. 1979), 385–408 at 405–6.

31 Paul Romney, Mr Attorney: The Attorney General for Ontario in Court, Cabinet and Legislature, 1791–1899 (Toronto: University of Toronto Press, 1986), 105, 155.

32 Journals of the Legislative Assembly, 2nd Session, 1838, Appendix 30, note 57.

33 7 Wm. IV, c. 29. See also T.E. Brown, 'Living with God's Afflicted,' note
57, 75.

34 Jameson, *Winter Studies and Summer Rambles*, 99–100.

35 AO, Ms. 180, Aggregate Census Returns, Upper Canada, 1824–1850.

36 AO, R.G. 22, Series 372, 31–9, grand jury presentment, 14 March 1838.

37 Ibid.

38 Ibid., 33–12, James Nicholls to Charles Richardson, 3 Oct. 1838; grand jury
presentment, 12 Dec. 1838.

39 2 Vict. c. 2 (1839).

40 D. Francis, 'The Development of the Lunatic Asylum in the Maritime
Provinces,' *Acadiensis* 6 (2) (1977), 23–38.

41 AO, Ms. 44, Robinson Papers, 'Draft of Address at the Laying of the
Foundation Stone of the Asylum for the Insane, 22 August 1846.'

42 David Howes, 'Property, God and Nature in the Thought of Sir John
Beverley Robinson,' *McGill Law Journal* 30 (3) (1985), 365–414 at 393.

43 Oliver, *'Terror to Evil-Doers,'* 47–8.

44 James E. Moran, 'Insanity, the Asylum and Society in Nineteenth-Century
Quebec and Ontario' (PhD thesis, York University, 1998), 317.

6 The Cold Hand of Charity

1 Susannah Moodie, *Roughing it in the Bush* (Toronto: McClelland and
Stewart, 1923), 226.

2 Brereton Greenhouse, 'Paupers and Poorhouses: The Development of
Poor Relief in Early New Brunswick,' *Histoire Sociale-Social History* 1
(April 1968), 103–26; James M. Whalen, 'Social Welfare in New
Brunswick, 1784–1900,' *Acadiensis* 2 (1) (Autumn 1972), 54–64; 'The
Nineteenth Century Almshouse System in Saint John County,' *Histoire
Sociale-Social History* 7 (April 1971), 5–27.

3 Richard Splane, *Social Welfare in Ontario, 1791–1893* (Toronto: University
of Toronto Press, 1965), 65–7; Stephen Speisman, 'Munificent Parsons and
Municipal Parsimony: Voluntary vs. Public Poor Relief in Nineteenth
Century Toronto,' *Ontario History* 65 (March 1973), 33–49 at 33–4.

4 Russell C. Smandych, 'Upper Canadian Considerations about Rejecting
the English Poor Law, 1817–1837: A Comparative Study of the Reception
of Law,' *University of Manitoba, Canadian Legal History Project* (1991), 1–59;
J.C. Levy, 'The Poor Laws in Early Upper Canada,' in D.J. Bercuson and
L. Knafla, eds., *Law and Society in Canada in Historical Perspective* (Calgary:
University of Calgary Studies in History, no. 2, 1979), 23–44.

5 Edmund Burke, 'Thoughts and Details on Scarcity originally presented to the Right Hon. William Pitt in the month of November, 1795, *Works*, vol. 6, (Oxford: Oxford University Press, 1907), 5. See also J.R. Poynter, *Society and Pauperism, English Ideas on Poor Relief, 1795–1834* (Toronto: University of Toronto Press, 1969) and Rainer Baehre, 'Paupers and Poor Relief in Upper Canada,' *Historical Papers* (1981), 57–80 at 57–9.

6 Splane, *Social Welfare in Ontario*, 67.

7 Speisman, 'Munificent Parsons and Municipal Parsimony,' 33.

8 Robert Gourlay, *Statistical Account of Upper Canada* reprint ed. (New York: Johnson Reprint Corporation, 1966), Intro., 7.

9 Rainer Baehre, 'Pauper Emigration to Upper Canada in the 1830's,' *Histoire Sociale-Social History* 14 (Nov. 1981), 339–67 at 340–2.

10 Margaret Angus, 'Health, Emigration and Welfare in Kingston, 1820–1840,' in Donald Swainson, ed., *Oliver Mowat's Ontario* (Toronto: MacMillan, 1972), 120–35 at 125.

11 Baehre, 'Paupers and Poor Relief in Upper Canada,' 57. One study of the poor in Kingston can be found in Patricia E. Malcolmson, 'The Poor in Kingston, 1815–1850,' in Gerald Tulchinsky, ed., *To Preserve and Defend: Essays on Kingston in the Nineteenth Century* (Montreal and Kingston: McGill-Queen's University Press, 1976), 281–97.

12 Ibid., 57–80.

13 AO, R.G. 22, Series 372, 1–13, Pauper List, April Sessions, 1828.

14 Ibid., 1–13, Pauper List, 12 July 1828.

15 Ibid., 1–13, R.D. Cockcroft to Niagara magistrates, 8 Apr. 1828.

16 Ibid., 2–34, Court order, 18 Apr. 1829.

17 Ibid., 1–13, Petition of Christopher Burt, 28 March 1828.

18 Ibid., 1–13, Petition of Mary Palmer, 7 Apr. 1828.

19 Ibid., 1–13, F.D. Converse and C. Beadle to Niagara magistrates, 5 Apr. 1828.

20 Ibid., 33–14, Petition of debtors, 11 Dec. 1838.

21 Ibid., 1–13, grand jury presentment, 14 Jan. 1828.

22 Ibid.

23 Ibid., 4–7, John Stevenson to Dr James Muirhead, 8 June 1829.

24 Ibid., 4–7, petition from George Russell, July 1829.

25 Ibid., 4–7, petition of Thomas Creen, 12 Oct. 1829; Sarah Ross to Niagara magistrates, 15 July 1829.

26 See above, 48–51.

27 AO, R.G. 22, Series 372, 3–5, grand jury presentment, Jan. 1829. In the period from April 1829 to April 1830, the Niagara district paid out just over £233 to twenty-four paupers.

28 Ibid., 3–8, court order, 16 Jan. 1829.

29 Ibid., 3–6, petition of Margaret Cantril, 15 Jan. 1829.

30 Ibid., 3–38, grand jury presentment, 16 Apr. 1829.

31 Reprinted in the *Farmer's Journal and Welland Canal Intelligencer*, 17 Sept. 1828.

32 AO, Ms 503, A2, Abraham Nelles Papers, Circular, 30 Jan. 1827.

33 Ibid., Abraham Nelles Papers, D1, Notice, 18 Sept. 1826; *Farmer's Journal and Welland Canal Intelligencer*, 4 Oct. 1826. For an example of another private subscription, mounted by Susannah Moodie and her husband, see AO, Ms. 74, Reel 8, #5, Merritt Papers, package 58.

34 Ibid., Abraham Nelles Papers, D1, Loyal Canadian Society, 8 May 1844.

35 Janet Carnochan, *History of Niagara (in Part)*, 277–8.

36 Edith Firth, *The Town of York, 1793–1815* (Toronto: Champlain Society, 1962), 98.

37 Richard Simmons, *From Asylum to Welfare* (Downsview, Ont.: National Institute on Mental Retardation, 1982), 7.

38 II Geo. IV c. 1 (1830).

39 AO, R.G. 22, Series 372, 4–40, Robert Addison to Niagara magistrates, Oct. 1829; For biographical information on Addison, see *Dictionary of Canadian Biography*, 6: 3–6; A.H. Young, 'The Rev. Robert Addison and St. Mark's Church,' *Ontario Historical Society, Papers and Records* 19 (1922), 158–91 and Rev. C.E. Smith, 'Rev. Robt. Addison, M.A.'; *Niagara Historical Society Transactions*, no. 35 (1923), 61–71.

40 Ibid., 8–5, Thomas Creen to Niagara magistrates, 12 July 1830.

41 Ibid., 11–1, Account of George Adams, 20 Oct. 1831.

42 Ibid., 8–32, grand jury presentment, 28 Jan. 1831.

43 Ibid., 11–6, grand jury presentment, 22 Oct. 1831.

44 Ibid., 11–41, petition of John and Deborah Bean, Jan. 1832.

45 Ibid., 11–39, grand jury presentment, 28 Jan. 1832.

46 Ibid., 1–13, petition of Mary Risinbarrick, 7 Apr. 1828.

47 Ibid., 4–40, petition of Mary Risinbarrick, 12 Oct. 1829.

48 Ibid., 8–5, petition of David Thompson, 27 Jan. 1831.

49 Ibid., 12–1, petition of David Bonesteel, 27 March 1832.

50 Ibid.

51 Ibid., 12–1, petition of David Bonesteel, 21 March 1833.

52 Ibid., 16–35, petition of David Bonesteel, 22 March 1834; grand jury presentment, 26 March 1834.

53 Ibid., 19–16, petition of David Robins, 20 March 1835; grand jury presentment, 25 March 1835.

54 Ibid., 22–2, petition of David Robins, 17 Jan. 1836; grand jury presentment, Jan. 1836.

55 II Geo. IV c. 20 (1830) and 3 Wm. IV c. 46 (1833). The statutory authority was extended for a further four years in 1837 by 7 Wm. IV c. 29 (1837).

56 AO, R.G. 22, Series 372, 17–21, attorney general Boulton to Charles Richardson, clerk of the peace, 3 Apr. 1833; Ibid., 17–24, grand jury presentment, 9 July 1834.

57 Ibid., 24–11, Petition of Isabella Evans, 12 July 1836.

58 Ibid., 24–11, grand jury presentment, 14 July 1836.

59 Ibid., 24–11, Petition of Leonard Heaslip and Stephen Roy, 11 July 1836.

60 Ibid., 29–14, grand jury presentment, 14 July 1837.

61 Ibid., 30–19, grand jury presentment, 8 Nov. 1837.

62 Ibid., 33–12, grand jury presentment, 12 Dec. 1838.

63 Ibid., 39–19, Petition of George Martin, 10 Sept. 1839. See also 57–1, account of E. King, 20 Feb. 1845.

64 Ibid., 15–13, Petition of Dwight Smith, 24 March 1833.

65 Ibid.

66 Ibid., 20–14, Petition of Thomas Angleman, 29 Jan. 1835; grand jury presentment, 17 July 1835.

67 Ibid., 21–4, Petition of Dr J.B. Matthews, 12 Oct. 1835.

68 Ibid., 25–17, Petition of Isaac Culp, 3 Oct.1835.

69 Ibid., 41–13, Petition of Nathan Beach and Jacob Stoner, 15 Feb. 1841.

70 Ibid., 42–4, John Sweet to chairman, quarter sessions magistrates, 19 Dec. 1840.

71 Ibid., 38–17, J. Black to Charles Richardson, 4 May 1840, with enclosure, Messrs. Tench, Slater, Sheehan, and Black to Elijah Day, 2 Sept. 1837; Richardson to Black, 8 May 1840.

72 Ibid., 33–12, grand jury presentment, 12 Dec. 1838.

73 Ibid., 33–12, grand jury presentment, 13 Dec. 1838.

74 Ibid., 33–14, court order, 13 Dec. 1838.

75 Ibid., 44–31, grand jury presentment, 14 Jan. 1842.

76 7 Wm. IV c. 24 (1837).

77 On the background to the House of Industry Act, see Baehre, 'Paupers and Poor Relief in Upper Canada,' Historical Papers, 1981, 73–6; J.H. Aitchison, 'The Development of Local Government in Upper Canada, 1783–1850' (PhD thesis, University of Toronto, 1953), 649–60; Splane, Social Welfare in Ontario, 70–2.

78 Judith Finguard, 'The Winter's Tale: The Seasonal Contours of Pre-Industrial Poverty in British America, 1815–1860,' Historical Papers, 1974, 83.

79 AO, R.G. 22, Series 372, 27–19, grand jury presentment,14 Apr. 1837.

80 Ibid., 39–19, grand jury presentment, 8 Nov. 1837.

81 Ibid., 30–19, court order, Nov. 1837.

82 See, for example, *The Brockville Recorder*, 23 Nov. 1837.
83 AO, R.G. 22, Series 372, 32–7, grand jury presentment, 13 June 1838; 36–15, grand jury presentment, 12 Dec. 1839.
84 Ibid., 40–14, grand jury presentment, 8 Dec. 1840.
85 Finguard, 'The Winter's Tale,' 82.
86 AO, R.G. 22, Series 372, 44–31, grand jury presentment, 14 Jan. 1842.
87 Ibid., 44–31, grand jury presentment, 14 Jan. 1842; 44–8, grand jury presentment, 12 Oct. 1841.
88 Ibid., 44–33, court order, 15 Jan. 1842.
89 Ibid., 45–33, grand jury presentment, 14 Apr. 1842.
90 Ibid., 44–8, grand jury presentment, 13 Oct. 1841; 44–31, grand jury presentment, 14 Jan. 1842; 45–33, grand jury presentment, 14 Apr. 1842.
91 Ibid., 49–25, grand jury presentment, 11 July 1843.
92 Aitchison, 'The Development of Local Government in Upper Canada, 1783–1850,' 653.
93 AO, R.G. 22, Series 372, 32–2A, Niagara district accounts for 1837, 12 June 1838.

PART THREE

1 NA, R.G. 5 A1, Upper Canada Sundries, vol. 124, pp. 68589–94, Justices Robinson, Macaulay, and Sherwood to Lt. Col. Rowan, 27 Dec. 1832.
2 AO, R.G. 22, Series 372, 21–15, draft of petition to Sir John Colborne, Sept. 1835.
3 Ibid., 24–8, Glenelg to Sir Francis Bond Head, No. 33, 2 March 1836 encl. in Bond Head to Charles Richardson, 9 July 1836.

7 Crimes and Punishments

1 *The Niagara Gleaner*, 18 Jan. 1823.
2 AO, R.G. 22, Series 372, 20–25, Warner Nelles to Charles Richardson, 7 July 1835; report of John Swan, surgeon, 7 July 1835; King vs Jeremiah Collins and others, July 1835.
3 For a discussion of this question, see Ann Alexandra McEwen, 'Crime in the Niagara District, 1827–1850' (MA thesis, University of Guelph, 1991), 58–60. The figures for the Gore district are found in John Weaver, 'Crime, Public Order and Repression: The Gore District in Upheaval, 1832–1851,' *Ontario History*, 78 (3) (Sept. 1986), 176–207 at 197.
4 The information in this table is taken from McEwen, 'Crime in the Niagara District, 1827–1850,' 142–4.

5 AO, R.G. 22, Series 372, 43–12, Conviction of James Smith for assault and battery, June 1841.
6 For the Gore district see Weaver, 'Crime, Public Order and Repression,' 176–207 and his book, *Crimes, Constables and Courts: Order and Transgression in a Canadian City, 1816–1970* (Montreal and Kingston: McGill-Queen's University Press, 1995), 23–50.
7 Ann Alexandra McEwen has compiled information on these cases in her 'Crime in the Niagara District, 1827–1850,' 141; she discusses them in 35–50. The information is based on the benchbooks from the Niagara assizes, but since half the benchbooks for the period are missing the total of criminal cases is certainly larger than represented here. I have discussed the case of Patrick Donnelly, who was declared insane, in chapter 5. See above, 90–106.
8 *Niagara Gleaner*, 20 Sept. 1823.
9 For the case of Angelique Pilotte see Constance Backhouse, *Petticoats and Prejudice: Women and Law in Nineteenth-Century Canada* (Toronto: Osgoode Society, 1991), 112–24.
10 *St. Catharines Farmer's Journal*, 11 Apr. 1839; McEwen, 'Crime in the Niagara District, 1827–1850,' 35–44.
11 Backhouse, *Petticoats and Prejudice*, 112–39.
12 McEwen, 'Crime in the Niagara District, 1827–1850,' 62–5.
13 John D. Blackwell, 'Crime in the London District, 1828–1837: A Case Study of the Effect of the 1833 Reform in Upper Canada Penal Law,' *Queen's Law Journal* 6 (2) (Spring 1981), 528–67 at 555; Constance Backhouse, 'Nineteenth-Century Canadian Rape Law, 1800–92,' in David Flaherty, ed., *Essays in the History of Canadian Law*, vol. 2 (Toronto: Osgoode Society, 1983), 200–47; Backhouse, *Petticoats and Prejudice*, 81–111.
14 AO, R.G. 22, Series 372, 25–22, King vs Samuel Farensworth, Oct. 1836.
15 Ibid., 47–41, Queen vs Andrew O'Marra, Jan. 1843.
16 McEwen, 'Crime in the Niagara District, 1827–1850,' 139–65.
17 In this change the Niagara district resembled the rest of the colony of Upper Canada. For a complete discussion see Peter Oliver, *'A Terror to Evil-Doers': Prisons and Punishments in Nineteenth-Century Ontario* (Toronto: Osgoode Society, 1998), 12–24.
18 *St. Catharines Farmer's Journal and Welland Canal Intelligencer*, 13 Jan. 1830; Oliver, *'A Terror to Evil-Doers,'* 97–105.
19 Frances Ann Thompson, 'Local Authority and District Autonomy: The Niagara Magistrary and Constabulary' (PhD thesis, University of Ottawa, 1996), 192.

20 AO, R.G. 22, Series 372, 47–40, note by Judge E.C. Campbell, 23 Dec. 1842.

21 McEwen, 'Crime in the Niagara District, 1827–1850,' 84–5.

22 AO, R.G. 22, Series 372, 63–1, Account of Patrick Finn, 2 June 1846.

23 *The Niagara Chronicle*, 10 Apr. 1844; McEwen, 'Crime in the Niagara District, 1827–1850,' 68–71.

24 McEwen, 'Crime in the Niagara District, 1827–1850,' 72–81.

25 AO, R.G. 22, Series 372, 54–1, Queen vs Benjamin Abbott, July 1844; petition of Crowland freeholders, 29 June 1844.

26 Thompson, 'Local Authority and District Autonomy,' 192. For a comparison with the Gore district, where the figures were similar at least until 1841, see Weaver, *Crimes, Constables and Courts*, 46–7.

27 NA, R.G. 5 A 1, Upper Canada Sundries, vol. 171, 93645–54, Alma to J. Joseph, 24 Oct. 1836; report of Robert Jameson, 26 Oct. 1836. See also Thompson, 'Local Authority and District Autonomy,' 49–50, and Oliver, '*A Terror to Evil-Doers*,' 44.

28 AO, R.G. 22, Series 372, 20–11, deposition of Corporal Hugh Byrnes, 12 May 1835; arrest warrant for Sarah Carter, Mary Macfarlane, Elizabeth Page, and Ellen Dennis, 12 May 1835.

29 Ibid., 53–34, grand jury presentment, 4 July 1844.

30 Ibid., 53–35, report of jail committee, 29 Apr. 1844.

31 Ibid., 22–11, grand jury presentment, 15 Jan. 1836; Tench to Charles Richardson, 7 Jan. 1836, deposition of David McAlpin, 5 Jan. 1836.

32 *The Niagara Gleaner*, 24 Sept. 1825.

33 AO, R.G. 22, Series 372, 29–13, deposition of Albert Goodenow, 26 Apr. 1837.

34 Ibid., 29–13, deposition of Joseph Morrison, 14 July 1837; grand jury presentment 14 July 1837.

35 McEwen, 'Crime in the Niagara District, 1827–1850,' 125–6.

36 AO, R.G. 22, Series 372, 1–38 and 1–39, King vs Thomas McMahon and King versus Jonathan Raymond, Apr. 1828.

37 Ibid., 4–29, King vs John McMonagle, July 1829.

38 Ibid., 15–11, deposition of Joseph Badgely, 29 June 1832. For the information on the long-running quarrel between the two men see 13–32, J.P. Black to James Muirhead, 3 Jan. 1833.

39 McEwen, 'Crime in the Niagara District, 1827–1850,' 82.

40 AO, R.G. 22, Series 372, 43–25, Queen vs Bernard McGann and Patrick Donnelly, Sept. 1841; deposition of Lachlan Bell, 19 July 1841.

41 Douglas Hay, 'War, Dearth and Theft in the Eighteenth Century: The Record of the English Courts,' *Past and Present* 95 (1982), 117–60; J.M. Beattie, *Crime and the Courts in England, 1660–1800* (Princeton: Princeton University Press, 1986), 199–264.

42 Beattie, *Crime and the Courts in England*, 263.
43 Donald Fyson, 'Criminal Justice, Civil Society and the Local State: The Justices of the Peace in the District of Montreal, 1764–1830' (PhD thesis, Université de Montréal, 1995), 326.
44 James Strachan, *A Visit to the Province of Upper Canada in 1819* (New York: S.R. Publishers Ltd., Johnson Reprint Corporation, 1968), 100.
45 John Goldie, *Diary of a Journey through Upper Canada and some of the New England States, 1819* (privately published, n.d.), 19.
46 John Duncan, *Travels Through part of the United States and Canada in 1818 and 1819*, 2 vols. (New York, 1823), 2:107–8.
47 J.C. Dent, *The Story of the Upper Canadian Rebellion* (Toronto: C.B. Robinson, 1885) 1:10–11.
48 Marion MacRae, *Cornerstones of Order: Courthouses and Town Halls of Ontario, 1784–1914* (Toronto: Clarke Irwin, 1983), 23–4.
49 Ibid., 25.
50 AO, R.G. 22, Series 372, 44–8, grand jury presentment, 13 Oct. 1841.
51 Ibid., 45–33, grand jury presentment, 14 Apr. 1842.
52 Ibid., 47–28, grand jury presentment, 10 Jan. 1843.
53 Ibid., 46–31, grand jury presentment, 13 July 1842.
54 Ibid.
55 Ibid., 49–25, grand jury presentment, 12 July 1843.
56 NA, M.G. 24 I 26, Alexander Hamilton Papers, vol. 46, C. Gamble to A. Hamilton, 10 Dec. 1834.
57 NA, R.G. 5 A1, Upper Canada Sundries, vol. 95, pp. 53000–1, Richard Leonard to Lt. Mudge, 14 July 1829.
58 AO, R.G. 22, Series 372, 58–37, John Clark to the Gaol Committee, 1 May 1845; court order, 22 May 1845.
59 W.J. Blacklock, 'The Prosecution of Crime in Upper Canada' (MA paper, University of Toronto, 1987), 72.
60 NA, M.G. 24 I 26, Alexander Hamilton Papers, vol. 47, Lt. Col. Booth to Alexander Hamilton, 25 July 1838.
61 Ibid., vol. 46, Draper to A. Hamilton, 28 June 1838.

8 Criminal Victims

1 W. Peter Ward, 'Unwed Motherhood in Nineteenth Century English Canada,' *Historical Papers* (1981), 34–56 at 35.
2 Lynne Marks, 'Christian Harmony: Family, Neighbours and Community in Upper Canadian Church Discipline Records,' in Franca Iacovetta and Wendy Mitchinson, eds., *On the Case: Explorations in Social History*

(Toronto: University of Toronto Press, 1998), 109–28; Bryan Palmer, 'Discordant Music: Charivaris and Whitecapping in Nineteenth Century North America,' *Labour/Le Travailleur* 3 (1978), 5–62.

3 Cynthia Comacchio, 'Beneath the "Sentimental Veil": Families and Family History in Canada,' *Labour/Le Travail* 33 (Spring 1994), 279–302 at 290, n 20; Kathryn Harvey, 'To Love, Honour and Obey: Wife-battering in Working-Class Montreal, 1869–79,' *Urban History Review* 19 (Oct. 1990), 128–40. See also André Lachance and Sylvie Savoie, 'Violence, Marriage and Family Honour: Aspects of the Legal Regulation of Marriage in New France,' in Jim Phillips, Tina Loo, and Susan Lewthwaite, eds., *Essays in the History of Canadian Law*, vol. 5, *Crime and Criminal Justice* (Toronto: Osgoode Society, 1994), 142–73; Terry Chapman, 'Till Death Do Us Part: Wife Beating in Alberta, 1905–1920,' *Alberta History* 36 (4) (1988), 13–22; James G. Snell, 'Marital Cruelty in the Nova Scotia Divorce Court,' *Acadiensis* 18 (1) (1988), 3–32; Annalee Golz, 'Uncovering and Reconstructing Family Violence: Ontario Criminal Case Files,' in Iacovetta and Mitchinson, eds., *On the Case*, 289–311.

4 Katherine McKenna, 'Lower Class Women's Agency in Upper Canada: Prescott's Board of Police Records 1834–1850' (unpublished paper, Canadian Historical Association, 1996), 9.

5 Ibid., 14.

6 Ibid., 8.

7 Elizabeth Jane Errington, *Wives and Mothers, Schoolmistresses and Scullery Maids: Working Women in Upper Canada, 1790–1840* (Montreal and Kingston: McGill-Queen's University Press, 1995), 29.

8 Ibid., 39.

9 Lori Chambers, *Married Women and Property Law in Victorian Ontario* (Toronto: Osgoode Society, 1997), 21.

10 Ann Alexandra McEwen, 'Crime in the Niagara District, 1827–1850' (MA thesis, University of Guelph, 1991), 36. This account is based on the judge's benchbook, Justice James Macaulay, AO, R.G. 22, Series 390, 1–3.

11 Jim Phillips, 'Women, Crime and Criminal Justice in Early Halifax,' in Phillips, Loo, and Lewthwaite, eds., *Crime and Criminal Justice*, 188–9; see also Allyson N. May and Jim Phillips, 'Homicide in Nova Scotia, 1745–1815,' *Canadian Historical Review* 82 (4) (December, 2001) 625–61.

12 Ibid., 191.

13 Anna Clark, *The Struggle for the Breeches: Gender and the Making of the British Working Class* (Berkeley and Los Angeles: University of California Press, 1995), 74.

14 Ibid.

15 Ibid., 79
16 Anna Clark, 'Humanity or Justice? Wife Beating and the Law in the Eighteenth and Nineteenth Centuries,' in Carol Smart, ed., *Regulating womanhood: historical essays on marriage, motherhood and sexuality* (London: Routledge, 1992), 187.
17 Clark, *The Struggle for the Breeches*, 74.
18 Constance Backhouse, *Petticoats and Prejudice: Women and Law in Nineteenth-Century Canada* (Toronto: Osgoode Society, 1991), 174.
19 Ibid., 175.
20 AO, R.G. 22, Series 372, 15–11, H. Nelles to Charles Richardson, 21 Jan. 1833; depositions of Rachel Anderson, Nancy Thompson, Mary Hill, 19 Jan. 1833.
21 *Colborne Chronicle*, 13 Jan. 1982, reproducing an article from *The Cobourg Star*, 16 July 1845. This article is taken from a manuscript in the Colborne Public Library by Percy Climo, 'From Pages of the Past. Part 11: Historical Items Relating to Colborne & Area, 1841–1849 from the Cobourg Star.' I am indebted to my colleague, Dr Catharine Wilson, for this reference.
22 AO, R.G. 22, Series 372, 34–8, statement of George Bradshaw and Jacob Misner, Wainfleet Town Wardens, 3 Dec. 1838; deposition of Elizabeth Cochrane, 29 March 1839.
23 Susan Lewthwaite, 'Violence, Law and Community in Rural Upper Canada,' in Phillips, Loo and Lewthwaite, eds. *Crime and Criminal Justice*, vol. V, 365.
24 Donald Fyson, 'Criminal Justice, Civil Society and the Local State: The Justices of the Peace in the District of Montreal, 1764–1830,' (PhD thesis, Université de Montréal, 1995), 393–8.
25 Golz, 'Uncovering and Reconstructing Family Violence: Ontario Criminal Case Files,' 293.
26 AO, R.G. 22, Series 372, 1–11, statement by Mary McMahon, 10 Apr. 1828.
27 John Weaver, *Crimes, Constables and Courts: Order and Transgression in a Canadian City, 1816–1970* (Montreal and Kingston: McGill-Queen's University Press, 1995), 55.
28 Ibid., 74
29 AO, R.G. 22, Series 372, 8–31, deposition of Jane Baker, 6 Dec. 1830.
30 Ibid., 9–15, deposition of Jane Baker, 21 March 1831 and trial of Daniel Baker, March 1831.
31 Ibid., 9–18, depositions of James Black, JP, Nathaniel Blackmer and Peter Cooper, 15 Feb. 1831.
32 NA, M.G. 24, I 26, vol. 44, Alexander Hamilton Papers, deposition of Jacob Misner the Younger, 23 June 1832.

33 AO, R.G. 22, Series 372, 12–28, 13–1, jail accounts, March–July, July–Oct. 1832.
34 Ibid., 8–31, deposition by Margaret Anderson, 12 Jan. 1831.
35 Ibid., 12–6, deposition of Elizabeth Lampman, 4 March 1832; Smith Griffin to Charles Richardson, 9 March 1832.
36 Ibid., 12–31, criminal calendar, July 1832, and 12–42, documents relating to the charge of assault and battery against Moses Goodfellow, July 1832.
37 Ibid., 14–22, documents in the case of William Rees, March, 1833, including letter from R.H. Dee to Charles Richardson, 25 March 1833.
38 Ibid., 19–27, depositions of Kenneth Reach and Cornelius Merrick, 28 Nov. 1834.
39 Ibid., 20–17, petition of Ellen Fitzgerald, 21 May 1835.
40 Keith Johnson, 'Claims of Equity and Justice: Petitions and Petitioners in Upper Canada, 1815–1840,' *Histoire sociale/Social History* 55 (May 1995), 219–40 at 231.
41 AO, R.G. 22, Series 372, 20–17, petition of Ellen Fitzgerald, 21 May 1835.
42 Ibid., 44–20, #13, recognizance of George Turney, 1 May 1841.
43 Ibid., 46–27, #2, recognizance of Wm. McKenzie, 1842.
44 Ibid., 25–7, conviction of James Mullingham, 26 May 1836.
45 Ibid., 21–9, summary convictions, Jacob Keefer, Thorold, Oct. 1835.
46 Ibid., 19–7, summary convictions, Ogden Creighton, Clifton, March 1835.
47 Ibid., 59–37, depositions of John Bunting and George Baker, Sept. 1845.
48 Ibid., 23–9, deposition of Mary Manly, 12 Feb. 1836.
49 Backhouse, *Petticoats and Prejudice*, 327.
50 McEwen, 'Crime in the Niagara District, 1827–1850,' 57 and 59.
51 Harvey, 'Wife-battering in Montreal, 1869–79,' 135–7.
52 Ibid., 137.
53 Judith Finguard, 'Jailbirds in Mid-Victorian Halifax,' in R.C. Macleod, ed., *Lawful Authority: Readings on the History of Criminal Justice in Canada* (Toronto: Copp Clark Pitman, 1988), 71.
54 This subject is dealt with more fully in chapter 10, where the case of Solomon Moseby is examined. For a study of the treatment of African Americans in the courts of Philadelphia see G.S. Rowe, 'Black Offenders, Criminal Courts, and Philadelphia Society in the Late 18th Century,' *Journal of Social History* 22 (1989), 685–712.
55 Jason H. Silverman, 'The American Fugitive Slave in Canada: Myths and Realities,' *Journal of Southern Studies* 19 (Fall 1980), 215–27 at 227.
56 AO, R.G. 22, Series 372, 2–9, precept, July 1828.
57 Ibid., 1–12, grand jury presentment, 12 Apr. 1828.

58 Ibid., 1–36, King vs. William Moffatt, Apr. 1828.
59 Ibid., 8–23, King vs. William Turman, Oct. 1830.
60 Ibid., 59–38, deposition of William R. Roberts, 24 Nov. 1845.
61 Ibid., 6–15, King vs. Harkless Livers, March 1830.
62 Ibid., 37–29, Queen vs. Reuben Gunn, March 1840.
63 *Niagara Chronicle*, 10 Apr. 1844.
64 NA, R.G. 8, Box 14, W.H. McEwan to D. Daly, 17 June 1846; John Jarron and Andrew Thompson to D. Daly, 13 July 1846.
65 AO, R.G. 22, Series 390, 38–2, Niagara assizes, 27 Oct. 1841; McEwen, 'Crime in the Niagara District, 1827–1850,' 39–40.
66 AO, R.G. 22, Series 372, 4–48, King vs Mary Fountain, Oct. 1829.
67 Ibid., 8–21. King vs. Adam Snyder, Oct. 1830.
68 Ibid., 37–31, John Clark to Charles Richardson, 10 March 1840.
69 *Niagara Chronicle*, 25 Nov. 1844.

9 Criminal Boundaries

1 Lieut. Col. A. Thorne to Col. Foster, 13 Sept. 1841, cited in Ernest Green, 'The Fearful Forties in Welland County,' *Welland County Historical Society, Papers and Records* (Welland, 1938), 5:164–5.
2 Jane Errington, *The Lion, the Eagle and Upper Canada: A Developing Colonial Ideology* (Montreal and Kingston: McGill-Queen's University Press, 1987); Reginald Stuart, *United States Expansionism and British North America, 1775–1871* (Chapel Hill, N.C.: University of North Carolina Press, 1988); Kenneth R. Stevens, *Border Diplomacy: The Caroline and McLeod Affairs in Anglo-American-Canadian Relations, 1837–1842* (Tuscaloosa: University of Alabama Press, 1989).
3 David Moorman, 'Where Are the English and the Americans in the Historiography of Upper Canada?' *Ontario History* 88 (1) (March 1996), 65–9 at 66. See also Jane Errington and George Rawlyk, 'The Loyalist-Federalist Alliance of Upper Canada,' *American Review of Canadian Studies* 14 (Summer 1984), 157–76 at 158–9.
4 Janet Baglier, 'The Niagara Frontier: Society and Economy in Western New York and Upper Canada, 1794–1854' (PhD dissertation, SUNY, Buffalo, 1993); Janet Larkin, 'The Canal Era: A Study of the Original Erie and Welland Canals within the Niagara Borderland,' *American Review of Canadian Studies* 24 (Autumn 1994), 299–314.
5 James G. Snell, 'The International Border as a Factor in Marital Behaviour: A Historical Case Study,' *Ontario History* 81, (4) (December 1989), 289–302.

6 Robert Lecker, ed., *Borderlands: Essays in Canadian-American Relations* (Toronto: ECW Press, 1991), viii.

7 John Weaver, *Crimes, Constables, and Courts: Order and Transgression in a Canadian City, 1816–1970* (Montreal and Kingston: McGill-Queen's University Press, 1995), 15 and 165.

8 Carl Berger, 'Internationalism, Continentalism, and the Writing of History: Comments on the Carnegie Series on the Relations of Canada and the United States,' in Richard A. Preston, ed., *The Influence of the United States on Canadian Development: Eleven Case Studies* (Durham, N.C.: Duke University Press, 1972), W. Swanson to Adam Shortt, 13 Jan. 1906 cited on p. 34, note 4.

9 Ibid., 47.

10 Marcus L. Hansen and J.B. Brebner, *The Mingling of the Canadian and American Peoples* (Toronto and New Haven: Carnegie Endowment for International Peace, 1940).

11 Berger, 'Internationalism,' 47 and *The Writing of Canadian History: Aspects of English-Canadian Historical Writing, 1900–1970* (Toronto: Oxford University Press, 1976), 137–59.

12 Stuart, *United States Expansionism*, 260.

13 Ibid., 135.

14 Philip Buckner, 'The Borderlands Concept,' in Stephen J. Hornsby, Victor A. Konrad, and James J. Herlan, eds., *The Northeastern Borderlands: Four Centuries of Interaction* (Fredericton, N.B: Acadiensis Press, 1989), 157.

15 S.F. Wise, 'Canadians View the United States: Colonial Attitudes from the Era of the War of 1812 to the Rebellions of 1837,' in A.B. McKillop and Paul Romney, eds., *God's Peculiar Peoples: Essays on Political Culture in Nineteenth-Century Canada* (Ottawa: Carleton University Press, 1993), 45–60.

16 Basil Hall, *Travels in North America in the Years 1827 and 1828* (New York: Arno Press, 1974), 1:193.

17 Patrick Shirreff, *A Tour through North America; together with a comprehensive view of the Canadas and the United States. As adapted for agricultural emigration* (Edinburgh, 1835; rep. New York: Benjamin Blom, 1971), 95–6.

18 NA, R.G. 5, A1, Upper Canada Sundries, vol. 117, pp. 65907–8, Hugh Richardson to Lt. Col. Rowan, 23 June 1832.

19 Ibid., vol. 118, pp. 66000–1, Charles Richardson to Lt. Col. Rowan, 4 July 1832.

20 Ibid., vol. 82, 44605–10, Joseph Adams to Commanding Officer, Royal Navy, Kingston, 12 Feb. 1827 and encl. statement, Kingsburg, 4 March 1820.

21 Ibid., vol. 124, pp. 68246–67, Daniel McDougal to Lt. Col. Rowan, 26 Dec. 1832, with enclosed affidavits.

22 Ibid., vol. 124, pp. 68185–6, Charles Eliot to Lt. Col. Rowan, 29 Nov. 1832.

23 Ibid. vol. 124, p. 68187, Attorney-General Boulton to Lt. Col. Rowan, 10 Dec. 1832.

24 For a brief biography of Macaulay see D.B. Read, *The Lives of the Judges of Upper Canada and Ontario from 1791 to the present time* (Toronto, 1888), 148–57.

25 R.G. 5 A1, Upper Canada Sundries, vol. 124, pp. 68614–27, Justice Macaulay's 'Notes on The King vs. James Bird and William Walker,' 29 Dec. 1832.

26 Samuel Flagg Bemis, *Jay's Treaty: A Study in Commerce and Diplomacy*, 2nd ed. (New Haven: Yale University Press, 1962), 482–3; A.L. Burt, *The United States, Great Britain and British North America: From the Revolution to the Establishment of Peace After the War of 1812* (New York: Russell Russell, 1961), 198.

27 NA, R.G. 5 A1, Upper Canada Sundries, vol. 125, pp. 68817–18, Solicitor-General Hagerman to Lt. Col. Rowan, 1 Jan. 1833. See also pp. 68842–3, Attorney-General Boulton to Lt. Col. Rowan, 3 Jan. 1833.

28 Ibid., vol. 125, pp. 69014–15, Charles Eliot to Lt. Col. Rowan, 14 Jan. 1833.

29 Ibid., vol. 125, pp. 69157–60, Charles Eliot to Lt. Col. Rowan, 24 Jan. 1833 and encl., W.H. Witherell, U.S. District Attorney, to Charles Eliot, 18 Jan. 1833.

30 Ibid., vol. 125, p. 69110, Attorney General Boulton to Lt. Col. Rowan, 19 Jan 1833.

31 Ibid., vol. 125, pp. 69157–8, Charles Eliot to Lt. Col. Rowan, 24 Jan. 1833.

32 3 William IV, c. 7, (1833), An Act to provide for the Apprehending of Fugitive Offenders from Foreign Countries, and delivering them up to Justice.

33 NA, R.G. 5 A1, Upper Canada Sundries, vol. 123, pp. 68159–60, Attorney-General Boulton to Lt. Col. Rowan, 26 Nov. 1832.

34 40 Geo. III c. 1 (1800), 'An Act for the further introduction of the Criminal Law of England into this Province and for the more effectual Punishment of certain Offenders.'

35 Weaver, *Crimes, Constables, and Courts*, 61; Oliver, *'Terror to Evil-Doers': Prisons and Punishments in Nineteenth-Century Ontario* (Toronto: Osgoode Society, 1998), 25–7.

36 NA, R.G. 5 A1, Upper Canada Sundries, vol. 116, pp. 65511–15, Jarvis to McMahon, 2 June 1832; Robinson to McMahon, n.d. 1832; pp. 65881–3, petition of prisoners in York gaol, 28 June 1832.

37 Ibid., vol. 122, pp. 67759–61, Sheriff Jarvis to Lt. Col. Rowan, 29 Oct. 1832.
38 Ibid., vol. 109, p. 62217, Magistrate Holme to Lt.-Gov. Colborne, 17 Oct. 1831.
39 Ibid., vol. 109, p. 62205, grand jury presentment, Gore District, 1 Sept. 1831.
40 Ibid., vol. 116, pp. 65179–81, petition of Francis Morgan, 12 May 1832.
41 Ibid., vol. 105, pp. 59259–63, petition of Samson Catlett, 3 Jan. 1831 and petition of inhabitants of Amherstberg, n.d. Jan. 1831.
42 Ibid., vol. 108, pp. 61330–2. Chief Justice Robinson to Edward McMahon, 7 July 1831.
43 Ibid., vol. 99, pp. 56093–7, John Ward to Schofield, 4 Apr. 1830, encl. in M. Burwell to Z. Mudge, 17 Apr. 1830.
44 Ibid., vol. 102, pp. 58264–6, petition of Abraham Welden, 23 Oct. 1830.
45 Ibid., vol. 101, pp. 57590–3, petition of Margaret Murtaugh, 16 Aug. 1830.
46 Ibid., vol. 107, pp. 61178–9, petition of David Underhill, 18 June 1831, and encl. John Willson to Z. Mudge, 13 June 1831.
47 Ibid., vol. 108, pp. 61751–55, Sheriff Jarvis to Edward McMahon, 27 Aug. 1831 and encl. coroner's report, 27 Aug. 1831.
48 *Journal of the House of Assembly* (1831) 'Report of a Select Committee on the expediency of erecting a Penitentiary,' Appendix, 211–12. It is reprinted in J.M. Beattie, *Attitudes Towards Crime and Punishment in Upper Canada, 1830–1850: A Documentary Study* (Toronto: Centre of Criminology, University of Toronto, 1977), 82.
49 AO, R.G. 22, Series 372, 14–34, petition of George Martin, 9 July 1832; 13–14, King vs George Martin, Oct. 1832.
50 Ibid., 20–13, James Macaulay to Sheriff of Niagara, 14 May 1835 in cases of James and Joseph Burniston and Aaron Roy.
51 Duc de la Rochefoucauld Liancourt, *Travels through the United States of North America, the country of the Iroquois, and Upper Canada, in the years, 1795, 1796 and 1797* (London, 1799), 1:256.
52 Ibid., 291.
53 NA, R.G. 5, A1, Upper Canada Sundries, vol. 9, p. 3651, 'A Friend of the British Constitution' to Lt. Gov. Gore, 4 Feb. 1809.
54 Harvey Strum, 'A Most Cruel Murder: The Isaac Underhill Affair, 1809,' *Ontario History* 80 (4) (1988), 293–310.
55 Burt, *The United States, Great Britain and British North America*, Baker to Monroe, 7 July 1815, cited 378–9.
56 Richard A. Preston, ed., *Kingston Before the War of 1812* (Toronto: Champlain Society, University of Toronto Press, 1959), lxxxiv.

57 Ibid., Mackenzie to Green, 8 Sept. 1801, 247.

58 John Richardson, *Eight Years in Canada* (New York: S.R. Publishers, Johnson Reprint Corp., 1967), 77.

59 Peter Burroughs, 'Tackling Army Desertion in British North America,' *Canadian Historical Review* 61 (1) (1980), 28–68. See Table 1, 30.

60 Arthur to Somerset, 24 Nov. 1838, *Arthur Papers*, I, 398, as cited by Burroughs, 'Tackling Army Desertion,' 34–5.

61 Burroughs, 'Tackling Army Desertion,' 36.

62 NA, M.G. 24 I 26, vol. 46, Hamilton to Lt. Col. Foster, 28 May 1832.

63 Reverend Isaac Fidler, *Observations on Professions, Literature, Manners, and Emigration in the United States and Canada, made during a residence there in 1832* (London, 1833), 215–16.

64 Ann Alexandra McEwen, 'Crime in the Niagara District, 1827–1850,' 108.

65 NA, R.G. 5 A1, Upper Canada Sundries, vol. 109, pp. 62053–54, L.P. Sherwood to Edward McMahon, 27 Sept. 1831.

66 Rochefoucauld Liancourt, *Travels through the United States ... and Canada*, 1:247.

67 William Lyon Mackenzie, *Sketches of Canada and the United States* (London: E. Wilson, 1833), 81–4.

68 Hill to William Duane, 29 July 1808, cited in Stuart, *United States Expansionism*, 51. For similar evidence from the Canadian side in the later colonial period, see E.A. Cruikshank, 'The Troubles of a Collector of Customs,' in *A Memoir of Colonel the Honourable James Kerby, His Life in Letters*, (Welland: Welland County Historical Society, 1931), 261–329.

69 Ibid., 106–16.

70 The documents on this case are found in NA, M.G. 24 I 26, vol 49, depositions dated 12 Dec. 1825 and court of quarter sessions decision 11 Jan. 1826.

71 J.A. Sharpe, *Crime in Early Modern England, 1550–1750* (London and New York: Longman, 1984), 122.

72 See especially some of the works on the English game laws, e.g., E.P. Thompson, *Whigs and Hunters: The Origin of the Black Act* (London: Allen Lane, 1975); Douglas Hay, 'Poaching and the Game Laws on Cannock Chase,' in Douglas Hay, Peter Linebaugh, and E.P.Thompson et al., eds., *Albion's Fatal Tree: Crime and Society in Eighteenth-Century England* (London: Allen Lane, 1975), 189–254.

10 Hands Across the Border

1 An earlier version of this chapter appeared in the *Canadian Review of American Studies* 30 (2) (2000), 187–209. For previous examples of the

historical treatment of this case see, among others, Jason Silverman, *Unwelcome Guests: Canada West's Response to American Fugitive Slaves, 1800–1865* (New York: Associated Faculty Press, 1985), 37–43; Roman J. Zorn, 'Criminal Extradition Menaces the Canadian Haven for Fugitive Slaves, 1841–1861,' *Canadian Historical Review* 38 (Dec. 1957), 284–94; Alexander L. Murray, 'The Extradition of Fugitive Slaves from Canada: A Re-evaluation,' *Canadian Historical Review* 43 (Dec. 1962), 298–314, and 'Canada and the Anglo-American Anti-Slavery Movement: A Study in International Philanthropy' (PhD dissertation, University of Pennsylvania, 1960), 125–8; Ged Martin, 'British Officials and their attitudes to the negro community in Canada, 1833–1861,' *Ontario History* 46 (June 1974), 79–88; W.R. Riddell, 'The Slave in Upper Canada,' *Journal of Negro History* 4 (4) (1919), 372–95. See also Michael Power and Nancy Butler, *Slavery and Freedom in Niagara* (Niagara: Niagara Historical Society, 1993), 49–53 for the best recent account of the Moseby affair. Another recent publication, Owen A. Thomas, *Niagara's Freedom Trail: A Guide to African-Canadian History on the Niagara Peninsula*, 2nd ed. (Niagara: Niagara Economic and Tourism Corporation, 1996) has a separate section on the Solomon Moseby affair, 30–1.

2 Anna Jameson, *Winter Studies and Summer Rambles in Canada* (Ottawa: New Canadian Library, 1990), 198–201; Janet Carnochan, 'Slave Rescue in Niagara Sixty Years Ago,' *Niagara Historical Society* #2 (Niagara, 1897), 8–18. Jameson reprinted her account in a later travel book, *Sketches in Canada, and Rambles Among the Red Men* (London, 1852), 55–8.

3 Allen P. Stouffer, *The Light of Nature and the Law of God: Antislavery in Ontario, 1833–1877* (Baton Rouge: Louisiana University Press, 1992), 12.

4 Power and Butler, *Slavery and Freedom in Niagara*, 20–31.

5 Ibid., 44.

6 William Lyon Mackenzie, *Sketches of Canada and the United States* (London: E. Wilson, 1833), 21–2.

7 Karolyn E. Smardz, '"There We Were in Darkness, – Here We Are in Light," Kentucky Slaves and the Promised Land,' in Craig Thompson Friend, ed., *The Buzzel about Kentucky: Settling the Promised Land* (Lexington: University Press of Kentucky, 1999), 240–58; and Silverman, *Unwelcome Guests*, 37.

8 NA, R.G. 5, A1, Upper Canada Sundries, 97819, James Boulton to J. Joseph, 28 Aug. 1837.

9 The details of Boulton's relationship with Alexander McLeod can be found in NA, Pamphlet #1982 (1845) 'Letter from Alexander McLeod to Sir Allan Napier McNab, Knight, Speaker of the Legislative Assembly of Canada, 4 Jan. 1845,' 9.

10 For documents on the Jesse Happy case, see J. Mackenzie Leask, 'Jesse Happy, a Fugitive Slave from Kentucky,' *Ontario History* 54 (2) (June 1962), 87–98. Neither Leask nor the other historians who have written about these cases have traced all the connections between the Happy and Moseby cases. The connections are integral to understanding what actually happened and why. One early account believed Happy and Moseby were one person with two different aliases: Charles Lindsey, *The life and times of Wm. Lyon Mackenzie: with an account of the Canadian rebellion of 1837, and the subsequent frontier disturbances, chiefly from unpublished documents* (Toronto, 1862), 160–1.

11 Jason H. Silverman, 'Kentucky, Canada and Extradition: the Jesse Happy Case,' *Filson Club History Quarterly* 54 (1980), 50–60.

12 NA, R.G. 1, E1, 49, Alexander Stewart to John Joseph, 5 Sept. 1837.

13 Ibid., Petitions of persons of colour, Niagara, 2 Sept. 1837 and petition of inhabitants of Niagara, n.d. 1837.

14 NA, C.O. 42/439, Bond Head to Glenelg, #112, 8 Oct. 1837, encl. p. 197, Bond Head to Niagara inhabitants, n.d. 1837.

15 Sir Francis Bond Head, *A Narrative* (London, 1839), 200–4.

16 The relevant documents are all printed in Leask, 'Jesse Happy.'

17 Ibid., 97–8.

18 The newspaper accounts are found in the *Niagara Reporter*, 14 Sept. 1837, *St. Catharines Journal*, 21 and 28 Sept. 1837 and the *Christian Guardian*, 27 Sept. 1837. For some of the legal records, see AO, R.G. 22, Series 372, 31–2 and 30–18. The judge's notes on the subsequent trials for riot can be found in AO, R.G. 22, Series 390, 4–1. See also Carnochan, 'A Slave Rescue in Niagara,' 8–18 and Jameson, *Winter Studies and Summer Rambles*, 198–201. The official Upper Canadian government records on the case are located in NA, Upper Canadian State Papers, vol. 40, 217–32 and C.O. 42/439, 170–3.

19 AO, R.G. 22, Series 372, 30–18, deposition of Henry Long, 15 Sept. 1837.

20 Ibid., deposition of William McIntyre, 15 Sept. 1837.

21 AO, R.G. 22, Series 390, 4–1, benchbook of Judge James Macaulay, 23 and 25 Oct. 1837. See also Ann Alexandra McEwen, 'Crime in the Niagara District, 1827–1850' (MA thesis, University of Guelph, 1991), 123–4.

22 NA, R.G. 5, A1, Upper Canada Sundries, vol. 209, pp. 115315–18, Alexander Hamilton to J. Joseph, 10 Nov. 1837. This document is filed with others for November 1838, suggesting that at some point it was misfiled. The error has never been corrected.

23 NA, M.G. 24, I26, vol. 48, A. McLeod to Alexander Hamilton, 22 Sept. 1837.

24 *St. Catharines Journal*, 28 Sept. 1837.
25 *Christian Guardian*, 27 Sept. 1837.
26 AO, R.G. 22, Series 390, 4–1, pp. 198–205, testimony of Dr Porter.
27 *Christian Guardian*, 27 Sept. 1837 and *St. Catharines Journal*, 21 and 27 Sept. 1837.
28 Jameson, *Winter Studies and Summer Rambles*, 200–1.
29 Ibid.
30 William Kirby, *Annals of Niagara*, 2nd ed. (Toronto: MacMillan, 1927), 278–9.
31 AO, R.G. 22, Series 390, 4–1, pp. 173–9, testimony of George Ball.
32 Jameson, *Winter Studies and Summer Rambles*, 198.
33 Carnochan, 'A Slave Rescue in Niagara,' 13–14.
34 Ibid., 16.
35 Stouffer, *The Light of Nature and the Law of God*, 52–7.
36 NA, C.O. 42/459, Memorial presented by Thomas Rolph to Earl Durham, 11 May 1839, encl. in Arthur to Normandy, #123, 23 May 1839. See also Stouffer, *The Light of Nature and the Law of God*, 58–62.
37 Kirby, *Annals of Niagara*, 279.
38 NA, M.G. 24 I26, vol. 48, Hamilton Papers, McLeod to Hamilton, 10 June 1834; W.G. Chisholm to Hamilton, 20 June 1834. Other biographical information on McLeod can be found in the *Dictionary of Canadian Biography* 10:481–2; Alastair Watt, 'The Case of Alexander McLeod,' *Canadian Historical Review* 12 (June 1931), 145–67 and Kenneth R. Stevens, *Border Diplomacy: the Caroline and McLeod Affairs in Anglo-American-Canadian Relations, 1837–1842* (Tuscaloosa and London: University of Alabama Press, 1989), 71–3.
39 NA, Pamphlet #1982 (1845) 'Letter from Alexander McLeod to the Honorable Sir Allan Napier McNab, Knight, Speaker of the Legislative Assembly of Canada, 4 Jan. 1845,' 7.
40 NA, R.G. 5 A1, Upper Canada Sundries, Hamilton to J. Joseph, 18 Sept. 1837.
41 NA, R.G. 5 A1, Upper Canada Sundries, vol. 209, pp. 115315–18, Hamilton to J. Joseph, 10 Nov. 1837.
42 Stevens, *Border Diplomacy*, 71.
43 John Ireland, 'Andrew Drew: The Man Who Burned the *Caroline*,' *Ontario History* 59 (3) (Sept. 1967), 137–56.
44 A.B. Corey, 'Public Opinion and the McLeod Case,' *Canadian Historical Association, Historical Papers* (1936), 53–64.
45 *Dictionary of Canadian Biography* 10:482. For an American account of McLeod's arrest and trial for the murder of Amos Durfee see Milledge L.

Bonham Jr, 'Alexander McLeod: Bone of Contention,' *New York History* 18 (1937), 189–217.

46 AO, MU 1964, F900, Alexander McLeod Papers, file 3, undated memoir.

47 NA, Pamphlet #1982 (1845), 'Letter from Alexander McLeod to the Honorable Sir Allan McNab'; *Parliamentary Papers*, 1844–45, IV, Appendix ZZ; NA, C.O. 42/458, McLeod to Bagot, 2 May 1842.

48 AO, MU 1964, F900, Alexander McLeod Papers, file 3, undated memoir.

49 Sir George Arthur, *The Arthur Papers,* ... ed. Charles R. Sanderson, 3 vols. (Toronto: Toronto Public Library, 1943–59), vol. 3, Arthur to Sir R.D. Jackson, 18 Jan. 1841.

50 Alexander L. Murray, 'The Extradition of Fugitive Slaves from Canada: A Re-evaluation,' *Canadian Historical Review* 43 (4) (Dec. 1962), 298–314 at 303–4.

51 Kirby, *Annals of Niagara*, 279.

52 Jason Silverman makes this point in 'Kentucky, Canada and Extradition,' 60.

53 For the story of Shadrach Minkins, see Gary Collison, *Shadrach Minkins, From Fugitive Slave to Citizen* (Cambridge, Mass.: Harvard University Press, 1997).

54 Ibid., 213–14.

55 Murray, 'Canada and the Anglo-American Anti-Slavery Movement,' 142.

56 *www.edunetconnect.com/cat/rebellions/index.html* – link to 'Other Reactions: Africans and First Nations.' The Solomon Moseby events are also included in the chronology of the 1837 rebellions in this site. I am indebted to Susan Glover for providing me with the reference to this site.

57 Ernest Green, 'Upper Canada's Black Defenders,' *Ontario History*, 27 (1931), 365–91.

CONCLUSION

1 Anna Brownell Jameson, *Winter Studies and Summer Rambles in Canada* (Ottawa: New Canadian Library, 1990), 43.

2 Lt. Col. G.T. Denison, 'Presidential Address,' *Transactions of the Royal Society of Canada*, 2nd Series, vol. 10 (Ottawa, 1904), xxv–xxxix. The address is reprinted in Leslie F.S. Upton, ed., *The United Empire Loyalists* (Toronto: Copp Clark, 1967), 139–44. See also W. Thomas Matthews, 'The Myth of the Peaceable Kingdom: Upper Canadian Society during the Early Victorian Period,' *Queen's Quarterly* 94 (2) (Summer 1987), 383–401 at 383–4.

3 Matthews, 'The Myth of the Peaceable Kingdom,' 399.

4 Barry Wright, 'Sedition in Upper Canada: Contested Legality,' *Labour/Le Travail* 29 (1992), 10. See also Paul Romney, *Mr. Attorney: The Attorney General for Ontario in Court, Cabinet, and Legislature, 1791–1899* (Toronto: Osgoode Society, 1986), 80–2 and his article entitled, 'From Constitutionalism to Legalism: Trial by Jury, Responsible Government, and the Rule of Law in the Canadian Political Culture,' *Law and History Review* 7 (1) (Spring 1989), 133–7 for an account of the trial of Robert Randal for perjury in 1825.

5 J.M. Beattie, *Crime and the Courts in England, 1660–1800* (Princeton: Princeton University Press, 1986), 15.

6 Robert Fraser, *Provincial Justice: Upper Canadian Legal Portraits from the Dictionary of Canadian Biography* (Toronto: Osgoode Society, 1992), lxii.

7 Sydney and Beatrice Webb, *English Local Government*, vol. 1, *The Parish and the County* (Hamden, Conn.: Archon Books, 1963), 605–6.

8 Romney, *Mr Attorney*, 115–21.

9 Ibid., 121.

10 Susan Lewthwaite, 'Law and Authority in Upper Canada: The Justices of the Peace in the Newcastle District, 1803–1840' (PhD thesis, University of Toronto, 2000), 276.

11 Donald Fyson, 'Criminal Justice, Civil Society, and the Local State: The Justices of the Peace in the District of Montreal, 1764–1830' (PhD thesis, Université de Montréal, 1995), 412.

12 Ann Alexandra McEwen, 'Crime in the Niagara District, 1827–1850' (MA thesis, University of Guelph, 1991), 138 and 33; Peter Oliver, 'The Place of the Judiciary in the Historiography of Upper Canada,' in G. Blaine Baker and Jim Phillips, eds., *Essays in the History of Canadian Law in Honour of R.C.B. Risk* (Toronto: Osgoode Society, 1999), 449.

13 Frances Ann Thompson, 'Local Authority and District Autonomy: The Niagara Magistracy and Constabulary' (PhD thesis, University of Ottawa, 1996), xii and 209.

Index

Turman, William, 170–1
Turney, George, 166
Turney, Mary Jane, 166
Twelve Mile Creek (later St
  Catharines), 44

Underhill, David, 188
Underhill, Isaac, 191
United States, 9, 11, 22, 51, 55, 71, 98–
  9, 101, 116, 121, 126, 149, 170, 175–
  9, 182–3, 186–94, 197, 200, 202, 210,
  212–14, 216, 219
Upper Canada, 3–4, 6, 11–12, 72–3,
  79, 81, 136, 149, 154, 160–1, 170,
  178, 183, 186–7, 196–8, 216, 219;
  Anti-Slavery Society, 210; districts
  of, 4–6, 222; executive council, 54,
  199, 201–4; historiography, 175–6;
  Houses of Industry, 126–9; legal
  system, 6, 22–3, 25; Legislative
  Council, 42, 52–3, 56; legislature, 4,
  23, 32, 53, 86–7, 89, 96–7, 99–102,
  107, 114, 119, 158, 185, 189, 197,
  213; lieutenant governors, 43;
  magistracy of, 32–4, 219; morality,
  74, 77; penal system, 150; treatment of insane, 90–106
Upper Canadian Rebellion, 97, 201
Utica (New York), 212

vagrancy, 144–5, 151. *See also*
  prostitutes
Vandecar, Silas, 110–11
Van Diemen's Land, 185
Vanfleet, Isaac, 81
Victoria, Queen, 86, 166
Vinica, Hiram, 98–9
Virginia, 207
Vrooman, William, 197

Wacousta, 191
Wadsworth, Chester, 71
Wadsworth, William, 70
Wafield, Barley, 172
Wainfleet, 9, 67, 88, 118, 159
Walker, Edward, King versus, 40
Walker, James, 182
Walpole, 36–7, 98
War of 1812, 10–12, 15, 18, 21, 34–5,
  38, 44, 113, 116, 149, 175, 177, 179–
  80, 191, 197, 219
Ward, John, 187
Ward, Peter, 154
Warwick, 67
Waterford (Ireland), 181
Watson, J. Wreford, 22
Weaver, John, 23, 79, 161, 176,
  185
Webb, Sydney and Beatrice, 27–8,
  221
Webster-Ashburton Treaty (1842),
  177, 184, 210, 215
Welch, Edward, 66–7
Weld, Isaac, 12
Welden, Abraham, 188
Welland Canal, 13, 20, 41, 60–1, 72,
  75, 79, 82, 87, 109, 112, 136, 175,
  216; cholera scare, 38–9; construc-
  tion of, 13–17, 69–70; police force,
  69–70; unemployment on, 70
Welland, county of, 9, 11
Welland, town of, 19
Wesley, John, 78
Western, district, 67
Westfall, William, 85
Wheeler, Edward, 69, 87
Wheeler, Peter, 62–3, 92
whipping, 140
White, Isaac, 172

1981 David H. Flaherty, eds., *Essays in the History of Canadian Law: Volume I*
1982 Marion MacRae and Anthony Adamson, *Cornerstones of Order: Courthouses and Town Halls of Ontario, 1784–1914*
1983 David H. Flaherty, ed., *Essays in the History of Canadian Law: Volume II*
1984 Patrick Brode, *Sir John Beverley Robinson: Bone and Sinew of the Compact*
David Williams, *Duff: A Life in the Law*
1985 James Snell and Frederick Vaughan, *The Supreme Court of Canada: History of the Institution*
1986 Paul Romney, *Mr Attorney: The Attorney General for Ontario in Court, Cabinet, and Legislature, 1791–1899*
Martin Friedland, *The Case of Valentine Shortis: A True Story of Crime and Politics in Canada*
1987 C. Ian Kyer and Jerome Bickenbach, *The Fiercest Debate: Cecil A. Wright, the Benchers, and Legal Education in Ontario, 1923–1957*
1988 Robert Sharpe, *The Last Day, the Last Hour: The Currie Libel Trial*
John D. Arnup, *Middleton: The Beloved Judge*
1989 Desmond Brown, *The Genesis of the Canadian Criminal Code of 1892*
Patrick Brode, *The Odyssey of John Anderson*
1990 Philip Girard and Jim Phillips, eds., *Essays in the History of Canadian Law: Volume III – Nova Scotia*
Carol Wilton, ed., *Essays in the History of Canadian Law: Volume IV – Beyond the Law: Lawyers and Business in Canada, 1830–1930*
1991 Constance Backhouse, *Petticoats and Prejudice: Women and Law in Nineteenth-Century Canada*
1992 Brendan O'Brien, *Speedy Justice: The Tragic Last Voyage of His Majesty's Vessel* Speedy
Robert Fraser, ed., *Provincial Justice: Upper Canadian Legal Portraits from the Dictionary of Canadian Biography*
1993 Greg Marquis, *Policing Canada's Century: A History of the Canadian Association of Chiefs of Police*
F. Murray Greenwood, *Legacies of Fear: Law and Politics in Quebec in the Era of the French Revolution*
1994 Patrick Boyer, *A Passion for Justice: The Legacy of James Chalmers McRuer*
Charles Pullen, *The Life and Times of Arthur Maloney: The Last of the Tribunes*
Jim Phillips, Tina Loo, and Susan Lewthwaite, eds., *Essays in the History of Canadian Law: Volume V – Crime and Criminal Justice*
Brian Young, *The Politics of Codification: The Lower Canadian Civil Code of 1866*

1995 David Williams, *Just Lawyers: Seven Portraits*
Hamar Foster and John McLaren, eds., *Essays in the History of Canadian Law: Volume VI – British Columbia and the Yukon*
W.H. Morrow, ed., *Northern Justice: The Memoirs of Mr Justice William G. Morrow*
Beverley Boissery, *A Deep Sense of Wrong: The Treason Trials and Transportation to New South Wales of Lower Canadian Rebels after the 1838 Rebellion*

1996 Carol Wilton, ed., *Essays in the History of Canadian Law: Volume VII – Inside the Law: Canadian Law Firms in Historical Perspective*
William Kaplan, *Bad Judgment: The Case of Mr Justice Leo A. Landreville*
F. Murray Greenwood and Barry Wright, eds., *Canadian State Trials: Volume I – Law, Politics, and Security Measures, 1608–1837*

1997 James W. St. G. Walker, *'Race,' Rights, and the Law in the Supreme Court of Canada: Historical Case Studies*
Lori Chambers, *Married Women and Property Law in Victorian Ontario*
Patrick Brode, *Casual Slaughters and Accidental Judgments: Canadian War Crimes and Prosecutions, 1944–1948*
Ian Bushnell, *A History of the Federal Court of Canada, 1875–1992*

1998 Sidney Harring, *White Man's Law: Native People in Nineteenth-Century Canadian Jurisprudence*
Peter Oliver, *'Terror to Evil-Doers': Prisons and Punishments in Nineteenth-Century Ontario*

1999 Constance Backhouse, *Colour-Coded: A Legal History of Racism in Canada, 1900–1950*
G. Blaine Baker and Jim Phillips, eds., *Essays in the History of Canadian Law: Volume VIII – In Honour of R.C.B. Risk*
Richard W. Pound, *Chief Justice W.R. Jackett: By the Law of the Land*
David Vanek, *Fulfilment: Memoirs of a Criminal Court Judge*

2000 Barry Cahill, *The Thousandth Man: A Biography of James McGregor Stewart*
A.B. McKillop, *The Spinster and the Prophet: Florence Deeks, H.G. Wells, and the Mystery of the Purloined Past*
Beverley Boissery and F. Murray Greenwood, *Uncertain Justice: Canadian Women and Capital Punishment, 1754–1953*
Bruce Ziff, *Unforeseen Legacies: Reuben Wells Leonard and the Leonard Foundation Trust*

2001 Ellen Anderson, *Judging Bertha Wilson: Law as Large as Life*
Judy Fudge and Eric Tucker, *Labour before the Law: The Regulation of Workers' Collective Action in Canada, 1900–1948*
Laurel Sefton MacDowell, *Renegade Lawyer: The Life of J.L. Cohen*

2002 John T. Saywell, *The Lawmakers: Judicial Power and the Shaping of Canadian Federalism*
Patrick Brode, *Courted Abandoned: Seduction in Canadian Law*
David Murray, *Colonial Justice: Justice, Morality, and Crime in the Niagara District, 1791–1849*
Barry Wright and F. Murray Greenwood, *Canadian State Trials, Volume II – Rebellion and Invasion in the Canadas, 1837–1839*